Killing Neighbors

Killing Neighbors

WEBS OF VIOLENCE
IN RWANDA

Lee Ann Fujii

Cornell University Press

Ithaca and London

First published 2009 by Cornell University Press

Printed in the United States of America

Library of Congress Cataloging-in-Publication Data

Fujii, Lee Ann.
  Killing neighbors : webs of violence in Rwanda / Lee Ann Fujii.
    p. cm.
  Includes bibliographical references and index.
  ISBN 978-0-8014-4705-1 (cloth : alk. paper)
  1. Genocide—Rwanda.   2. Violence—Rwanda.   3. Ethnic
conflict—Rwanda.   4. Political violence—Rwanda.   5. Rwanda—
History—Civil War, 1990-1993—Atrocities.   6. Rwanda—History—
Civil War, 1994—Atrocities.   7. Rwanda—Ethnic relations.   I. Title.

  DT450.435.F85 2009
  967.57104'2–dc22

2008034134

Cornell University Press strives to use environmentally responsible
suppliers and materials to the fullest extent possible in the publish-
ing of its books. Such materials include vegetable-based, low-VOC
inks and acid-free papers that are recycled, totally chlorine-free, or
partly composed of nonwood fibers. For further information, visit
our website at www.cornellpress.cornell.edu.

Cloth printing   10 9 8 7 6 5 4 3 2 1

Contents

Acknowledgments		vii
List of Abbreviations		xi
	Introduction: Genocide among Neighbors	1
1	Conducting Fieldwork in the Aftermath of War and Genocide	23
2	Violence and Identity in Historical Perspective	45
3	Local Narratives and Explanations	76
4	The Enigma of Ethnicity	103
5	The Power of Local Ties	128
6	The Logic of Groups	154
	Conclusion	180
	Dramatis personae	191
	Glossary of Kinyarwanda Terms	193
	References	195
	Index	203

Acknowledgments

This book is born from the support of many. I must first thank the funders who made the project possible. Fellowships from Fulbright; The Africa Program at the Woodrow Wilson International Center for Scholars; The Institute for European, Russian, and Eurasian Studies at George Washington University; and the Dean's Office of the Columbian College of Arts and Sciences at George Washington University provided support for fieldwork in Europe and Rwanda and for the drafting of early versions of the manuscript. Michael Moses and Iva Beatty in the dean's office also provided moral and financial support during the very early stages of this project while Carol Sigelman, chief research officer, provided generous support during production. In Rwanda, the Ministry of Local Government, Community Development and Social Affairs, the Ministry of Internal Security, and the Office of the Proceurer Général de la République kindly granted me permission to conduct fieldwork in two provinces and two central prisons.

Stateside, I was fortunate enough to have the support of a diverse group of people who read drafts of chapters, lent an ear, and provided wise counsel at critical moments. This group includes Deborah Avant, who has been a constant source of encouragement and insight; and Bidisha Biswas, Stephen Lubkemann, and David Newbury whose valuable comments on early drafts of chapters helped to steer me in the right direction. For their methodological mentoring from afar, I owe a special thanks to Kristen Monroe, who was a huge help to me long before we had ever met in person, and to Dvora Yanow, who, at later stages, helped me to articulate my methods and approach more clearly and I hope, more convincingly. For her able research assistance in both French and English while I was a fellow at the Woodrow Wilson Center, I wish to thank Marie-Pierre Dunand, who was also a wonderful teacher when it came to answering my many questions about language and translation.

For making sure I made it to and from Rwanda in one piece, I thank Susan Wiley, Patrick Bond, Cristin Guinan-Wiley, Zeinab Said, and Sunni Khalid, who all know Rwanda now, even if they have not yet been there. For their friendship, I thank Theresa and Paul DeGeest who always knew the right thing to say to make me laugh and keep a proper perspective. For her ace proofreading and for knowing more about the genocide than anyone else in Seattle through her own reading, I thank my mother, Mitsie Fujii. The fact that this project sparked her interest in a country that most, including myself, could not have located on a map before 1994, reminded me of the importance this project has had in drawing attention to events and places that most of us might prefer to forget or ignore.

I am also grateful to the many people who helped me on my way to Rwanda and after my return. For early guidance on sources and other foundational questions, I thank Filip Reyntjens and Danielle de Lame, who were both extremely welcoming to this first-timer to Belgium. I also wish to thank Catherine André for our email and phone conversations and for sending me articles. For her advice on finding the right interpreter and other concerns in the field, I thank Jennie Burnet. For his assistance with my very first trip to Rwanda in 2002 and all his accumulated wisdom and advice since then, I thank Scott Straus whose own work has set the bar extremely high for every researcher who has followed him. On my return, I was lucky enough to meet Major Brent Beardsley, former ambassador to Rwanda David Rawson, and fellow researchers Omar McDoom and Eugenia Zorbas at various conferences. I spent many enjoyable hours with all these people hearing new and fascinating details about the genocide and their own personal experiences in the country. I look forward to many more such conversations in the future.

A special indebtedness goes to the people who made my stay in Rwanda so pleasant, especially in those moments when it was difficult to be there: An Ansoms, Heather Baldwin, Anne Brandstetter, Sue McLain, Betsy Levy Paluck, Lars Waldorf, and Sarah Wells. A special thanks to Sue and Ben for their hospitality in "Roo" and to Sue, for her help with last-minute translation questions and for sharing her photos with me. I also wish to extend my gratitude to John Donaldson, Stephanie McNulty, and Michelle Moyd for their steadfast friendship during our respective time in the field emailing across four continents (Asia, Latin America, Africa, and Europe). All these people helped me in innumerable ways during my time in Rwanda, through endless conversation, ongoing moral and logistical support, and kind encouragement. I cannot imagine how I could have survived my time there without them.

I also thank the Rwandan friends and colleagues I made during my stay. These people treated me with generous hospitality and helped me in both large and small ways. They include the staff of the Political Affairs Office at the United States Embassy as well as friends from outside the embassy: Antoine, Immaculée, Védaste, Richard, Théogène, Katos, Féfé, and Geoffrey. A special thanks to Védaste Kabasha for his assistance in helping me secure all the necessary permissions from the various ministries and for his helpful input on the use of certain Kinyarwandan words. My thanks also to Marie Claire for last minute corrections and translation help. I also wish to thank my two language teachers, Louise Nibagwire (in Maryland) and Geneviève Mukandekezi (in Rwanda), with whom I spent countless hours conversing in rusty French and beginner Kinyarwanda.

The person most responsible for the success of my fieldwork was my interpreter and research assistant, who prefers that I not use her name. Her hard work, dedication, professionalism, and kindness were invaluable every step of the way. Whether helping me navigate rural life in Rwanda or finding me fast and reliable braiders, she was there as both able resource and reliable friend. The afternoons she and I spent with our friend, Immaculée, in my cozy apartment, reviewing field notes and sharing a meal, were some of the happiest moments during my time in Rwanda.

The people most responsible for the quality of this book were those who read the entire manuscript (sometimes more than once) and offered incredibly smart and insightful comments. This group includes Nathan Brown, Danielle de Lame, Alison Des Forges, Martha Finnemore, Richard Grinker, Charles King, René Lemarchand, Mark Lichbach, David Newbury, Libby Wood, and one other (still anonymous) reviewer from Cornell University Press. I am honored by the generosity and encouragement all these scholars have shown me and only hope that I did justice to their fine comments and suggestions.

Finally, I wish to extend my heartfelt thanks to the Rwandans who gave so generously of their time to talk with me over many months, patiently answering all my questions and even asking some of their own. I dedicate this work to these people as well as all the Rwandans I will never know because they perished in the genocide.

Abbreviations

APROSOMA	Association pour la promotion sociale de la masse
CDR	Coalition pour la défense de la république
CNS	Commission Nationale de Synthèse
FAR	Forces armées rwandaises
MDR	Mouvement démocratique républicain
MDR-Parmehutu	MDR-Le parti du mouvement de l'émancipation Hutu
MRND	Mouvement révolutionnaire national pour le développement
MRNDD	Mouvement révolutionnaire national pour le développement et la démocratie
MSM	Mouvement social muhutu
PL	Parti libéral
PDC	Parti démocrate chrétien
PSD	Parti social démocrate
RADER	Rassemblement démocratique rwandais
RPF	Rwandan Patriotic Front
UN	United Nations
UNAMIR	United Nations Mission to Rwanda
UNAR	Union nationale rwandaise

Map of Rwanda with shaded circles indicating approximate location of research sites

Introduction

Genocide among Neighbors

Édouard did not look the part. None of the rural men and women who participated in the Rwandan genocide did. Their lives revolved around work, chores, children, and church, not mass murder. Édouard was typical in this regard. He was born in a rural community rung by the Virunga Mountains, the range made famous by Dian Fossey's gorillas. He grew up to become a farmer, married, had four children. Among his neighbors was a Tutsi family. He and his neighbor were not close, but each "still played the role of neighbor," helping one another and sharing good times. After the Rwandan Patriotic Front (RPF), a guerrilla army comprised of mostly Tutsi refugees, invaded Rwanda on 1 October 1990, Édouard began to hear rumors that his own Tutsi neighbor—and indeed, everyone's Tutsi neighbor—were secretly supporting the RPF. For Édouard, the RPF threat had become all too real. In January 1991, the rebel army had launched an attack on the nearest town, less than twenty kilometers away. To help protect his community, Édouard and a dozen other men arranged to go to his Tutsi neighbor's house to root out the RPF accomplices the man was allegedly hiding. When the group arrived, several men surrounded the house. Édouard threw rocks on the roof to make the man come out. The man emerged, brandishing a machete, and managed to strike the first blow. The group killed him instantly. Inside they found no accomplices, only the man's frightened sisters and mother.

The murder of Édouard's neighbor at the hands of other neighbors was no isolated incident. In a wholly different part of the country lived Olivier, a man who spent his childhood years in Kigali. His family eventually moved south, to the center of the country, where Olivier grew up to become a mason. He married and had seven children. Though his own wife was Hutu, other members of his family had married Tutsi. Olivier also had several Tutsi neighbors. Close interrelations with Tutsi were typical for the region. When the war began in October 1990, daily life continued as before. Political parties were starting to form, which threatened the one-party state that had ruled Rwanda for nearly two decades. The emergence of new parties created palpable tensions, even violence, in many parts of the country, but Olivier's family steered clear of politics and experienced no problems. Everything changed on 6 April 1994, when assailants shot down the plane carrying President Habyarimana as it tried to land at the airport in Kigali. Almost immediately, a new authority took over Olivier's *secteur* and began organizing local men to burn and loot Tutsi homes. Olivier was among those recruited. He was a particularly active recruit, never hesitating to carry out any order the new authority issued. Even when the order came to kill all the Tutsi, Olivier obliged. He obliged so often that by his own estimate, he took part in nearly every killing in his community.

What made Édouard and Olivier turn on their Tutsi neighbors? What made these men kill?

The genocide was no homegrown project. It was sponsored and conceived from above, by a small group of powerful extremists in President Habyarimana's regime. These mighty few objected to the power-sharing terms of a recently signed peace agreement between Habyarimana and the RPF. Through genocide, they sought to maintain their monopoly on power.

The slaughter began on 6 April 1994, shortly after assailants shot down the plane carrying the president. Within hours, specially trained militia, soldiers, and Presidential Guard began going door to door with lists of targets, which included anyone—Hutu or Tutsi—not firmly in the extremists' camp. The killers dispatched their victims with gruesome efficiency. Militia simultaneously set up roadblocks across the city to prevent escape, killing anyone with a Tutsi identity card and anyone who "looked" Tutsi.

Outside the capital, the violence followed a different path. Killings began at different times in different regions (Straus 2006, 53–64). Soldiers, professional militia, and National Police continued to play a leading role in perpetrating violence, but rural residents also did their part. Local elites and political entrepreneurs used the crisis of the president's assassination to seize power in their communities and began enlisting residents into genocide. Some people refused. Others found ways to avoid participating. Many, however, joined in the killings. Despite long-standing, mostly amicable, relations with their victims, these peasant-killers went about their task in determined fashion. They trapped victims at road-blocks, lured them to public buildings, and descended on their homes and hiding places. They killed the young and old, the healthy and infirm, men as well as women, mostly Tutsi but thousands of Hutu as well. What explains this transformation from peasant to *génocidaire*? How do ordinary people come to commit mass violence against their own neighbors, friends, and family?

The question of intimate mass violence constitutes a central puzzle in the study of political violence (Fearon and Laitin 2000, 846). The question is even more puzzling in the African context since most African states lack the ability to mobilize outside capital cities or other urban centers (Straus 2004b, 12).

From a rationalist perspective, popular participation in mass slaughter is puzzling because people are better off under conditions of peace than violence. It makes no sense for masses to support elite projects of genocide or ethnic cleansing, when it is the masses who incur most of the costs, and elites, most of the benefits (de Figueiredo and Weingast 1999, 262).

The puzzle becomes even more disturbing when the targets of violence are people whom the killers have known as friends, neighbors, and family. Neighbors are not supposed to kill neighbors, let alone commit genocide against them. Indeed, long-standing, interethnic ties of the sort that typified relations in Rwanda should preclude, not facilitate, participation in mass violence (Coleman 1988; Putnam 1993; Varshney 1997).[1] Killing at close range, moreover, is grisly work, as the ordinary men of Police Battalion 101 knew firsthand after marching thousands of Jewish civilians into the forest and shooting them in the back of the neck (Browning 1992). So, too, is killing a person one sees as occupying the same "moral universe" as oneself, and thus entitled to the same norms of protection (Fein 1979).[2] What is perhaps most difficult of all is to kill a person one knows and regards in positive terms, for killing kith and kin is more than just a physical act; it is an act of social violation. It destroys not just bodies, but bonds.

---

1. Scholars have also noted social capital's "dark side" (Portes 1998, 15–18; Colletta and Cullen 2000; Mann 2005, 21; Kalyvas 2006, 14).

2. A clear example of Fein's notion of "moral universe" is found in Walzer (1977), where he quotes from memoirs of soldiers who refrained from shooting an enemy combatant when the enemy soldier did something that made him look "human," such as lighting a cigarette or pulling up his pants. As Walzer (1977, 139) explains: "A soldier who looks funny is not at that moment a military threat; he is not a fighting man but simply a man, and one does not kill men."

Foils and Foibles: A Second Look at
Ethnicity-based Approaches

The usual approach to resolving this puzzle is to point to ethnicity as the key driver of violence. In ethnicity-based approaches, violence is the outcome of ethnic group relations, which are inherently competitive and often antagonistic. The type of violence that occurs, such as atrocities or mass murder, are supposed indicators of the power of ethnic levers at work. The more extensive or brutal the violence, the greater the antagonisms must have been. Ethnicity-based approaches thus locate causes in the nature of ethnic groups themselves—the collective attributes or tendencies that unite people under a common ethnic label. These attributes and tendencies may be constructed or ancient. They may be modern or old, real or imagined. No matter their origin, they turn Serbs, Sunni, and Hutu into clearly bounded ethnic groups. Under the right conditions, these approaches assert, ethnic groups will commit violence against "enemy" groups.

Two of the most commonly posited pathways to mass-based violence are "ethnic hatreds" and "ethnic fears."[3] For purposes of clarity, I treat these two approaches as distinct though some scholars combine the two. The "ethnic hatred" thesis views collective hatreds as an integral part of ethnic group identities. According to this thesis, ethnic hatreds can persist over generations, even centuries, through myth, memory, or both. Despite the passage of time, these hatreds do not necessarily lessen or alter but remain dormant and even "simmer" until something or someone pushes the lid off the pot, at which point, they may "erupt" or "explode" into mass-led violence against the hated group (Goldhagen 1996; Kaufmann 1996; Kaufman 2001; Petersen 2002).

The "ethnic fear" thesis focuses not on cultural constants, but on elite ambitions and moves. According to this model, elites foment mass fear of the ethnic "other" using extremist media, organized riots, arbitrary arrests, and other known techniques, in pursuit of their political goals. Ethnic fears are not an extant feature of group identities, but a resource that political entrepreneurs exploit to their own advantage. Ethnic publics heed calls to support violent campaigns because it is rational for them to

---

3. Scholars have also devised explanations for specific cases of mass killing or genocide. Explanations for the Rwandan genocide cover a wide range of explanatory factors, including structural violence (Uvin 1998); the effects of media (Chalk 1999; Chrétien et al. 1995); identities created under colonialism (Mamdani 2001), to name a few. These explanations are generally not proffered as general theories of mass or ethnic violence, however.

do so. The basis of that rationality depends on the theory. In Barry Posen's (1993) framework, it is rational for ethnic groups to try to increase their security when the state has collapsed or can no longer guarantee all citizens' well-being. According to Rui J.P. de Figueiredo and Barry Weingast (1999), it is rational for masses to accept what elites say because the risk of possible annihilation is too great should elite exhortations turn out to be true. For Russell Hardin (1995), it is rational for people to identify with their ethnic group because ethnic groups provide coordination power, which enables groups to attain their goals. In all three scenarios, no counterdiscourse or countermovement exists that can offer people an alternative set of frames or options; this leaves ethnic groups no other choice but to line up behind their ethnic leaders.

In both the ethnic fear and ethnic hatred approaches, the causal chain works as follows. When crises occur, the insecurity (and opportunity) of the moment inflames people's fears and hatreds. Once activated, these emotions drive Serbs to kill Muslims, Muslims to kill Hindus, and Hutu to kill Tutsi. Each step leads inexorably to the next. Individual motives and interests are immaterial to the outcome, because under crisis conditions, motives and interests converge. They become shared by all members of the same ethnic group. The result of this convergence is precisely what the architects of these projects intend: masses of one group go after masses of the other.

Both approaches offer intuitively compelling explanations for mass violence. Large-scale crises, such as war, do seem to bring out people's latent prejudices and fears which, in turn, do seem to push people to line up with their own against the perceived enemy or threat. In the wake of Japan's surprise attack on Pearl Harbor, for example, the Roosevelt administration authorized the forced relocation of all United States residents of Japanese ancestry, the majority of whom were American citizens, to "internment camps" in the country's interior. There was no public outcry or protest against this mass deportation, evidence perhaps of white America uniting behind its leaders against a threatening racial group.

Facile readings of history, however, rarely hold up to closer scrutiny. While war may indeed generate widespread fears and prejudices, violence does not become the only or inevitable outcome. Even in wartime, ethnic masses do not act as a single unit, but as a variety of groups and groupings that do not always follow ethnic lines. Indeed, the most common strategy that people follow during wartime is neutrality, not unequivocal support for one side over another (Kalyvas 2006). Neutrality often manifests as acquiescence to whichever side is in power. Such acquiescence is not an indicator of tacit support of those in power, but may be a function of other factors. As Ian Kershaw (1987, 372) argues in the case of ordinary Germans during World War II, for example, the lack of public protest against deportations of Jews to the East did not signal the public's support for these policies, but rather, its indifference to them, an indifference borne of people's "concern for matters only of immediate and personal relevance." As Chip Gagnon (2004, 27) similarly points out in the case of the Balkan wars of the early 1990s, many people chose silence as "the least evil" option. As these and other scholars point out, fear and insecurity do not always push all, or even most, people to violence. In fact, fear can have just the opposite effect, leading people to retreat further "into the private sphere" (Kershaw 1987, 372).

Responses to other genocides also seem consistent with the findings of Kalyvas, Kershaw, and Gagnon. Even during campaigns of genocide, people do not necessarily act as ethnic blocks. The ethnic hatred and ethnic fear theses do not anticipate this level of fragmentation. As a result, both models end up raising more questions than they answer when applied to the Rwandan case. First, if it was overwhelming hatreds or fears that drove hundreds of thousands of ordinary Hutu to participate in the genocide, then what explains the hundreds of thousands who did not participate?[4] Second, if collective hatreds and fears were powerful enough to motivate ordinary people to kill, then why did local leaders have to force so many to participate in the violence? Why did everyone not join in the slaughter willingly? Third, if crisis really does push people to line up with their own, then what explains all the instances in which Hutu crossed ethnic lines to help Tutsi? Or cases where killers targeted other Hutu? Neither approach can answer these questions because neither expects such patterns to arise in the first place.

In addition to raising questions they cannot answer, both approaches have little to say about the specific form that genocidal violence took in Rwanda. So consistent was the manner in which killers carried out their murderous task that Scott Straus (2004b; 2006), in a masterful analysis of the genocide, is able to use these features to distinguish genocidal violence from other forms of violence that were occurring at the same time. As Straus (2004b, 86) writes: "Genocidal violence is characterized by public, indiscriminate attacks against Tutsis, often in broad daylight and by large numbers of attackers. Isolated, sporadic, surreptitious attacks do not

---

4. Straus (2004a, 94–95) estimates between 175,000 and 210,000 total perpetrators, of whom 90 percent would have been "non-hardcore civilian perpetrators." More recently, *gacaca* (local court) proceedings have led to accusations against half a million people (Waldorf 2007, 267).

constitute genocidal violence." What Straus does not tell us, however, is why genocidal violence would have these characteristics in the first place. Why would the killings be public? Why would they be performed by large numbers of attackers, especially in cases where the number of victims was relatively small? And why would these types of attacks constitute genocidal violence while "sporadic, surreptitious attacks" do not?

For some types of political violence, form is what defines them. By definition, riots need crowds and lynchings a target. It would make little sense to analyze either type of violence without taking into account the public nature of the acts, the way rioters choose their targets and sites (Horowitz 2001), and in the case of lynchings, the public display of the victim's body and the severing of body parts for souvenirs (McGovern 1982; Tolnay and Beck 1995).

Unlike riots and lynchings, however, there is nothing inherent in the definition of genocide that would warrant one method of mass murder over another. This leaves Straus to derive his definition inductively—from the evidence. His definition is consistent with his own data as well as that of other studies of the genocide (e.g., Mironko 2004). The killings in Rwanda were committed by groups, not individuals. These groups were large, oftentimes much larger than what was required to kill the victims at hand, who, in many cases, were too young or too old to flee. The killings were also public, not private affairs, involving large numbers of onlookers.

The form that killings took in Rwanda is not typical of other genocides. During the Holocaust, genocidal violence was rarely on public display. The structure and location of concentration camps kept the gruesome reality of mechanized mass killing out of view of local residents. Similarly, in the Nazi-occupied East, executioners marched their victims deep into the forests to kill and bury them out of public view (Browning 1992). In Cambodia, Khmer Rouge cadre tortured and killed accused enemies in a secret facility known as S-21; in rural areas, they took their victims to remote sites to kill them, out of sight of other villagers (Chandler 1999; Hinton 2005). In all these cases, the number of killers was usually no more than what was required to complete the task in efficient manner. Why would the killings in Rwanda take such different form? Neither the ethnic hatred nor ethnic fear model helps to answer this question. Yet, answers to this question, I will argue, are directly germane to the core puzzle of this study—why ordinary people would participate in extraordinary crimes in the first place.

Limitations of Standard Analytic Categories

The problem begins not with theories, but categories. To analyze violence, scholars rely on a standard set of categories to sort actors and the messy reality they inhabit. When analyzing genocide, analysts generally rely on the categories "perpetrator," "victim," "bystander," and "rescuer." Membership in these categories is assumed to be exclusive and stable. In this scheme, a perpetrator cannot also be a rescuer; and once a perpetrator, always a perpetrator.

The problem with this system of categorizing, however, is that it "fixes people in a way that is not borne out by the realities of genocide."[5] Genocides are dynamic, while categories are static. In dynamic settings, contexts and conditions change, sometimes in an instant. These changes, in turn, can shift actors' relations, perspectives, motives, and identities. Static categories cannot capture these shifts. Neither can they capture endogenous sources of change—transformation that occurs through the unfolding of the process itself. Participating in violence or watching others commit violence can also change people's relations, perspectives, motives, and identities. For example, people may initially join in the violence because of external pressures, but continue their participation for reasons that arise from their initial actions. Indeed, many elites banked on this process of change, mobilizing people at lower thresholds of participation, such as looting and pillaging, before escalating activities to killing (Des Forges 1999, 90).

Another problem with standard categories is that they smooth over tensions that exist both within and between categories. In the present case, actors did not confine their activities to one category; rather, they often moved back and forth between categories, or straddled multiple categories at the same time. Others hovered in the margins, such as those recruited for violence but able to pay others to go in their place. These actors did not participate in the killings directly but nevertheless played a part in them. How should we categorize them? As victims? Bystanders? Or perpetrators with an asterisk? Standard categories cannot capture, let alone account for, these ambiguities, yet the data suggest ambiguity and contradiction were central features of the violence in rural areas.

What we need is a way to engage these complexities directly. By ignoring them, we risk building theories around skewed understandings of the phenomena we are trying to explain. If the same person was capable of killing and saving, for example, then explanations based on motive would be indeterminate, since the motives for one set of actions (say, killing) would not preclude or subsume motives for the other (say, saving). Analyzing the full range of people's actions is also crucial for theorizing the

---

5. Vicki Barnett, discussant comments, United States Holocaust Memorial Museum, 24 May 2005.

agency of these actors. If we were to base theories of agency on only one set of actions—the set that most easily fits an existing analytic category—our theories would be at best, partial, and at worst, wrong. The answer is not to jettison typologies, but to take special care to ensure that the categories do not speak for the data, rather, that the data speak for themselves, no matter where that leaves them on the grid.

Limitations of Macro-level Concepts and Perspectives

In addition to the limitations of standard categories, there are also limitations to the way the ethnic hatred and ethnic fear models treat key concepts, such as "the masses," "elites," and "ethnicity."

The first is a problem of perspective. Both approaches take a bird's eye view of the dynamics that presumably undergird the violence. From afar, it is easy to mistake causes for consequences and political divisions for cultural inevitabilities. From a distance, it is easy to view all political conflicts as ethnic in nature, and hence, to seize on ethnicity as a primary source of violence, rather than one possible factor among many.

Another problem with the view from on high is the treatment of the "masses" as an undifferentiated whole. No distinction is made between those who are more ambitious versus those more passive, or those who have ties to elites versus those who do not. Treating the masses as an undifferentiated whole exaggerates the level of volition, with the ethnic hatreds model assigning too much agency (since people are driven by their own hatreds), and the ethnic fear, too little (since people are simply following their leaders).

A third problem arises from the second. The expectation that masses will follow elites under the right conditions leads analysts to generalize what goes in the capital to the rest of the country, as if structures, interests, identities, and beliefs flow from the center to the periphery in unmitigated form. As Stathis Kalyvas (2003; 2006), Norbert Peabody (2000), and others have pointed out, however, violence in the periphery does not always follow the master narrative of elites in the center. Indeed, as numerous ethnographies of violence have shown, violence in the periphery tends to hew to local politics and relations (see, e.g., Bax 1995 in the Bosnia-Herzegovinian context; Brass 1997 in the Indian context; and Lubkemann 2005 in the Mozambican civil war).

A fourth limitation to these approaches is the way they treat the concept of ethnicity. Both approaches assume ethnic groups to be unitary actors in the sense that members of the same group share the same interests and goals, particularly under conditions of threat or insecurity (Brubaker and

Laitin 1998, 438). Treating ethnic groups as unitary actors leads to privileging conflicts between ethnic groups over conflicts within groups or outside the ethnic group construct altogether. This is a potentially costly move, since it assumes a priori that conflicts between groups will always be the most important type of conflict to examine. In Rwanda, this assumption proves tenuous. Since Rwanda's independence in 1959–61, political conflicts have been entrenched in regional rivalries that pitted Hutu elites from the north against Hutu elites from the center-south. This north-south rivalry did not abate in the 1990s, but continued apace, such that the main threat to Habyarimana's northerner regime was not the Tutsi masses or a Tutsi-led political party, but a party founded by Hutu elites from the central province of Gitarama (Reyntjens 1995a; Bertrand 2000; Gasana 2002).

Privileging ethnic divisions over other types of cleavages not only risks missing more important fault lines, it also comes dangerously close to accepting the pronouncements of hypernationalist leaders who want outsiders to believe the main conflict in their country is ethnic, rather than political. Leaders' attempts to reframe political problems as ethnic issues have clear motive. Deeply entrenched ethnic problems require radically different solutions than political contests. Ethnic conflicts call for partition, annexation, irredentist policies, ethnic cleansing, and even genocide as "solutions." Political conflicts, on the other hand, invite no such drastic measures, but entail the more mundane arts of politics, such as bargaining and negotiation. Analysts should remain ever wary of mistaking the rhetoric of elites—particularly threatened elites—for accurate depictions of the political situation in their countries. Falling into this trap makes the analyst complicit in elite projects that seek to turn political contests into ethnic realities, for scholars, too, promote certain understandings of complex situations over others.

What the limitations of the ethnic hatred and ethnic fear models point to is the need to investigate how violence interacts with ethnicity and how ethnicity, in turn, interacts with violence, without assuming that each exists separately from the other in premade or stable form. We need to investigate how exactly the conflict or violence is, or becomes, ethnic, rather than assuming it to be such from the start. As Rogers Brubaker and David Laitin (1998, 427) write: "*That* political violence can be ethnic is well established, indeed too well established; *how* it is ethnic remains obscure. The most fundamental questions—for example, how the adjective 'ethnic' modifies the noun 'violence'—remain unclear and largely unexamined" (emphasis in original). Understanding this grammatical link is the goal of this book.

A Dynamic Approach to Explaining
Genocidal Participation

To move beyond the limitations of standard approaches, I propose an alternative lens, one that can take moving pictures, rather than just static snapshots. This lens is trained on the dynamism of actors and their actions during violence. It seeks to capture how contexts, identities, and motives shift or transform through the unfolding of violence across time and space.

This alternative lens begins by viewing genocide as a process, not a clearly bounded event. As a process, genocide ceases to be a clearly demarcated temporal period of mass slaughter and becomes instead a messy agglomeration of actions taken and not taken, decisions made and unmade, perceptions reinforced and transformed. Genocide as process becomes a temporal and spatial unfolding of ambiguous actions, shifting contexts, and actors with multiple and contradictory motives. This process, moreover, need not be linear, for the violence can speed up, slow down, claim new targets, and abandon the old.[6]

Viewing the genocide as a process generates different expectations than viewing it as a discrete event. If genocide is a process, then we would expect actors to move between categories or to occupy multiple categories at the same time. Viewing actors dynamically allows us to probe a broad range of people's behavior during the genocide, with its attendant contradictions and ambiguities, without the need to box actors into the standard categories of "victim," "perpetrator," "bystander," or "rescuer." Indeed, one of the objectives of this study is to understand the ways in which these actors do not fit these categories neatly or nicely.

This alternative lens also views ethnicity much differently than standard approaches. When standard, ethnicity-based approaches refer to "ethnicity," they are referring to a specific set of constructions, which depict ethnic group identities in terms that are meant to occlude regional differences and smooth over local variations in an effort to achieve some larger political goal. The reasons for this practice may not be mobilization for mass murder, but simply the state's need to make its populations "legible" (Scott 1998). In any case, the goal is the same—to fashion a singular understanding of what it means to be Serb, Sunni, Tutsi, or Tamil through official institutions and practices. I call this set of constructions "state-sponsored ethnicity."

Rather than assuming that state-sponsored ethnicity represents the sum total of ethnic meaning in all of social and political life, as standard

6. I thank Alison Des Forges for this point.

approaches tend to do, I assume it to be one set of meanings among many that exist at the same time. Most of these alternative meanings remain invisible to outsiders, because they are rooted in cultural forms and local knowledge, which are, by definition, beyond outsiders' grasp. Their invisibility to outsiders, however, does not mean they do not exist. The key is finding ways to detect these less visible, but no less important, sets of meaning.

What I propose is to view state-sponsored ethnicity not as an external force that acts on people, but as a "script" for violence that people act out. I do not use the word *script* in the cognitive sense to refer to a "schema" that makes behavior in "predictable, conventional, or frequently encountered situations" automatic or unthinking (Gioia and Poole 1984, 450), for there was nothing conventional or predictable about wartime or genocide. Neither do I mean it in the sense of daily impression management as theorized by Erving Goffman (1959). Whereas Goffman is concerned with the stage management of everyday life—the myriad ways in which people adjust and attune their behavior to create and maintain certain images of themselves in front of others, such as patients, colleagues, or clients—I am interested in how people cope during crisis, when existing social orders have been upended or are threatened. During crisis and war, the rules and expectations for normal behavior change, sometimes in radical ways. Thus, I use the term *script* not to evoke habitual or everyday practices, but to refer to a play or piece of theater, the performance of which constitutes an event or moment out of the ordinary.

In its most basic form, a script is a dramaturgical blueprint for an imagined world, one that is self-contained and populated by specific characters who say and do specific things at specific moments in time. The script for genocide follows this model; it begins with a scene of apocalyptic proportions—the threatened existence of the group deemed innocent and good. The level and immediacy of mortal danger steadily increases, culminating in the heroic defense of the threatened group through annihilation of the group's greatest enemy.

The creators of this script are usually threatened elites in the capital who come to see genocide as their best strategy for staying in power. Through this text, they are able to summon a new political and social order, one that ensures attainment of their political goals. By diffusing this text through elite-controlled channels, such as meetings, rallies, and mass media, they attempt to make others see this world as well.

For local power holders and power seekers, the script does not represent a set of instructions they must follow to the letter, but rather an opportunity to apply their own interpretation to the text. Local leaders are the directors of their local productions. As such, they are in charge of casting and adapting the text to fit local needs and requirements. Directors do not work in a vacuum, however. They must answer to powerful patrons and producers who create incentives for realizing certain interpretations over others. By pleasing patrons and producers, directors garner rewards in the form of recognition, promotion, and authority. Conversely, displeasing their patrons and producers can put them out of a job. Directing the script thus provides local leaders with the opportunity to express and consolidate power in their communities.

No director's vision is ever hegemonic. Realization of the director's ideas depends on the actors themselves—their skills, interests, and commitment level. Actors join the production for different reasons; some because they truly support the project, some because it is easier to go along, and others, for yet different reasons. The director's vision is therefore dependent on how the actors perform their roles.

Viewing state-sponsored ethnicity as a script for violence, not a cause, alters our expectations for how ethnicity operates during genocide. If ethnicity operates as a script, then we would expect actors' performances to vary. We would expect performances to vary between actors such that some actors adhere to the text more faithfully than others. We would also expect performances to vary by individual, such that the same actor's performances might be more convincing in some instances than in others. We would also expect actors to know the difference between the world of the play and the world outside the play, even during a "performance." We would expect that inhabiting one world would not obviate actors' awareness of the other. In other words, we would expect actors to be able to maintain both their onstage and offstage worlds simultaneously.

The result of this creative process is not a single performance or outcome, but a welter of diverse performances. Some actors will follow the text closely, such as when killers go after Tutsi and only Tutsi. Some will stray from the text as when killers target Hutu as well as Tutsi for killing. Some may abandon the script altogether as when killers help Tutsi instead of hurt them. The advantage of conceptualizing state-sponsored ethnicity this way is that it leads us to disaggregate the violence and to investigate the complexities and ambiguities embedded within the genocide.

Through this alternative lens, state-sponsored ethnicity ceases to be some monolithic "thing" that leads inexorably to violent end, but one set of constructed meanings, among multiple possibilities, and one that remains open to interpretation. This alternative lens shifts the focus away from ethnicity as an external force to those who interpret, direct, and perform the script. It shifts attention to the directors and actors, and by doing so, provides the possibility for agency at every level, not only on the part of leaders, but also among their supposed followers.

Defining Key Concepts and Terms

In addition to ethnicity, I use other key concepts that require explicit definition. The first is the concept of violence. Violence can be physical (Riches 1986), structural (Uvin 1998), symbolic (Nagengast 2002), or spiritual (Ellis 1995). For this study, I define "violence" in physical terms—as the act of harming or attempting to harm a person's body or material property. I define "genocidal violence" as any action undertaken in support of an extermination campaign of the targeted group. In the Rwandan case, genocidal leaders defined the target in ethnic terms, but other definitions are possible as well.[7]

I define "participation in genocide" in broad terms—as anyone who took part in any activity that related directly to the genocide (as opposed to the civil war). These activities include denouncing the hiding places of Tutsi, raping Tutsi, pillaging Tutsi property, or searching for Tutsi to kill. They do not include such activities as carrying supplies for the RPF or fleeing one's home because of war-fighting. I make the definition broad to capture all the different ways people participated in the genocide, but narrow enough to differentiate genocidal violence from war violence, despite the fact that genocidal leaders did their best to link the two into a seamless whole. Because of its broadness, this definition does not distinguish between different levels of moral or legal culpability. Such questions, while critically important, remain beyond the scope of this book.

Before continuing, it is important to reiterate that genocidal violence took place concurrently with a civil war between the RPF and Rwanda government forces, known by their French acronym, FAR (Forces armées rwandaises). Thus, when I speak of the "war" or "civil war," I am referring to a guerrilla-style war that took place from 1 October 1990 through 18 July 1994, when the RPF declared victory in the country. Insofar as the genocide was closely intertwined with the civil war, I will often speak of the period of 1990–94 as "the period of the civil war and genocide." Those I interviewed, however, use their own words to talk about this period. The most common word that people used to refer to the period of

---

7. For a more extensive discussion of scholarly debates surrounding the proper definition for genocide, see Fein (1993), Alvarez (2001), Straus (2001), and Sémelin (2005, chap. 6).

1990–94 is *intambara,* which means "war." People seemed to use this word most often despite there being multiple ways to refer to "genocide" in Kinyarwanda (e.g., *itsembatsemba, jenoside, itsembabwoko*), indicating perhaps a shared understanding of how closely linked the two forms of violence were. This discursive practice undoubtedly says quite a bit about how language shapes the way people construct the past, but I leave such analyses to those more expert than I in linguistic analysis. Suffice it to say that when I refer to the "war," I am referring to the civil war between the RPF and FAR. When respondents refer to the "war," they are usually, but not always, referring to the civil war between the RPF and FAR and/or the genocide of Tutsi and moderate Hutu.

Because the war began before the genocide, it is also important to clarify how I treat the temporal boundaries of the genocide proper—its beginning and end. Generally, scholars treat the start of the Rwandan genocide as the president's plane crash of 6 April 1994, since this was the event that triggered the first massacres of political moderates—both Hutu and Tutsi—in the capital. I follow this practice, but argue, at the same time, that episodes of Tutsi-targeted violence that preceded the plane crash also formed an integral part of the overall process of genocide, even if these episodes fall outside the temporal bounds of the genocide proper. I do not mean to imply that these prior episodes led inevitably to genocide—to the contrary. I would argue there was no point at which the genocide became unavoidable or unstoppable. I only wish to emphasize that because some regions experienced killings of local Tutsi long before the president's plane crash, I do not restrict my analysis to the one-hundred-day period that followed the president's plane crash. Rather, I speak of the "killings" of Tutsi in my northern research site that took place in January 1991 (following an RPF attack in the area), and then restarted "during the genocide," to acknowledge that the president's plane crash triggered yet another round of Tutsi-targeted massacres in that particular community, not the first or only round. In other communities, by contrast, the plane crash triggered the first violent attacks against Tutsi and shortly thereafter, the genocidal killing of Tutsi.

Finally, I eschew the term *the masses* and instead attempt to identify key sets of local actors. The main actors I identify and investigate are local leaders, their collaborators, and a group I call "Joiners." Joiners were the lowest-level participants in the genocide. They did not lead or organize the genocide but were responsible for carrying out much of the violence against Tutsi in their communities. Joiners had no prior military or police training but went about their task in organized fashion. Joiners did not always gain any special privileges or protections from participating in the violence, yet continued to participate over time. Joiners were, in every sense of the term, "ordinary" men and women of their communities.[8] As ordinary members of their communities, Joiners had the most to lose and least to gain from participating in the genocide, because it was they who stood to suffer the most from the destruction of their communities. Thus it is they who represent the core puzzle of this study.

Unlike many studies of perpetrators, this book does not examine Joiners as strictly "perpetrators" but looks at the range of actions they took, both in support and defiance of the genocide. Similarly, this study does not examine Joiners in isolation but against a range of different behaviors people from the same community exhibited during the genocide. Thus, in addition to Joiners, leaders, and collaborators, I also reference those who did not lead, collaborate, or join in the violence in any way. These actors include those who were the primary targets of violence (survivors); those who helped to save Tutsi (rescuers); those who evaded participation (evaders); those who witnessed but did not take part in the genocide (witnesses); and people who refused or resisted pressures to participate in the violence (resisters). The multiplicity of responses was perhaps a natural consequence of the multiplicity of roles that people inhabited in their daily lives. This link between social life and people's responses to the genocide, I will show, was no accident; it shaped how actors performed genocide in two small communities. I do not seek to explain all these diverse behaviors; rather, I use this range of responses as context for understanding how and why Joiners came to participate in the genocide while others chose much different paths. As Kalyvas (2006, 48) points out, "Instances of violence cannot be considered independently of instances where violence does not occur." I argue similarly that we cannot adequately explain those who join in violence without also examining those who do not.

Collecting and Analyzing Interview Data from Two Research Sites and Prisons

The data for this study come from nine months of fieldwork in Rwanda, the majority of that time spent in two rural communities and central prisons: "Kimanzi" in the northern province of Ruhengeri and "Ngali" in the central province of Gitarama. I use pseudonyms to refer to the two research

---

8. While small in number relative to men, women also participated in the genocide; see, e.g., Landesman (2002) and Hogg (2001). In my two research sites, however, there were no women who had confessed to participating in the genocide. One woman had been imprisoned for five years as a *génocidaire*, but she denied any involvement in the genocide.

sites to protect identities. The map at the beginning of this chapter shows the general location of the two research sites.

In each community and prison, I conducted semistructured, intensive interviews with the help of a French-Kinyarwanda interpreter. My goal was to speak with a wide range of people who lived through or participated in the genocide in different ways. The sample included confessed killers (still imprisoned at the time of fieldwork), incarcerated prisoners who maintained their innocence, former prisoners, survivors, resisters, witnesses, and rescuers. I used a strategy of repeat visits to talk with a core subset of people multiple times. This strategy enabled me to probe sensitive issues in depth, follow up similar themes with multiple people, and cross-check people's responses against one another. The questions I asked concerned what people saw and did during the genocide and how they explained their own and others' actions. I also asked people about specific domains of daily life before the genocide, such as choosing marriage partners and raising children. These life history narratives provide insight into the logics people used to make sense of the world before and during the genocide.

The theoretical framework I use to analyze the data come from multiple disciplines and literatures. To theorize the social dimensions of violence, I draw on the work of anthropologist Paul Richards (1996; 2005) and sociologist Mark Granovetter (1985). Richards argues that violence is organized social action. To call violence "social" means that its activities are oriented toward others (Hedström and Swedberg 1998, 13). Because it is oriented toward others, violence is expressive, not just instrumental. Specific acts of violence can carry specific meanings. Cutting off the arms or hands of villagers in Sierra Leone, for example, might serve the goal of social control, but these acts also convey graphic warnings to villagers not to vote in upcoming elections or harvest their fields (Richards 1996, xx). To call violence "organized" means that it is ordered, not chaotic or random, though the basis for that order may be opaque to outsiders. Analysts should not assume, therefore, that that which does not make sense on the outside lacks any strategic calculation on the inside.

Related to these insights is the work of Granovetter and in particular, his concept of social embeddedness. Granovetter's argument is simple but powerful. He argues that most behavior is embedded in social relations. This approach, he argues, "avoids the extremes of under- and oversocialized views of human action" (Granovetter 1985, 504). Undersocialized views treat actors as pure agents, unfettered by social ties or structures; while oversocialized views assume structure determines all. For Granovetter, the notion of "social embeddedness" strikes a more convincing middle ground. Social relations, he argues, have an independent effect on actors, one that is neither merely "frictional" nor overly deterministic. Actors pursue specific courses of action within the set of social relations in which they are embedded. These networks offer opportunities as well as constraints.

For Granovetter, systems of social relations can and do act as sites of trust-building (as the literature on social capital teaches), but this does not preclude the possibility that distrust and malfeasance can arise at the same time. Granovetter identifies two reasons for this seeming paradox. The first is that by trusting someone, a person becomes more, not less, vulnerable to betrayal. The second is that malfeasance—particularly of the more ambitious variety—generally requires teams or groups of bad-doers. Simply put, large-scale bad deeds cannot be done alone. Thus the "extent of disorder resulting from force and fraud" depends on how social relations are structured or organized (Granovetter 1985, 492). While an elaborate heist might require a small group of thieves, a war requires much larger numbers of people organized into social units called armies. As Granovetter (1985, 492) explains: "More extended and large-scale disorder results from coalitions of combatants, *impossible without prior relations*" (emphasis added).

Applying these insights to the question of how neighbors turn into genocidal killers is useful from several angles. First, it invites the analyst to disaggregate the masses to identify key actors. Second, it invites the analyst to investigate the various acts and activities these key actors undertake in different contexts. Third, it leads the analyst to explore the structure and content of relations that tie these actors to one another. Fourth, it suggests linking the configuration of social relations to people's actions not in a mechanical or deterministic way, but in a way that takes social relations seriously as sites and mechanisms that pattern behavior in specific ways.

Looking at the effects of social relations does not rob actors of their agency—to the contrary. Social relations provide the immediate context in which people act and interact for, against, and toward others. Social relations thus provide the basis for locating agency at "neighbor" level. How these relations define and structure contexts, perspectives, identities, and actions allows us to situate actors and the different possibilities for acting in precise moments. Agency, I will show, was not a binary state that was either "off" or "on," but a shifting set of possibilities that had as much to do with objective realities as subjective and intersubjective understandings of changing conditions and pressures.

Argument and Audience

In the pages to follow, I lay out an argument that challenges standard ethnicity-based approaches and more specifically, the two main foils of this study, the ethnic hatred and ethnic fear theses. In their place, I offer a "social interaction" argument, which, I contend, better explains ordinary people's participation in mass violence. By focusing on the dynamics of social interaction, I do not mean to negate or minimize the importance that ethnicity—or hatred and fear for that matter—played in the violence. Ethnicity was critically important, just not in the way that the ethnic hatred or ethnic fear models assume or expect.

According to my social interaction argument, state-sponsored ethnicity operated not as an external causal force, like gravity, but as an endogenously generated "script" for violence. As a script, state-sponsored ethnicity was not some "thing" inscribed in people's cultural DNA or collective histories; it was a set of constructions that were intended for performance but remained open to interpretation.

What mediated between the script for genocide and people's actual performances in a given moment were local ties and group dynamics. Prior ties shaped how people saw and reacted to their situation. In certain circumstances, they enabled Joiners to continue to see Tutsi as friends, not targets, and some Hutu as targets, not friends. Ties also served as mechanisms for recruitment and initiation into the violence, binding Joiners to leaders and their killing groups in powerful ways. Once initiated, Joiners continued their participation because killing in large groups conferred powerful identity on these actors, which led the groups to reenact the violent practices that were consistent with the group's identity. As Charles Tilly (1985) argues with respect to European state formation—that wars make states—I argue that killing produced groups and groups produced killings.

This study follows the recent "micropolitical turn in the study of social violence" (King 2004, 432). Its findings are not necessarily unique to Rwanda or the two small communities on which they are based. In fact, the findings are quite consistent with the multitude of ethnographic and microhistorical accounts of civil war violence that Kalyvas (2006) surveys in remarkable breadth and depth. As Kalyvas (2006, 9–10) argues, violence is a "universal process formed by recurrent elements and organized in systems with regular structural features." Thus, "while contexts may differ, mechanisms recur." Pace Kalyvas, I argue that mechanisms understood in depth in one setting, such as Rwanda, are of theoretical import for three reasons. First, they can help to confirm or disconfirm hypotheses derived from more general theories of violence. Second, they help to identify any misspecified assumptions or logics that underlie existing theories. Third, they suggest the micromechanisms that are at work in genocidal contexts which may or may not be similar to civil war or other forms of organized violence. In short, findings from cases in Rwanda are both validating and additive. This book thus contributes to an emerging literature that seeks to understand and explain violence in its multiple dimensions. This literature distinguishes violence from conflict, rejects facile explanations based on surface understandings, and takes seriously the role that "the local" plays in large-scale processes, such as genocide and war (Browning 1992; Bax 1995; Richards 1996; Brass 1997; Hinton 2002; Kalyvas 2003, 2006; Wood 2003; Dean 2004; Lubkemann 2005; Richards 2005; Straus 2006).

The present study contributes to this literature in two ways. First, it raises new questions about the nature of violence that political scientists do not normally ask. Among the questions the book raises is why violence takes the form it does, the answers to which, I argue, help to explain how such violence occurs at all. Second, the book highlights the importance of analyzing the social dimensions of violence as a way to gain a better understanding of the complexities and ambiguities embedded in all political violence. Examining the social dimensions of genocide also helps to locate agency at the microlevel, rather than assuming it away or assigning it to whole groups of actors, such as "the Hutu" or "the masses."

Because this book sheds light on the nature of violence and the actors who commit that violence, it should be of interest to any scholar who seeks better answers to the disturbing question of "why people kill each other in large groups outside the context of a declared intensified war" (King 2003, 432). Because such large-scale forms of killing show no signs of abating in the twenty-first century, policymakers should also be interested in the book's findings. The shocking efficiency with which neighbor-level violence unfolded during the Rwandan genocide suggests that political violence can be deeply embedded in local relations and knowledge, yet at the same time, be highly efficient in its overall destructiveness. Thus, far from acting as a restraint on killing, social ties and interactions can act as propulsion mechanisms, pushing the violence forward by pulling in new participants, creating new targets, and engaging people in public, theatrical forms of killing. The challenge for scholars is to theorize how these processes work at base, not just in the Rwandan context but across settings. Such insights could help to direct policy discussions in more promising directions, since they offer a more accurate view of the dynamics driving violence than macrolevel studies.

The foundations for making theoretically valid comparisons and cogent policy recommendations, however, rest in deep, not surface, understandings of messy and complex realities. Political scientists often underestimate the value of knowledge about the "particular" or "local," assuming such findings to be too closely tied to specific times and places to be generalizable. This assumption is false. Superficial knowledge about such a complex phenomena as genocide leads to cursory comparisons, which in turn, give rise to mistaken conclusions and wrongheaded policies. Understanding the particular, by contrast, is precisely what leads to valid comparisons across cases. Such comparisons promise new and important insights about the nature of mass-level violence in general.

Organization and Scope

To present my argument and findings, I begin at the highest level of analysis and drill down to greater levels of granularity in subsequent chapters. The chapters proceed as follows. Chapter 1 discusses the methods and strategies I used to collect my data and the conditions I encountered in the field. Chapter 2 analyzes the national and international politics that preceded the genocide and situates the meaning of the terms *Hutu* and *Tutsi* in historical context. Chapter 3 examines how local residents in the two research sites describe and explain what occurred in their communities during the period of 1990–94. Chapter 4 examines how ethnicity operated in people's everyday lives as well as during the genocide. Chapter 5 analyzes the configuration and content of social ties in the two research sites and how these ties mediated between the script for genocide and Joiners' performances. Chapter 6 examines how group dynamics pulled Joiners into violence and how killing in groups conferred new forms of identity. The Conclusion outlines the contours of a constructivist theory of mass violence.

No study can hope to explain all the complexities of a single phenomenon. The real world is too big and messy to fit into any single analysis. This book is no different. It offers no grand theories of genocide (if such a thing were even possible), but rather, "neighbor-level" insights that scholars can use to build better theories of ethnic violence and genocide. The book does not explain all behaviors during genocide. It does not explain why some rescued or why some resisted. Neither does it explain why one member of the same family opted to help Tutsi while another opted to kill them. Instead, the book references a range of responses to genocide to craft a clear and compelling argument about the actions of one specific group of actors—Joiners—since it was Joiners who had the most to lose by mass murdering their neighbors and friends. If this book helps to deepen our understanding of this one group, without skirting the complexities and ambiguities embedded in their actions, it will have done its job. For understanding what moves Joiners to violence is an important step in keeping them from joining in the first place.

1

Conducting Fieldwork in the Aftermath of War and Genocide

Different interests tell untruths in different ways, and it is a standard part of the anthropological method to reconstruct a more "objective" picture through careful cross-referencing of "versions" and "interests."

—PAUL RICHARDS, *No Peace, No War*

The community of "Ngali" lies in the southern portion of Rwanda. Its landscape is low rising hills, dotted with thin clumps of trees and fields of coffee, bananas, corn, and other crops. Key vantage points offer panoramic views of the network of back roads and modest homes that fill out the picture. Admiring this landscape in 2004, I found it hard to fathom that only ten years earlier, these same hills were the site of genocide, carried out by local bands of killers who sought to kill every Tutsi in the community and any Hutu trying to help Tutsi. At the same time, it was difficult to imagine how anyone could have escaped the carnage, so unforgiving was the terrain as to render all movement visible.

To the north of Ngali, toward the Virunga mountain range that marks the boundary between Rwanda, Uganda, and the Democratic Republic of the Congo, lies the community of "Kimanzi." Lava from the mountains makes the soil in this region extremely rich and fertile. As is typical for mountainous regions, the climate is cold. Even in the dry season, morning temperatures often call for multiple layers of clothing, at least until the sun comes out and even then, the chilly mountain air cuts through each layer. People from this region are used to the cold and prefer it to the heat of Kigali—those who have actually been to Kigali, that is, for as some residents will tell you, they have never ventured that far south in their lives.

The terrain of Kimanzi is strikingly different from that of Ngali. Where

Figure 1.1 "Ngali" secteur, Rwanda, 2004. Photo by Lee Ann Fujii

Ngali is compact, Kimanzi is spacious. Houses, roads, and fields spread out across a much larger expanse. Indeed, in Kimanzi, it is even possible to achieve that rarest commodity in this, one of the most densely populated countries in the world—privacy. Many houses, for example, are not visible from the nearest road or the closest neighbor's house.

The nearest urban centers to Ngali and Kimanzi are the main provincial towns of Gitarama and Ruhengeri. Each town features an array of small businesses, government offices, banks, post offices, and a central prison, the only "gift," a Rwandan friend joked, the Belgians left behind when they departed the country.

The Belgians built the prison system in the 1930s and the buildings appear to have changed little since that time. One or two guards, sporting rifles that look like they came from the same era, man the main gate where

Figure 1.2. "Kimanzi" secteur, Rwanda, 2004. Photo by Lee Ann Fujii.

vehicles and pedestrians enter. A simple brick wall extends from the main portal, but does not always extend all the way around the prison grounds. At the main prison in Ruhengeri, for example, the brick wall ends where the prison's fields begin, providing unimpeded access to the land where prisoners grow crops for food.

Once inside the gate, one enters the main courtyard, where a variety of activities are usually in progress: a game of volleyball, the odd English lesson, prisoners going to and from their jobs in various prison workshops, while a few others unload supplies from the back of a truck. The most obvious difference between the world behind the gate and the one in front is that those engaged in these various tasks are all dressed in the blush pink uniform of a prisoner. The style and quality of uniforms vary. Most men wear shorts with a short-sleeved, buttoned-down shirt, oftentimes visibly worn. A select few, however, sport uniforms that appear to have been professionally tailored and cleaned, all the way down to their cuffed hems and smartly creased pant legs. It is men in the latter category who greet me in impeccable French.

Inside the courtyard sits an interior building, cut off from the outside world by a windowless steel door. This is the building that houses the inmate population. Since I obtained permission to conduct interviews in the prison courtyard only, I never saw inside this interior space.[1]

Among the imprisoned population are former residents of Kimanzi and Ngali, accused of having been génocidaires. Some have voluntarily confessed to participating in the genocide in the hope of garnering a reduced sentence, while others maintain their innocence. Both confessed and non-confessed prisoners are subject to the same dire living conditions, which include a constant shortage of food, sanitation, and medical care. As more than one prisoner told me, were it not for the assistance of the Red Cross, many prisoners would not even have access to a bar of soap.

In 2004, I spent nine months in Rwanda, the majority of that time in one or the other research community and central prison, asking people what they saw and did during the period of the civil war and genocide (1990–94). I also asked people about their lives before the genocide to understand the broader social context in which the events of 1990–94 took place. Because these interviews provided the bulk of the data for this book, the methods I used to collect the data merit extended discussion.

Selecting Sites and Respondents

In 1990, Rwanda's official population of 7,157,551 was spread out across 10 *préfectures*, 145 *communes*, and 1,490 secteurs (République rwandaise 1994, 8, 12). The government added an eleventh préfecture in 1992, turning the capital city of Kigali into its own administrative unit (Des Forges 1999, 41). The vast majority of the country's 7 million inhabitants lived in the rural hills outside Kigali and made their living as subsistence farmers, cultivating an assortment of staple and cash crops. Some people made extra money working as day laborers in brick factories (André and Platteau 1998, 14; Jefremovas 2002) or as local merchants selling traditionally brewed beer. Fewer still had salaried jobs as teachers or clerks or as low-level bureaucrats in the large party-state apparatus (de Lame 1996).

To understand how ordinary Rwandans made sense of what happened in their communities during the period 1990–94, I chose two rural communities in two different regions of the country: Ngali in the central province

---

[1] For an in-depth look at daily life inside these interior walls, see Tertsakian (2008).

of Gitarama and Kimanzi in the northern province of Ruhengeri. I selected these two communities to capture important historical differences that have long distinguished north from south in Rwanda. The northern préfectures have always had the smallest percentage of Tutsi in the country. The provinces in the center and south of the country, by contrast, have generally had higher proportions of Tutsi than in the north. Each region has also been the home base for a president. Grégoire Kayibanda, Rwanda's first president, heralded from Gitarama, while Juvénal Habyarimana, Kayibanda's successor (through a coup), came from Gisenyi in the northwest.

In addition to historical, political differences, the two regions also had very different experiences of the war and genocide. People in Ruhengeri (in the north) experienced the civil war between the RPF and Rwandan government forces (FAR) firsthand, and from the very beginning of the conflict. The first mass killings of Tutsi in Ruhengeri took place in January 1991 after an RPF attack on the main town. People in Gitarama, by contrast, had no direct experience of the war or mass killings of Tutsi until the plane crash that killed President Habyarimana on 6 April 1994.

Because of these differences, I expected the two sites to provide diverse, perhaps even competing, accounts and explanations of the period 1990–94. My field research, in many ways, confirmed this expectation.

The selection of the precise sites where I conducted my interviews was based on two factors, one methodological, the other practical. Because I was interested in violence committed by neighbors against other neighbors, I sought communities that were mostly rural, since urban centers tend to be dominated by higher-level authorities, such as *préfets*, who, in turn, have access to different types of armed resources (such as communal police). To help to ensure that my research sites were not dominated by provincial-level authorities or elites, I chose communes within each province that were located outside the main provincial town. While this strategy did not guarantee that the two sites were more rural than urban in their orientation (since the remotest hills in Rwanda still maintain connections to urban centers, including the capital [de Lame 1996]), it helped to focus attention on local, and not just town, elites.

Within the two selected communes, I chose two secteurs (the administrative unit just below a commune as shown in figure 1.3) that were within a thirty-minute drive of the main paved road. I call the two secteurs I chose "Kimanzi" and "Ngali." I use pseudonyms for most place names below préfecture and for all the people who talked to me to protect their identities.

The most significant demographic difference between Kimanzi and Ngali is the relative and absolute number of Tutsi in each locale. As table 1.1 shows, the number of Tutsi in Kimanzi was extremely small—around

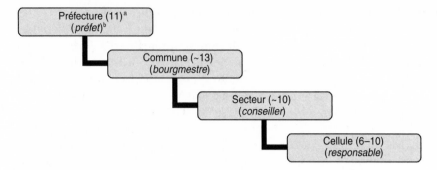

Figure 1.3 Administrative hierarchy in Rwanda in 1990–94
[a]Number of units contained in the unit above. Thus the number "11" next to "Préfecture" means that in 1994, the country was comprised of 11 préfectures, each of which included approximately 13 communes.
[b] Head of the administrative unit.

twenty-five or so people according to the 1991 government census. This figure also matched residents' estimates. The small number of Tutsi in Kimanzi necessitated going beyond the immediate research site to talk with Tutsi survivors from neighboring secteurs in order to obtain a more detailed picture of what occurred in the area. Tutsi from neighboring secteurs were fair proxies for Tutsi from Kimanzi in terms of their experiences during the period of the civil war and genocide (1990–94), since most Tutsi fled in similar directions and at similar times. In Ngali, the number of Tutsi was much larger, but even here, I included three people who fled to Ngali from other secteurs. Having fled to Ngali, these people could also provide an important vantage point on how violence unfolded in Ngali and neighboring areas.

Ngali and Kimanzi secteurs were each made up of six to seven *cellules.* A cellule is comprised of roughly one hundred households. Because of the small number of Tutsi in Kimanzi, there were cellules that had no Tutsi whatsoever. In Ngali, by contrast, there were Tutsi in all six cellules.

Across the two sites, I conducted 231 semistructured, individual interviews with 82 different people (37 people in Kimanzi and 45 in Ngali).[2] In addition to one-on-one interviews, I conducted two group interviews, one in each research site.[3] (See table 1.2 for the breakdown of interviews in

2. In reality, the number of interviews and interviewees was slightly higher. In my data analysis, however, I excluded six interviews with six different people because the six did not live in or flee to the two research sites during the period of the war and genocide (1990–94).
3. In one group interview, there were six men; in the other, there were three. The first took place in Kimanzi secteur and the second in the central prison for Ngali.

Table 1.1 Official 1991 population figures for the two research sites

	Kimanzi (Ruhengeri)	Ngali (Gitarama)
Préfecture population	767,531[a]	851,288[b]
Commune population	55,000[a]	75,000[b]
Secteur population	5,000[a]	3,500[b]
Number of households in *secteur*	900[a]	700[b]
Average household size for *secteur*	5[a]	5[b]
Percentage of Tutsi in *préfecture*	0.5[c]	9[c]
Number of Tutsi in *secteur*	25[d]	315[d]

Source: *Recensement général de la population et de l'habitat au 15 août 1991, Résultats provisoires* (République rwandaise, décembre 1991); *Résultats définitifs* (République rwandaise, avril 1994). Figures below *préfecture* are rounded to protect identities.
  [a] Tableau 4.2.15. Répartition de la population résidante selon le sexe et le secteur, le nombre et la taille moyenne des ménages (1991), 79–84.
  [b] Tableau 4.2.15. Répartition de la population résidante selon le sexe et le secteur, le nombre et la taille moyenne des ménages (1991), 58–63.
  [c] Tableau 4.2. Répartition (en %) de la population de nationalité rwandaise selon l'ethnie, la préfecture ou le milieu de résidence (1994), 124.
  [d] Calculation based on percentage of Tutsi in *préfecture* × population of the *secteur*.

Table 1.2 Breakdown of interviews by research site

	Kimanzi (north)		Ngali (center-south)	
	Number of interviews	Number of informants	Number of interviews	Number of informants
Secteur	67	26	78	28
Prison	41	11	45	17
Total	**108**	**37**	**123**	**45**

each site.) All of the people I interviewed had lived in one or the other community (or neighboring community in the case of "Kimanzi" respondents) at the start of the civil war in 1990, except for three people who fled to Ngali at the start of the genocide.

Of the eighty-two people I interviewed, twenty-eight were in prison at the time of my field research, all accused of having participated in the genocide. Sixteen of the twenty-eight prisoners I interviewed had taken part in a government program that offered the possibility of a reduced sentence to prisoners who voluntarily confessed their participation in the genocide. At the time of my fieldwork, none of the confessed prisoners I spoke with had had his dossier processed, so all had yet to benefit from the program. Of the twelve prisoners who did not confess, two had already been sentenced (one to life in prison and the other to death); the remaining ten maintained their innocence and thus elected not to confess.

Rescuing   Resisting   Witnessing   Evading   Pillaging   Denouncing   Killing

Figure 1.4 Spectrum of responses to genocide

The research design drew its inspiration from Kristen Monroe's (1991; 1996) work on altruism. To investigate altruistic behavior, Monroe constructed a continuum of rational behavior, anchored by self-interested actors at one end and selfless (altruistic) actors at the other. To study mass-level participation in violence, I constructed a spectrum of responses to genocide. At one end of the spectrum, I placed the least or anti-violent response, which I identified as "rescuing," and at the other, the most violent, which I identified as "killing." In between those two poles I hypothesized a wide range of responses, including refusing to participate in the violence (resisting); witnessing without taking part in the violence (witnessing); avoiding participation in the violence (evading); turning people in to authorities (denouncing); and pillaging property (pillaging). I arrived at some of these categories prior to going to the field; others emerged during the course of the fieldwork, as I learned from people's testimonies the kinds of actions people actually took during the genocide. What the spectrum provided was a way to think both deductively and inductively about the actions people took or could have taken during the genocide. Figure 1.4 shows the spectrum of responses to genocide that guided the research.

I used a purposive selection strategy to find people whose experiences represented as much of the spectrum as possible. The people I interviewed included those who killed, rescued, and resisted as well as those who pillaged, profited, and protested; people who fled the violence as well as those who stayed put; prisoners who confessed their participation in the genocide and those who maintained their innocence; people imprisoned during the war and genocide (1990–94) and those imprisoned afterward; people who claimed to know little about what happened and those who claimed to have seen everything. Missing in this group were some local leaders of the genocide, many of whom were already dead by the time of my fieldwork or living in exile. In these cases, I queried others about them. The goal of these and other strategies (discussed below) was to capture a wide range of vantage points to ensure that the data did not privilege any single perspective, such as, for example, the perspective of survivors, who had but one view of the violence. A random selection strategy could not guarantee this type of broad perspective.

Among the people with whom I spoke, I tried to achieve a balance of men and women and a diversity of ages. I was only partially successful at achieving gender balance. In both research sites, male respondents outnumbered female respondents by four to one. The reason for the gender imbalance is that many women did not volunteer to be interviewed, claiming they were too busy to talk or had nothing to say. Men, by contrast, were generally, though not always, more available and willing to talk with me.

Respondents' ages ranged from thirty to eighty at the time of interviews, making the youngest person I interviewed twenty-one and the oldest in her seventies at the time of the genocide. Ages are imprecise because some respondents gave different birthdates at different interviews.

One age cohort I sought out specifically was those born before 1950. I wanted to talk to people who were old enough to remember the seminal events of 1959–61, when political violence first took center stage in Rwanda. Older people, I reasoned (and my interviews confirmed), had lived history and thus had more stories to tell. I was also interested to see if those who lived through past periods of violence drew links from past events to the more recent genocide. Some people made a link, though others did not. Age seemed to be a defining factor as no one born after 1950 ever drew a link. As one younger respondent told me, for example, comparisons of the RPF invasion to cross-border raids by Tutsi exiles in the 1960s meant nothing to him, since the war with the RPF was the first he had ever known. Thus, in order to probe the extent to which people linked past episodes of violence to genocide, I had to find people who were old enough to have lived through these events, or alternatively, find people who were familiar with past episodes through stories passed down from older people. I found few of the latter, which suggests that older people do not generally pass down stories of past violence, or, if they do, that the younger generation did not think to share them with me or did not think of them when talking to me about the genocide.

One criteria that I did not use for selecting people was ethnicity. One reason was that government policy at the time forbade any talk of Rwandan ethnicity publicly and privately. This meant it was not possible to ask a person directly if she was Hutu or Tutsi, or to ask for people by ethnicity when asking local authorities to suggest people who might be willing to talk with me. And because Rwandans all speak the same language (Kinyarwanda), live in the same face-to-face communities, dress similarly, share the same names, it is not possible to deduce a person's ethnicity from looking or talking to her or knowing her name. In addition, religious identity does not coincide with ethnic identity in Rwanda. Put simply, choosing people according to their ethnicity was not possible had I wanted to do so.

The other reason for not using ethnicity as a selection criteria was methodological. Because I was interested in understanding participation in the genocide, my priority was to gain the widest representation of responses possible—regardless of the actors' ethnicity. Not knowing people's ethnicity also had its advantages. It forced me to ask questions I would not otherwise have asked. The fact that no one told us up front what their ethnicity was did not mean that I and my interpreter did not make assumptions about people's ethnic identity. In fact, we made assumptions all the time. It was through asking a person about a topic other than ethnicity that I would discover my assumptions were wrong. Not knowing helped to unmask mistaken assumptions. This process of unmasking, in turn, gave rise to richer forms of data than those I would have collected had I simply known the person's ethnicity beforehand.

Choosing an Interpreter

To conduct the type of fieldwork I set out to do required finding the right research assistant who would serve not only as a French-Kinyarwanda interpreter during interviews, but just as important, as a cultural translator and guide in all phases of the research. Based on consultations with numerous colleagues and friends, both *muzungu* (foreigner) and Rwandan, I decided that my ideal candidate would be someone whose ethnicity was not obvious from appearances so that neither Hutu nor Tutsi respondents would feel reluctant to talk with us.[4] I also needed someone who had lived through the war and genocide. After the RPF victory, hundreds of thousands of Rwandans who had been living abroad since the 1950s and 1960s returned to live in Rwanda. Hiring a returnee presented many potential problems. A returnee would have been identifiable as an outsider by all sorts of visible cues, such as mannerisms, dress, and even language (since many returnees speak languages other than Kinyarwanda and are sometimes more comfortable in these other languages). As an outsider, a returnee would not have been familiar with the political terrain in Rwanda, particularly at the local level. A returnee may also have been exposed to ideologies espoused by those in the larger

---

4. *Muzungu* is a term that originally meant "European" or "white person" but over the years, has come to take on broader meaning. It can be used to refer to any Westerner, white or nonwhite. It can also be used to refer to a Rwandan or African who is rich or presumed rich because of his or her connections to Westerners. As one respondent, for example, described a wealthy neighbor: "He was a *muzungu* who lived in Kigali."

exile community, which may have biased him or her against certain segments of the Rwanda population.[4] Potential respondents, in turn, were likely to view a returnee (and by extension, the researcher) as aligned with the RPF-led government.

Other considerations mattered as well. Based on the advice of one colleague, I tried to find someone who would be comfortable working in a rural setting; this meant finding someone who had grown up in the countryside and not in Kigali. I also wanted someone who had life experience of his or her own and was not right out of college. Older women, one colleague explained, will feel more comfortable talking to someone closer to their age. Finally, I wanted to find someone who was adept at navigating the bureaucratic and administrative relations necessary to do my research. I was extraordinarily lucky to find a person who fit all these criteria and more. My interpreter was a Rwandan woman (who prefers to remain anonymous) in her thirties who had grown up in the countryside and had worked in all parts of the country. She came to me through a referral, but it was clear from all the interviews I conducted with potential interpreters that she was the best fit for me and my project.

From our earliest moments together, my interpreter showed herself to be quite skilled at putting people of all backgrounds at ease, through a deft combination of friendly humor and professionalism. In addition, her ethnicity was not obvious from her appearance. She fit none of the stereotypes of Hutu or Tutsi (see chapter 4 for a discussion of stereotypes). Since I could not ask my interpreter her ethnicity directly, a Rwandan colleague suggested that I ask her how she lived through the period of the war and genocide. My interpreter answered that she had lost family on her mother's side during the genocide and family on her father's side after the genocide. The combination of losses indicated that she was of mixed parentage, which made her an ideal interpreter for this project.

Hiring the right interpreter was critical because the quality of data depended almost completely on the types of relationships we were able to build not only with respondents but also local officials, who could either facilitate or hamper our access to the community. People's difficulty at pinpointing various elements of her identity, not only her ethnicity but also her age and marital status, was a good indicator that her comportment during interviews did not betray any sympathies or prejudices she might have had for one group or segment over others. This neutrality was

---

4. See, for example, the memoir of Béatrice Marie Umutesi (2000), who encounters some of these ideologies and prejudices when she meets other Rwandans while studying in Brussels.

crucial to her ability to gain people's trust and was therefore critical to the success of the project as a whole.

Confronting Subjectivity

In addition to the importance of people's perceptions of my interpreter and her identity, I quickly became aware of how my own subjectivity shaped the kinds of questions I was able to ask and the kind of access I was able to gain with certain people. By subjectivity, I mean my own background and status vis-à-vis the people in my two research sites—the fact that I was American and female, for example—and the ways in which people, in turn, perceived and constructed my identity, including my ethnicity.

Being an obvious outsider allowed me to ask questions that might have seemed too obvious, and thus suspicious, if posed by a Rwandan. In the aftermath of the genocide, talking about the past was a dangerous act. People were afraid of being falsely accused and imprisoned. One woman I talked to was still visibly angry about having been imprisoned on charges that she had participated in the genocide. When I asked her why she had fled as the RPF was advancing toward Ngali, she snapped back angrily at my interpreter, "Don't you know?" This show of emotion was extremely rare for Rwandans who value keeping their emotions inside. My interpreter replied that the questions were coming from me, not her. Hearing this, the woman calmed down and began answering my questions. As this example illustrates, people did not expect an outsider like myself to know the same things as an insider. This assumed ignorance allowed me to ask the most basic kinds of questions, which enabled me to probe the foundational logics underlying people's understandings of the world—how things were and how they were meant to be. Asking the obvious helped to bring these logics to light.

Being a woman working with a female interpreter also helped me to establish certain forms of rapport that would not have been possible had I been working with a male interpreter or had I been a male researcher myself. After talking to some women multiple times, for example, the interviews ceased being structured, formal enterprises and took on the quality of friendly conversations among a group of women friends or acquaintances. At the start of one interview, for example, the respondent asked me whether I had ever tried a particular Rwandan dish. When I said I had not, she left the room and promptly returned with a large helping, which the three of us proceeded to devour, all the while chatting in a mixture of Kinyarwanda and French.

I do not mean to exaggerate this aspect, as this shift in tone and atmosphere did not happen often; but neither do I mean to dismiss it, for I took any level of rapport as an indication that we were collecting data that would have been beyond our reach had the relationship remained exclusively formal. For example, the same woman who fed us our impromptu lunch also commented that I was not like other *bazungu* (plural of muzungu), whom she then parodied with a vivid impression of a fastidious and standoffish foreigner. We all laughed at this display. Laughing over a common joke and sharing a meal were indicators that we were building relationships. The payoff often came right before or right after the start of the interview, when respondents would share gossip with us about their closest neighbors or additional details about themselves. It is hard to imagine these moments arising without having established some level of rapport beforehand.

In addition to perceiving me as an outsider, people often perceived me as being half Rwandan (or *métisse* in French). Being métisse did not constitute me as an insider by any means, for my status as a muzungu, or Westerner, far outweighed any possible Rwandan parentage. What it did do, however, was make my identity a source of wonder or curiosity for respondents. In some research settings, such ambiguity might have had a distancing effect as people would have wanted to know the precise identity of the researcher and researcher's assistant before talking with them.[6] In my case, however, my dual status as muzungu and possible *umunyarwanda* (Rwandan) opened the door to questions that related directly to the kinds of data I was seeking—questions about what constitutes identity, in general, and what constitutes Rwandan identity, more specifically. The only difference is that it was my identity that served as the focal point for these discussions, not the identity of the respondent. By referencing my identity, I was able to ask different questions than if I were talking about the respondent's identity. I could ask people, for example, what they thought my ethnicity was (apart from being a muzungu) and why they thought I was one ethnicity and not another. Because these discussions often came up in a lighthearted or joking manner, I felt freer to probe people's ideas about ethnicity at length, without worrying about whether the topic was making them wary of me, given the government's ban on talk of ethnicity.

Interview Protocol

Before starting my fieldwork, I obtained official permission from the Ministry of Internal Security and the Ministry of Local Government,

6. I thank Richard Grinker for this point. See, too, Tone Bringa's (1995) discussion about her need to live with a single family during the duration of her research in a mixed Croat-Muslim village in Bosnia-Herzegovina, rather than splitting her time between one Catholic and one Muslim household.

Community Development and Social Affairs. Following protocol, my interpreter and I then introduced ourselves to authorities at each administrative level for our research sites and left copies of our letters of authorization with each official or his or her representative. We began by introducing ourselves to the préfet of each province, then proceeded to the *maire* of each district (formerly the *bourgmestre* of the commune), and finally to the *conseiller* of each research site. Though we always introduced ourselves to the conseiller, we did not always meet with every *responsable* for the six to seven cellules that made up each research site.

To locate people to interview, we worked through local authorities and other long-time residents. Based on very general criteria I specified, these people would recommend and facilitate introductions to individuals to whom we might talk. After completing the first round of interviews, we also began seeking out people whose names had come up repeatedly during interviews, without divulging how we had come across their names. The rare occasions when people asked, my interpreter responded that the local responsable had given us their name. Since the responsable is supposed to know everyone in his or her cellule, it would not come as a surprise to anyone that he or she suggested names to us.

Oftentimes, men whose names came up repeatedly in interviews were dead or living in exile. In some of these cases, I used a second-best strategy of interviewing the wives, assuming the wives were in a privileged position to know about their husband's activities during the genocide, and perhaps, had even participated in them directly.

Working through intermediaries meant that no one ever turned us away when we arrived for our first interview (since the intermediaries had already gained initial consent). I was not concerned that the intermediaries were pressuring people because in at least one case, the person declined the intermediary's invitation to talk with us.

In only one case did a respondent avoid us after the first interview. Ironically, this man was a Tutsi genocide survivor, so I assumed he had nothing to hide, but as often occurred, my assumption turned out to be wrong. During our first interview, the man greeted us with a show of hospitality. After that, he avoided us, despite our repeated attempts to track him down through his wife and the local responsable. I finally gave up trying to find the man and started asking others about him. By all reports, the man was not well-liked, even before the genocide. After the genocide, the new RPF-backed authorities named him the new conseiller of the community. Using his newfound authority, the man worked with former Interahamwe to have many people, both Hutu and Tutsi, imprisoned and killed. His victims included family members as well as friends. The man also threatened other genocide survivors if they refused to make accusations against people he was targeting. His motive, everyone told me, was greed, not revenge. What this experience taught me was the importance of not assuming (as I often did) that "genocide survivors" had nothing to hide, for here was a genocide survivor who had as much, if not more, to hide than many of the confessed killers we had interviewed.

We conducted all interviews in Kinyarwanda, the native language of all Rwandans. I posed my questions in French; my interpreter then translated them into Kinyarwanda and the respondents' answers back into French. While a few respondents did speak French fluently, we opted to do all interviews in Kinyarwanda because Kinyarwanda is the language in which everyone, even the most educated, thinks and feels. In addition, my own basic understanding of Kinyarwanda, from private lessons with a Rwandan teacher before I left for the field and from working exclusively with Rwandans while in the field, helped me to recognize key words and expressions, which I tried to use in my own questions whenever possible.

We conducted interviews in people's homes or in the home of a centrally located resident where people knew to find us. In the prisons, we conducted interviews in a private room or a private area in the main courtyard. No matter the location, we always asked anyone within earshot (including household members and other prisoners) to leave, a request people always honored. Everyone seemed to understand our need for privacy; our high social status may also have made it difficult for people to refuse.

We worked weekdays only and avoided market days because people were usually not at home on those days. We split our time evenly between each site, spending one week in one location and the following week in the other. By dividing our time this way, people could expect to see us as regular fixtures for a certain period, but also count on regular breaks from our visits.[7]

At the start of interviews, my interpreter gave a full introduction of both of us as well as a detailed explanation of our project. She introduced me as an American Ph.D. student working on her doctoral dissertation and herself as my interpreter. She then explained the entirety of the project, not just the portion of which the respondent was a part. This explanation took several minutes and included assurances that we would not share the person's testimony with any authority or reveal their identity in any piece of writing. One reason for giving such a lengthy explanation up front (besides to obtain informed consent) was to demonstrate that we had nothing

---

7. I thank Danielle de Lame for this excellent suggestion and the reasoning behind it.

to hide—that we were who we said we were. Accurate and detailed self-pre-sentation is especially important in conflict settings where suspicions of others, particularly outsiders, can run very high (Peritore 1990; Sluka 1990)

At the end of these introductions, we asked for the person's consent and after obtaining verbal consent, I always asked the person if she or he had any questions for us. At subsequent interviews, we always reobtained consent. So strict were we about obtaining consent at every interview that some respondents nearly took offense. At the third interview with one prisoner, for example, the prisoner responded with palpable exaspera-tion: "If I didn't want to talk to you, I wouldn't be here!"

Gaining the cooperation of local authorities and the consent of respon-dents was particularly important in light of my overall research strategy. My strategy was to go back to the same people and talk to them multiple times over the course of the six-month interview period.[8] I used a "funnel" method to whittle down the number of people with whom we spoke at each round of interviews since time constraints did not make it possible to speak with all eighty-two people multiple times. In the first round, we spoke with eighty-two people; in the next round, we spoke with a subset of that original number; in the next round, a subset of the previous subset, until, by the end, we had spoken to a handful of people (seven to nine) in each research site multiple times (five to nine).

I used multiple criteria to decide with whom to continue interviews. At each round, I tried to make sure that I was talking to people whose expe-riences covered a broad range of responses to the genocide. If a person's experiences matched those of others I had already interviewed, I would not continue with that person. I used other criteria as well. Some people were difficult to find or seemed bored by the interview process. In these cases, I decided not to expend too much time or energy pursuing these people. At the same time, I tried not to use "ease of interview" as my cri-teria for continuing with people as that would have steered me toward only the most outwardly articulate or likable. And articulateness or likabil-ity did not necessarily indicate any level of forthrightness on the part of the respondent.

The reasoning behind the strategy of multiple interviews was that over time, people would become more comfortable with us, and thus more forthcoming. The strategy seemed to pay off. In later interviews, I was able

---

8. I was in Rwanda a total of eight and a half months. The first two months were spent se-lecting research sites, obtaining permissions from ministries, hiring an interpreter, taking language lessons, and working out the logistics of conducting fieldwork in two different sites.

to probe sensitive topics in detail, such as issues of ethnicity. With multiple interviews, I was able to glean information that I could not have collected in a one-shot interview or through survey questions, such as crimes to which confessed killers had not formally confessed. Another key advantage of this strategy was that I was able to apply what I learned from one interview to other interviews. This process of learning sometimes involved discovering a better way to phrase a question or, other times, pursuing the same line of questions with multiple people as a way to triangulate responses and to ferret out more details.

My goal in triangulating people's responses, however, was not to adjudicate between competing versions of events to determine which version was true and which was false, but to determine areas of convergence, overlap, or disagreement. Convergence did not necessarily indicate greater veracity, as collective memories often coalesce around a consensus version of events (Portelli 1991). With prisoners, especially, I expected prison culture to give rise to a stock account of events, particularly since most of the prisoners with whom we spoke had been in prison at least eight years, some nearly ten.[9] What is more, at the time of my fieldwork, the government had begun cracking down on people who it believed were espousing a genocidal ideology, or *divisionisme*. In such a milieu, people likely thought twice about saying anything that could be construed as *divisioniste*. This political reality meant that while the government may have encouraged prisoners to confess to their participation in the genocide (as a way to relieve the immense backlog of genocide cases), it may have also discouraged any talk of ethnic hatred or divisions, past or present.[10] The advantage of the strategy of repeat visits was that it could get beyond any consensus narratives that existed and perhaps bring to light areas of consensus silence as well.

Another advantage of the strategy of repeat visits was that at subsequent interviews, I would ask people if they had any questions for us before starting. Often these questions were requests for assistance of some kind. Prisoners often asked us, for example, whether we could help expedite the prosecutor's review of their legal dossiers. People living in the two research sites often requested financial aid to pay for medicine, school fees for their children, or household items they needed. I refused all requests, many with great reluctance. My interpreter did a masterful job of explaining that my university as well as Rwandan authorities did not authorize me to engage in such activity. To the prisoners, I explained further that I was not a lawyer and had no connection to the legal system in their country

9. I thank David Newbury for this point.
10. I thank Alison Des Forges for this point.

and hence, had no authority to help them with their dossiers. After explaining why I could not help them, I often reobtained consent to make sure people were not talking to us only because they believed they would be rewarded in some way. No one ever refused to talk to us after we explained that we could not help them, which assured me that their participation in the interviews had not been forced on them by their personal circumstances.

Some of the richest data we collected came from the questions people asked us about who we (my interpreter and I) "really" were. In the two research sites as well as the prisons, rumors about my interpreter and me were rife. They ranged from entertaining to serious. The most Hollywood-worthy was that I was the long, lost daughter of a local woman who had had a baby with a muzungu (Western) man. This woman had since died and I was supposedly the prodigal daughter returning to her natal hill.[11] Other rumors were more serious, however, and indicated the level of fear and mistrust that permeated my research sites (and presumably all parts of the country). One woman with whom we spoke several times told us that both she and her neighbors believed we were there to question people for the *gacaca* process that was scheduled to commence shortly throughout the country.[12] People were afraid of the gacaca, she told us, because they feared they might be imprisoned for what they did or did not say, or what they did or did not do during the genocide. After observing me and my interpreter make our bimonthly trek to the woman's house over several months, her neighbors, the woman later told us, came to see us not as threatening officials, but as friends dropping by for a visit. The woman herself likened our interviews to talking to a pastor or priest (a much less menacing analogy), because we always came for short visits, then left, then came back again. Being aware of the suspicions our presence raised made us look for ways to allay people's fears whenever we could. One way to do this was to keep showing up when we said we would. The regularity of our visits seemed to make our presence less remarkable, and hence less worrisome, to respondents as well as their neighbors.

Finding ways to allay people's fears and to build a measure of trust and rapport was crucial to the kinds of questions I wanted to ask people. The

11. Hill, not village, is the common referent for a person's place of origin in Rwanda (De Lame 1996; C. Newbury 1988).

12. The Rwandan government introduced *gacaca* as a form of community-based justice in which a panel of locally elected judges and the community at large would try those accused of genocide who came from the same community. The initiative began in June 2002 with a pilot program of select communities. It was scheduled to begin nationwide in 2004. Neither research site participated in the pilot program, and the program had not yet started in the rest of the country by the time of my fieldwork in 2004. For background on gacaca, see Waldorf (2006).

focus of my interviews was twofold. First, I asked people what they remembered about the period of 1990–94 and why they thought people behaved the way they did. "Why did your neighbors help your family hide while other neighbors did nothing?" was a question I asked one survivor in Kimanzi, for example. Answers to these questions provided insight into what these events meant to those who experienced them. Too often studies of ethnic violence impose meaning onto complex situations, rather than explore what the events mean to the people who lived through them. Through these interviews, I sought to move beyond imposed or assigned meanings to find out how the people themselves constructed the past and where and how they placed themselves in these narratives. Did the people who lived through these events see the killings as acts of hatred, for example (as countless observers had argued), or did they see them as a manifestation of some other force?

The second set of questions I asked related to key domains of daily life. These domains included how people were disciplined as children, how they were treated at school, how they chose their marriage partners, and how they made or lost friends. I focused on these everyday domains because they involve nearly universal human experiences and because they provided a window into people's personal histories—how social relations of various kinds shaped and formed them. Because telling one's "life history" is not a cultural form in Rwanda, I chose to focus on a common set of life domains for purposes of comparability. These narratives of daily life highlight what the speaker takes for granted and what she thinks is unusual. People remark on the unusual; what they take for granted, by contrast, literally goes without saying. This juxtaposition between what is said and what is left unsaid points to the importance of the "white spaces," or silences, in the data. While we can never be sure what the silences represent, we must nonetheless try to analyze what they might be "saying," for the silences can evoke as much information about the juxtaposition or continuities between daily life and the genocide as the words themselves. Silences can give a clue as to which parts of daily life were subsumed by the violence and which parts continued in a different guise. Throughout the chapters that follow, I try to interpret these silences in the context of what people do say.

Interpreting Narratives of Violence and Daily Life

Interpreting narrative data or any kind of text, as historians and anthropologists know all too well, is not about determining Truth with a capital T. It has to do, instead, with contextualizing the data or placing them in a larger picture. In the present study, my strategy for contextualizing the data is to examine one set of narratives against the backdrop of other narratives. These other narratives might include other interviews with the same person or interviews with a specific group of actors, such as Joiners. Contextualizing the data also involves examining their meaning or possible meanings within the framework of historical conditions and institutions.

Contextualizing the data is crucial to understanding the range of possible answers people could have given to a particular question. This range is not boundless; it is circumscribed by cultural norms and understandings, which make certain scenarios imaginable and others beyond imagining. (Indeed, it was the limitations of my own imagining that often led to my faulty assumptions.) Understanding this range, in turn, helps to identify patterns in the answers people do give.

Contextualizing, however, does not tell us anything about the quality of the data themselves. As one colleague asked me, Why would people talk to you? While the question is apt, I would rephrase it to read: What reason did people have to say one thing to me instead of another? The answer to this question is different for different people. Many people like to talk about themselves while others do not. Many like to gossip about others, while others prefer to remain circumspect. Those who like to talk about themselves might volunteer more details than a person who does not. There is also the factor of time. Ten years after the events in question, people get things wrong. They forget. They embellish. They lie. They equivocate. In fact, everyone with whom I spoke had good reason to do any or all these things—not just those people who had obvious reason to lie or withhold, such as suspected génocidaires. In my experience, there was no group of people who had nothing to hide, just as there was no group who had reason to hide everything. Most, if not all, people fell somewhere in between these two extremes.

Because of the vagaries of memory, the passage of time, and incentives to deviate from or adhere to certain narratives, we cannot judge the quality of the data by the truths or accuracies contained within them (Fujii forthcoming). Instead, we must treat the data as repositories of shared meanings and understandings about how the world works. Interpreting these data thus involves identifying patterns of meaning or what I call the "logics" that underlie people's statements about the genocide as well as daily life. How people talk about the world—whether true or not—gives clues as to how they make sense of that world—how it is and how it ought to be. These logics form a type of causal knowledge. They reveal themselves through repetitions as well as contradictions and silences. Even when people lie, they do so based on the same basic understanding of how the world works and what should or should not happen. Thus, even within the bounds of the data, it is possible to identify and analyze the system of meaning that people used to navigate daily life as well as the extraordinary events of 1990–94. Understanding people's logics helps to explain why they did what they did, for as Monroe (2004, 276) points out: "How we make sense of the world and our place in it guides how we act and how we understand other actors in our world."

Interpreting silences is but one step in that process. Silences may indeed embody "the speaker's view of what is canonical" (Monroe 2001, 494)—something so obvious that it goes without saying. Silences, however, can also signal the need for the speaker to keep certain things to herself. As Kay Warren (1998) points out, "strategic ambiguities" always arise in narratives about war and violence. Often, such ambiguities are not invitations to probe more deeply, but rather subtle admonishments to the researcher to respect certain topics as "off limits." As Liisa Malkki (1995, 51, citing Feldman 1991, 12) remarks about her own fieldwork experience in the 1980s interviewing Burundi refugees living in Tanzania:

> The success of the fieldwork hinged not so much on a determination to ferret out "the facts" as on a willingness to leave some stones unturned, to listen to what my respondents deemed important, and to demonstrate my trustworthiness by not prying where I was not wanted. The difficult and politically charged nature of the fieldwork setting made such attempts at delicacy a simple necessity; like Feldman, I found that "in order to know, I had to become expert in demonstrating that there were things, places, and people I did not want to know."

Like Warren, Malkki, and others who have studied war and violence up close, I, too, never pressed anyone to talk about anything he or she did not want to discuss. When I encountered hesitation or resistance, I used the opportunity to ask questions about entirely different topics to demonstrate my willingness to respect the respondent's boundaries. By doing so, I hoped that the respondent would begin to trust that I would leave it up to her to revisit these topics in her own time. This is precisely what happened with one woman. She was the wife of the leader of the genocide for Ngali. I interviewed her only because her husband had already died. Throughout our many interviews, she refused to say anything about the period of the genocide, insisting she took to bed the whole time until the family fled to the Congo. At first, I thought her refusal to talk about the genocide was because she did not want to implicate herself or her husband. Over time, however, I came to believe that her refusal was bound up in a palpable fear of what her neighbors would find out and what the impending gacaca trials would reveal. Everyone was afraid, she told us, of being falsely accused and sent to prison. At our very last interview, however, as she walked my interpreter and me to the car, she started to talk about the period of the genocide with my interpreter. What she said was not filled with any new details; yet, the gesture gave me confidence that she had come to trust us and that what she had told us up until that moment was also an expression of that trust.

This example is a reminder that despite the reasons people had to lie or withhold, they nonetheless did agree to talk with me, many multiple times, knowing there was no payment or reward for them and that they risked raising the suspicions or jealousies of their neighbors by doing so. The task of the researcher, then, is to sift through and analyze the data as they come, while keeping in mind the particular circumstances in which they arose.

It is to an analysis of these data that we now turn.

2

Violence and Identity in Historical Perspective

L'ethnie n'est pas éternelle, elle est historique.
—DANIELLE DE LAME, *Une colline entre mille ou le calme avant la tempête*

There is a common assumption that underscores much of the literature on ethnic and mass violence—that ethnicity is the master cleavage that structures political and social relations. The ethnic hatred and ethnic fear models work directly from this tenet. Both assume the primacy of ethnic division and conflict in causing violence. Applied to the Rwanda case, both would expect the cause of the genocide to reside in the conflict between Hutu and Tutsi. This logic would lead the analyst to look for some fundamental, perhaps insurmountable, ethnic divide that precipitated and eventuated in genocide. For why else would one group try to exterminate the other?

In this chapter, I argue against a strictly ethnic reading of events and put forth a more nuanced story of the macroprocesses and conjunctures that led extremists to seize on genocide as a strategy for holding on to power. In this alternative version, the principal conflict is not between Hutu and Tutsi as corporate entities, but between elites of the same ethnicity who use violence to divert attention away from the real threats to their power. I situate this argument historically to show how even in the past, before and during the period of colonialism in the first half of the twentieth century, ethnicity was not the ever-present master cleavage standard approaches assume it to be. Rather, I show how "Hutu" and "Tutsi" started out as social labels and gradually took on ethnic meaning under a process of state expansion, which did not originate with European colonizers, but came to full flower under colonial force.

The emergence of ethnic identities, however, did not overtake other equally important cleavages. Throughout the colonial and postcolonial period, regional identities continued to be important. In the 1980s and 1990s, political divisions pitted those committed to democratic reform against those adamantly opposed to such change. These political alle-agiances were cross-cut by a complex and sometimes unexpected combi-nation of ethnic and regional interests, such that political moderates (the majority of whom were Hutu) initially opposed the Tutsi-led RPF, but later, allied with it. Rather than being a simple conflict between Hutu and Tutsi, the real contest was between those who wanted to hoard power and those willing to share it. The story of genocide was thus not one of ethnic conflict—old or new—but an even older tale of power and politics.

Prelude

Rwanda was not an obvious place for genocide to take place. Under the stewardship of President Juvénal Habyarimana, who had come to power in a coup in 1973, the country had become a model for African develop-ment. It was orderly, safe, and relatively free of corruption. The people were hard-working, churchgoing, and "suitably" grateful for any and all outside assistance (Prunier 1995, 81). From 1975 to 1980, the economy grew at the impressive rate of 8 percent per annum as measured by GDP (United Nations Department of Economic and Social Affairs nd, 325), a remarkable feat given that 95 percent of the population made its living as farmers in one of the most densely populated countries in the world. For its many successes and attributes, Rwanda became the darling of interna-tional donors. In a period of twenty years, the amount of aid flowing to the country grew tenfold (Bertrand 2000, 22).[1]

In addition to a sound economy, ethnic relations, too, were peaceful under Habyarimana. On taking power, the new president put an end to anti-Tutsi violence. Many Tutsi businessmen even flourished under Habya-rimana, so much so that some even saw Habyarimana as favoring Tutsi (Reyntjens 1994, 35–36).

Crisis and Decline

By the late 1980s, Rwanda's model image was beginning to fall apart. World prices for coffee, the country's main export, fell precipitously, re-sulting in famine, widespread unemployment, a severe drop in govern-ment revenues, and the bitter medicine of structural adjustment.[2] Worse, democracy had become the new *cause célèbre* for Western states, which, hav-

1. Citing a 1998 Belgian government report, Bertrand (2000, 22) notes that aid to Rwanda grew from $35 million in 1971–74 to $343 million in 1990–93. On the role that in-ternational donors unwittingly played in "aiding violence" in Rwanda, see Uvin (1998).
2. As David Newbury (1999, 33) notes, coffee prices on the world market fell by over 50 percent in the 1980s. The fall in prices drastically reduced government revenues, which, in

ing just witnessed the end of communist rule in Eastern Europe and the fall of the Berlin wall, began adding conditions to their aid. Where before, money and arms flowed freely to the Rwandan government, a one-party state since its inception, donor countries began calling for political reform and liberalization. Even France, Habyarimana's staunchest ally and supporter, began attaching democratic strings to its packages of aid.[3]

At the same time, calls for democratization began mounting within the country. A small but growing number of elites began calling for Habyarimana to open up the political space to multiple parties. The first public call for democratic change was a letter entitled "Pour le multipartisme et la démocratie," signed by a group of thirty-three prominent individuals, which included journalists, engineers, bankers, and lawyers (Bertrand 2000, 52). The drafters sent their letter to the president in September 1990 (Reyntjens 1994, 104, Bertrand 2000, 50). In the letter, the authors never spoke of "Hutu" and "Tutsi" but argued instead that the only division the Rwandan people were suffering was socioeconomic, the result of the regime's hoarding of power (Bertrand 2000, 55).

Habyarimana, aware of the mounting discontent with his regime, tried his best to steer the reform process himself. In July 1990, Habyarimana announced an "aggiornamento politique," a policy shift that would result in a new constitution to be unveiled on 1 July 1992, the thirtieth anniversary of Rwanda's independence (Reyntjens 1994, 90–91). A few months later, on 24 September 1990, Habyarimana formed the Commission Nationale de Synthèse (CNS). Two of the commission's tasks were to identify how the Rwandan population understood the concept of democracy and to draft an outline of the new constitution (Bertrand 2000, 44; Reyntjens 1994, 91). On 11 November 1990, Habyarimana announced he would begin allowing opposition parties to form (Prunier 1995, 122). On 10 June 1991, parliament passed a new constitution, which officially granted people the right to form political parties (Prunier 1995, 126; Reyntjens 1995a, 266).

All these moves were intended to show the people that the "father of the nation" had been reborn a democrat (Gasana 2002). By controlling the process of reform, Habyarimana hoped to forestall the demise of his nearly

---

turn, reduced the amount the government paid farmers for raw coffee, thereby cutting the income of the average coffee farmer. Economic decline and increasing poverty was also perceptible at the microlevel. As André and Platteau (1998, 28–29) found, for example, growing inequalities and increasing levels of absolute poverty (as measured by daily caloric intake) were detectable even over a relatively short period of time, from 1988 to 1993.

3. France held an Afro-Franco summit in La Baule (France) in June 1990, where it announced that henceforth, French foreign aid would depend on the recipient country's progress toward democratization (Bertrand 2000, 20).

twenty-year reign. A move towards multipartyism would mean the end of the MRND, the party that Habyarimana not only created, but embodied. This made the personal and political stakes one and the same. So as Habyarimana gave with one hand, he took with the other. After forming the CNS to chart a new political path for the country, the president stacked the commission with close allies. In spite of these efforts, the CNS released a report in December 1991 that supported the widespread calls for political reform (Bertrand 2000, 47).

Despite Habyarimana's attempts to thwart change, a vibrant opposition emerged quickly. The party that posed the greatest threat to the president was the MDR (Mouvement démocratique républicain), a reincarnation of PARMEHUTU, the party founded by Rwanda's first president, Grégoire Kayibanda. Like Kayibanda's original party, the new MDR was founded by Hutu elites from the central province of Gitarama. This was no accident. Ever since the northerner Habyarimana had ousted Kayibanda in a coup in 1973 and banned Kayibanda's original party, southern and central Hutu were looking for the next opportunity to regain their former position of power and privilege. The historical north-south rivalry was emerging once again.

In contradistinction to the original PARMEHUTU, which Kayibanda had fashioned as a fundamentally Hutu party, the new MDR tried to present itself as a party for all Rwandans (Bertrand 2000, 94). The party's stated position was to move beyond the ethnic and regional politics of the MRND and address the issues that affected everyone. As one MDR founder explained: "For the reformers of the MDR-Parmehutu, it was obvious that the current political problem was not the oppression of the Hutu by the Tutsi, but the oppression of the Rwandan people of all ethnicities by a group that had acceded to power by force and was determined to stay there" (Nsengiyaremye 1995, 249).

In addition to the MDR, other opposition parties began to form. They included the PSD (Parti social démocrate), a center-left party based in the southern préfecture of Butare, and the PL (Parti Libéral), a center-right, urban-based party that attracted many businesspeople, including several prominent Tutsi. While many parties were rooted in specific regions of the country, all shared one goal—to bring an end to the one-party rule of the MRND. Through a newly emerging free press, the parties began voicing their criticisms of the regime, drawing new supporters along the way.

Amidst rising activity in the political sphere and shrinking activity in the economic, a new crisis erupted. On 1 October 1990, the Rwandan Patriotic Front (RPF), a rebel army comprised of mostly Tutsi exiles whose families had fled Rwanda in the late 1950s and 1960s, invaded from

Uganda.[4] With the help of French, Belgium, and Zaïrean troops, Rwandan government forces were able to push the invaders back into Uganda by the end of the month. Despite what appeared to be a quick victory for the regime, the war revealed yet another flank where Habyarimana was vulnerable.

Notwithstanding the shock of the invasion, the war (which the RPF continued to prosecute guerrilla style) did provide the regime with opportunities it would not have otherwise had to bring the reform process to a halt and to keep itself in power. The regime cast the invasion as an "ethnic war" (Bertrand 2000, 99) and used every weapon in its arsenal, from mass arrests to political assassinations and organized massacres, to refocus people's attention on the "real" enemy—the RPF.

At the same time, however, the war also helped to strengthen the opposition in its stance against the regime. While the MDR initially gave unanimous support to the government's fight against the RPF, it refused to go along with the government's framing of the conflict as an "ethnic war" (Bertrand 2000, 100). Instead, the MDR cast the war as part of a broader set of long-standing political problems that the Habyarimana regime had badly mismanaged. According to the MDR, the war was further proof of the regime's incompetence at dealing with the most pressing issues facing the country, not the least of which were the 600,000 or so Rwanda refugees living in neighboring countries and demanding their right of return.[5] Over the years, Habyarimana had either denied a refugee problem existed or refused to allow a mass return, agreeing to individual resettlement only.

The MDR also continued to exert pressure on the regime. When the party held its first public rally on 11 August 1991 at the stadium in Nyiramirambo in Kigali, more than four thousand people gathered to hear MDR leaders extol their party's ideas for reform and change. The proposal for a National Conference, where the nation could openly debate the

---

4. The justification the RPF gave for the armed invasion was the overthrow of a corrupt and authoritarian regime in the name of all Rwandans. As Mamdani (2001, chap. 6) argues, however, the reason for and timing of the RPF's invasion had less to do with corruption in Rwanda, and more to do with internal politics in Uganda, which had made the Banyarwanda ("Rwandan people") in Yoweri Museveni's regime a political liability, despite the key role they played in helping to bring Museveni to power in 1986. For insight into the timing of the invasion, see Gasana (2002, chap. 3).

5. The figure is Prunier's (1995, 63) estimate. Newbury and Newbury (1999, 302) cite 400,000 to 600,000 refugees living in neighboring countries. See, also, Mamdani's (2001, 160–61) discussion of the range of estimates of Rwandan refugees living in the Great Lakes region in the 1990s.

problem of ethnic and regional cleavages and the prospects for democracy, garnered the loudest applause (Bertrand 2000, 103).

The MDR also began to move away from its position of nominal alliance with the government in its fight against the RPF, as it became clear to MDR leaders that the regime was using the war as a pretext for silencing the opposition in order to halt the reform process altogether. Two of the regime's preferred methods were extremist media and organized violence.

Shortly after the RPF's invasion on 1 October 1990, the regime sought to make "ethnicity" the sole lens through which people viewed the country's problems. In public speeches, radio programs, newspaper articles, and vulgar political cartoons, the regime sought to paint the RPF, and by extension all Tutsi, as a foreign race bent on retaking the country by force. As early as 22 November 1990, for example, only six weeks after the RPF's invasion, Radio Rwanda, the state-run radio station and the only station in the country, warned listeners that "since their [Tutsi's] goal is to exterminate and enslave us, we must not feel any mercy towards them" (Article 19 1996, 29).

A second method for silencing the opposition involved the use of organized violence. The targets were invariably political opponents of the regime, both Tutsi and Hutu. Days after the RPF invasion on 1 October 1990, the regime staged a fake attack on Kigali. Shooting took place throughout the early morning hours of 4 October 1990, though there were no casualties and only little damage. The regime pinned the supposed attack on the RPF and cited this breach of security as the pretext for arresting four to eight thousand political opponents as "accomplices" (Bertrand 2000, 58).[6] Among those arrested were many Tutsi intellectuals whom the justice minister at the time characterized as enemy accomplices, reasoning that "for an attack of this scale to take place you have to have people you can trust. Only through Rwandans belonging to the same ethnic community could this possibility materialize" (Lemarchand 2000, 7).

A week after the faked attack, the regime organized a massacre in the commune of Kibirira in the northern préfecture of Gisenyi. Under orders of local leaders, residents killed more than three hundred Tutsi and burned five hundred houses to the ground (Fédération Internationale des Droits de l'Homme 1993; Prunier 1995, 110). In January 1991, following an RPF attack in the area, another massacre of Tutsi occurred, this time in the adjacent préfecture of Ruhengeri. More civilian attacks followed in 1992 and 1993. The regime carefully planned and organized all the mas-

---

6. Reyntjens (1994, 94) estimates 6,000 to 7,000 detained; Prunier (1995, 108) and Braeckman (1994, 113–15) 10,000. Des Forges reports that one FAR police major told her that the number was closer to 13,000 (personal communication, 2 February 2008).

sacres, which took place in well-chosen sites, usually Habyarimana strongholds where the regime could be "sure of success" (Des Forges 1999, 87). Perpetrators were rarely punished, and when they were, the sentences were relatively mild. In one case, for example, a gendarme was found guilty of involvement in the murder of an Italian aid worker who had lived in the region of Bugesera for twenty years. For his role in the woman's murder, the man was sentenced to one year in prison (Reyntjens 1995a, 268–69). An atmosphere of impunity only served to heighten people's fears.

The government framed the killings as spontaneous and angry attacks by locals on their Tutsi neighbors who were allegedly supporting the RPF (Prunier 1995, 139, 143). The massacres enabled the government to characterize any further moves toward democratization as a "slide toward anarchy" (Prunier 1995, 144).[7]

The MDR and other opposition parties, however, refused to relent in their criticism of the regime. On 17 November 1991, the main opposition parties signed a common memorandum that outlined the regime's intransigence in enacting real democratic reforms (Prunier 1995, 134). Habyarimana parried by asking his new justice minister, Sylvestre Nsanzimana, to form a new cabinet (Reyntjens 1994, 109). On 31 December 1991, Nsanzimana was sworn in as the new prime minister, along with a new cabinet that featured only one person from the opposition, a member of the PCD (Parti chrétien démocrate), which, at the time, was a satellite party of Habyarimana's own MRND (Nsengiyaremye 1995, 253).

Dissatisfied with the new cabinet, the opposition took to the streets and began organizing mass protests in cities throughout the country—a first for the country. The first march took place in Gitarama on 7 January 1992. The next day, more than fifty thousand people marched in Kigali. On 11 January 1992, there were more protests in Butare (Bertrand 2000, 141). Another protest was planned for 15 January 1992 in Kigali. Local authorities tried to stop the march, but organizers were still able to mobilize some twenty thousand people. The sheer size of this gathering made the president realize that "his power really was contested by a majority of the population and that authoritarian pressures would no longer work" (Bertrand 2000, 142).

Under these growing pressures, Habyarimana accepted an agreement with the main opposition parties, now united in a common front against the regime, in March 1992. The agreement called for a new government to form, with the premiership going to the MDR, the largest of the

7. There is evidence that the government's tactics were working as planned. Results from a survey students took in Kabgayi (Gitarama) in September-October 1991 showed that multipartyism was not the priority for people, but rather, finding a way to end the war and the economic crisis (Bertrand 2000, 124–25).

opposition parties. The agreement also called for the government to begin peace talks with the RPF. On 7 April 1992, a new cabinet was sworn in under the new prime minister, Dismas Nsengiyaremye, a prominent member of the MDR (Prunier 1995, 145; Nsengiyaremye 1995, 254). In the following months, government representatives also began talks with the RPF (Prunier 1995, 150).

All was not smooth sailing. The Habyarimana regime, and in particular, the tight inner circle centered around Habyarimana's wife, Agathe, nicknamed the *akazu*, or "little house," in Kinyarwanda, was not going down so easily. In March 1992, a new party formed called the CDR (Coalition pour la défense de la république), which was overtly racist and adamantly opposed to the peace talks that had begun with the RPF. As the peace talks continued throughout the second half of 1992 and into 1993, the MRND and CDR protested how the negotiations were going (Prunier 1995, 163), at one point calling the agreement "a plan for treason" (Des Forges 1999, 96).

For its part, the RPF did little to counter extremist messages about its true aims. On 8 February 1993, the RPF violated a cease-fire, attacking along the northern front in the region of Byumba (Des Forges 1999, 109; Prunier 1995, 174). The opposition, which had been cooperating with the RPF since May 1992, felt betrayed. To its erstwhile allies, the RPF seemed more intent on exacting victories on the battlefield (to gain leverage at the bargaining table) than negotiating in good faith. The RPF's relentless aggressions gave further credence to extremist message that the rebel army was not out to share power, but to seize it by force.

On 4 August 1993, under intense international and regional pressure, Habyarimana signed a peace agreement with the RPF. The Arusha Accords, as the agreement came to be known, ended the three-and-a-half-year civil war. The accords set the terms for integrating the two armies and for power sharing among the major, political parties. It also laid out an ambitious timetable for installation of a broad-based transitional government to be comprised of members from all political parties, except the CDR, which the RPF argued was not, properly speaking, a political party but simply the extremist wing of the government's MRND party.[8] As with most major points in the agreement, the RPF prevailed.

---

8. Ironically, outside mediators pressed the RPF to compromise on this issue. The Americans and Tanzanians, in particular, argued that it was better to bring hardliners inside the government where they could be managed, than leave them outside where they could wreak havoc (Jones 1999, 70–71). Even the Ugandans, the RPF's main backer, supported the American and Tanzanian position and urged the RPF to accept the hardliners into the transitional government and to cede less control over the armed forces. The RPF, however, held firm. For an excellent analysis of the peace process, see Jones (2001).

Despite constituting a victor's peace for the RPF, the Arusha Accords marked a milestone. For the Rwandan population, peace and democracy seemed, at long last, to be within reach. Any optimism would be short-lived, however. Two months later, events in neighboring Burundi would eviscerate any hopes that the Arusha Accords would bring lasting peace and stability to Rwanda. On 21 October 1993, Tutsi army officers in Burundi assassinated their country's first democratically elected Hutu president, Melchior Ndadaye. The force of this event reverberated across the political spectrum in Rwanda. The immediate impact was to split all opposition parties into pro-extremist "Hutu Power" factions and moderates. Moderates and hardliners within each party then fought over the seats the accords had assigned to their party, which delayed installation of the transitional government by several months.

In the meantime, political moderates started moving toward the extremists' camp, which painted the assassination in apocalyptic terms, arguing that it stood as undeniable proof that Tutsi were the same everywhere and would do anything to regain power (Jones 2001). The RPF's bland statement of regret over Ndadaye's murder and the warm welcome it gave to Ndadaye's assassins in Kampala (Uganda) fed into the extremist's depiction and alerted once moderate politicians that their alliance with the RPF was no more than a marriage of convenience for the rebel army, and a very temporary one at that (Prunier 1995, 201–2).

In the wake of the Burundian president's assassination, the first contingent of United Nations (UN) peacekeepers arrived to oversee implementation of the Arusha Accords. In the following months, both Habyarimana and the RPF continued to find reasons to delay installation of the transitional government, which caused UN Force Commander Roméo Dallaire to threaten withdrawal. Finally, in early April 1994, President Mwinyi of Tanzania persuaded Habyarimana to attend a summit in Dar es Salaam, ostensibly to discuss the crisis in Burundi. Habyarimana's fellow heads of state, however, used the opportunity to convince the Rwandan leader to implement the peace accords for the sake of regional stability.

Trigger for Violence

Whether Habyarimana had planned on heeding his colleagues' advice remains unknown. On the evening of 6 April 1994, Habyarimana was arriving home from Dar es Salaam in his private Falcon jet, a gift from the French government. On board was a small coterie of the most powerful men in his regime as well as the new Burundian president, Cyprien Ntaryamira, who had been attending the same meeting. As the plane made its final descent to the main airport in Kigali, the runway lights suddenly went out. The French pilot immediately aborted the landing but as he began to pull the plane up, assailants fired two missiles from a nearby hill. One missile was a direct hit. The plane crashed, killing everyone on board.[9]

The shooting down of the president's plane was, to put it mildly, a momentous event. It set in motion violent responses from both the hardliners and RPF. Presidential Guard, an elite force trained and armed by the French, secured the crash site, forcing a stand-off with the Belgian troops that Dallaire had sent to investigate. The next day, 7 April 1994, the six hundred RPF troops that had been cantoned at the Parliament building, awaiting installation of the transitional government, took defensive positions in a few locations. The civil war would soon start in the capital. In the northern provinces of Ruhengeri, Byumba, and the eastern region of Gabiro, fighting broke out immediately (Dallaire 2004, 269).

Within hours of the crash, specially trained militia,[10] soldiers and Presidential Guard began going to door-to-door with lists of targets. At the top of the lists were Hutu opposition leaders, including the prime minister, Agathe Uwilingiyimana (Des Forges 1999, 188–89). Others on the list included journalists, human rights activists, and anyone—Hutu or Tutsi—not firmly in the extremists' camp. State agents killed those on the list and anyone else who happened to be home at the time. As Jean-Pierre Chrétien (1997, 92) describes:

> It was a veritable St. Bartholomew of all those, Hutu as well as Tutsi, who represented the opposition and the logic of peace of Arusha: ministers of the transitional government, judges, priests, journalists, democratic activists not won over by the logic of "Hutu power," all duly noted on the lists and slaughtered, often with the rest of their family.[11]

So efficient were the killers in eliminating the opposition—the majority of whom were Hutu—that within twenty-four hours of the crash, there were no prominent opposition figures left to help steer events in a more moderate and less violent direction. This left Dallaire to negotiate with the self-appointed interim government, led by hardliners from Habyari-

9. This version of events came from a personal communication (6 June 2004) with Major Brent Beardsley, who served as executive assistant to Dallaire in UNAMIR, the UN peacekeeping force for Rwanda.

10. The two main militia groups trained and recruited in Kigali were the Interahamwe, formed by the MRND, and the Impuzamugambi, formed by the CDR. Interahamwe recruits had received training the previous summer and were armed with grenades as well as kalishnakov rifles (Chrétien 1997, 94).

11. All translations from French language sources are my own.

mana's inner circle—the same people many suspected were behind the president's assassination.[12] Whatever the real truth, one thing was clear to Dallaire. This was the group that was now firmly in charge and behind the massacres taking place all over Kigali. As Dallaire (2004, 232) summed up: "In just a few hours the Presidential Guard had conducted an obviously well-organized and well-executed plan—by noon on April 7 the moderate political leadership of Rwanda was dead or in hiding, the potential for a future moderate government utterly lost."

Within hours of the crash, militia and soldiers set up roadblocks throughout the city to inhibit movement and prevent escape. Armed with an assortment of weapons, including machetes, clubs, rifles, and "even the odd AK-47" (Dallaire 2004, 253), those manning the roadblocks killed any and all Tutsi and anyone who "looked" Tutsi (Des Forges 1999).[13]

A week after the assassination, killers began using a new tactic—luring or collecting Tutsi in a single spot, like a church, school, or government building, where killers could attack their victims en masse (Des Forges 1999, 209–10). Though this tactic ostensibly made for more efficient killing (since a single grenade could kill many at once), it actually enabled the killers to kill their victims more slowly, in deliberately painful and humiliating ways. One commonly reported atrocity was the severing of Achilles tendons, a practice supposedly intended to prevent escape, but clearly meant to torture victims, a great many of whom were too young or too old to run (Taylor 2002; Physicians for Human Rights [UK] nd).

Outside the capital, the genocide followed a different path. Violence began at different times in different regions. Those leading the charge included soldiers and militia but just as often, local authorities who used the opportunity of the president's assassination to assert their own authority through violence (Straus 2006, chaps. 2–3). The regions where genocide began earliest were those where support for the president's MRND party was strongest: Gisenyi and Ruhengeri in the north and the capital of Kigali (Straus 2006, 60–61). Other regions, by contrast, particularly those in the south, held off for days, even weeks, due in large part to local leaders who

12. The identity of the assailants remains unknown but at the time, many believed that hardliners were the likeliest culprits (see, e.g., Prunier (1995, 213–29)). I now believe the evidence points more strongly toward the RPF. According to this view, Paul Kagame, then leader of the RPF and current president of Rwanda, ordered the plane shot down as a way to hasten the "transition" (Reyntjens 1995b; Ruzibiza 2005). As Straus (2004b, 57) explains: "A military victory may have seemed more likely and more appealing than a political one."

13. The most common physical stereotype of Tutsi was that they were tall and had long, thin noses, but at the roadblocks, a person's "Tutsiness" was firmly in the eye of the beholder. For a more in-depth discussion of ethnic stereotypes, see chapter 4.

preached calm and unity. In Butare, the préfet was so effective at maintaining calm that the interim government had to replace him with a more genocide-friendly personality and bring in professional killers from outside the region to jump-start the killings. As a result of these concerted efforts, the south, which had always had the highest percentage of Tutsi in the country and reputedly the highest levels of integration between the two groups, experienced some of the worst violence of the genocide.[14]

The genocide ended on 18 July 1994 when the RPF took Gisenyi and declared victory in the country (Prunier 1995, 299). Between 6 April and 18 July 1994, killers succeeded in slaughtering more than half a million Tutsi and some fifty thousand Hutu, a killing rate one observer calculated at "333⅓ deaths per hour" (Barnett 2002, 1).

As this gloss of events shows, contrary to the expectations of the ethnic fear and ethnic hatred theses, the principal cleavage preceding the genocide was not ethnic, but political. It was between those opposed to multiparty democracy and those firmly committed to this aim. A second cleavage was regional, which pitted Hutu elites from the north against rivals from the center-south. Hutu and Tutsi were found on all sides of these divides. Even the mostly Tutsi RPF did its part to confuse ethnic lines. Instead of aligning itself with political moderates to bring down the authoritarian regime of Habyarimana (its stated objective), the rebel army seemed bent on the same goal as the extremists—to seize total power at any price. The political battle thus came down to moderates versus extremists. In this matchup, politics and power trumped ethnic loyalties every time.

Origins of *Hutu* and *Tutsi*

While elites in the capital may not have always followed ethnic lines in their fight for power, perhaps the masses did. Perhaps the Hutu masses, unlike Hutu elites, were more easily drawn to ethnic appeals because of pent-up hatreds they felt toward Tutsi, which had lingered from the past. To search for evidence of such hatred, let us examine the historical origins of the terms *Hutu* and *Tutsi*.[15]

14. For a closer look at the violence in the south, see Des Forges's (1999, 303–591) chapters on Gikongoro and Butare and Guichaoua's (2005) study of Butare.

15. There is a third group in Rwanda called the Twa. Their numbers are extremely small (about 1 percent of the population). The group is largely marginalized in mainstream politics, and Hutu and Tutsi have both treated this group with racist disdain. Because of space considerations, I do not discuss the Twa in any depth.

Official versus Lived History

To inquire into Rwandan history is to wade through an historiography dominated by statist accounts that exaggerate the continuities and reach of Rwanda's royal court. Official oral histories (*ibiteekerezo*), issued by the court, were vehicles for glorifying the Nyiginya dynasty. These were stories of unending conquest and expansion by the Nyiginya, many of which were pure imagination, "cobbled together from a collection of fictitious tales in order to legitimize the Nyiginya dynasty" (Vansina 2004, 44). By conflating the history of Rwanda with the history of the Nyiginya, official accounts served to justify and preserve a social order that placed absolute power and authority in the hands of a single clan.

To preserve this order, official histories claimed a primordial basis for Tutsi rule and superiority. These accounts cast the three groups, Hutu, Tutsi, and Twa, in specialized roles that emanated from each group's unique background. The basic story was that before the arrival of Tutsi, the area was inhabited by scattered groups of cultivators (the Hutu) and forest dwellers (the Twa) and hence had little historical significance or importance. When a group of pastoralists called Tutsi arrived from the north, they quickly conquered the region and its peoples. The Tutsi proceeded to introduce pastoralism, ironworking, culture, and other technological advances, and established a centralized (monarchic) form of government. Hutu were assimilated into this newly ordered state through a system of vassalage that granted Hutu the use of cattle in exchange for labor and gifts. Thus it was the Tutsi—more specifically, the Nyiginya clan—that turned a scattered number of Bantu-speaking peoples into a powerful and cohesive state. As this narrative shows, official histories promulgated a highly biased view that celebrated Tutsi as the group responsible for domesticating, civilizing, then ruling the region we know today as Rwanda. In truth, these histories were more myth than fact (D'Hertefelt 1964, 222; Rennie 1972).

With the arrival of the first European explorers and missionaries in the late nineteenth century, the Tutsi-centric history of Rwanda found a new and receptive audience. It also found a new medium for diffusion—the written word. One of the earliest and most prolific writers was Abbé Alexis Kagame, a Rwandan priest with a passion for history and an equal passion for upholding the ideology of the court. Kagame claimed knowledge of the inner workings of the court, including the ritual codes that defined kingship or the cosmic order on which the people's well-being rested (Newbury 1981). Kagame's writings were highly influential, so influential that European writers failed to take note of the biases replete in his work

(Vansina 1962, 7–9; Newbury and Newbury 2000, 854). While prolific, Kagame failed to take into account competing versions of Rwandan history, particularly regional histories that cast doubt on "the 'migration and conquest' model of kingship" to which Kagame subscribed (Newbury 2001, 279).

Official histories fit European expectations and outlook. From the perspective of these powerful outsiders, Tutsi were indeed fit to lead and Hutu only fit to follow. What Europeans added to this discourse was "scientific" basis for their racialized worldview. Drawing from the Hamitic hypothesis, a pseudo-scientific theory that ranked all races according to each group's innate—that is, biologically determined—intelligence and abilities, Europeans saw themselves at the top of the pyramid and black Africans, at the bottom. In between those two poles were races that approximated European superiority, thereby indicating Hamitic or Caucasian origins traceable to Ethiopia. As Edith Sanders (1969, 530) explains, "Every trace and/or sign of what is usually termed 'civilized' in Africa was attributed to alien, mainly Hamitic, origin." Through this Hamitic lens, Europeans saw undeniable proof of Tutsi superiority in their natural ability to lead, their leaner and taller builds, their longer noses, and lighter skin. From these observed traits, it seemed patently clear to these newcomers that Tutsi were closer to the industrious, intelligent European than to the supposedly dumber, lazier Hutu.

Contemporary historians have debunked this heavily distorted, statecentric reading of the past. In his 1962 essay, "L'Évolution du royaume du rwanda des origines à 1900," Jan Vansina finally put the Hamitic history of Rwanda to rest. As Vansina points out, the content of official histories was always suspect because the standard practice among the *abiru*, the official interpreters of Rwandan history, was to rewrite the past according to present conditions (Vansina 1962, 21). Excised from official accounts were the incessant internal coups and assassinations at the court that belied claims to a long and uninterrupted rule (Newbury and Newbury 2000, 849); the "fundamentally 'Hutu' nature" of many of the court rituals and institutions" (Des Forges 1995, 45); the forms of social and political organization that Hutu kingdoms had established long before the enthronement of the Nyiginya clan (Rennie 1972); and the presence of cattle long before the arrival of Tutsi to the region (Newbury 1995, 4; 2001, 268–69).

European collaboration in maintaining a statecentric history was due not only to a racialized worldview, but also to the skewed sample from which they drew their observations. Many of the physical characteristics and cultural practices missionaries and colonial administrators observed, then generalized to Tutsi and Hutu as a whole, were unique to members of the royal court, who accounted for no more than 10 percent of all Tutsi in the country (Newbury and Newbury 2000, 839). The Nyiginya clan, moreover, had dynastic claim but was not a ruling clan. Not all members of the Nyiginya were royalty just as not all Tutsi were part of the political elite (Newbury 2001, 294n86). The vast majority were farmers and herders, like their Hutu counterparts. In truth, neither Hutu nor Tutsi were homogeneous groups with discrete and stable boundaries, and distinct ethnic histories. Rather, internal variation was the rule.

As this brief overview of Rwandan historiography shows, ideology has been the hallmark of Rwandan history.

Regional Variations in Usage and Meaning. Scholarly work conducted in the 1960s onward challenge official stories of the past. One of the key findings of this recent work is the extent to which the meaning and use of the labels *Hutu* and *Tutsi* varied by region and context. This variation was largely a function of a region's ties to the central court. In areas that had fairly loose or nonexistent ties, locals may not have used the terms at all. In the mountainous regions of the north, for example, where people jealously guarded their autonomy from the central court and all potential "colonizers," inhabitants referred to themselves not as Hutu, but as Bakiga, that is, as a group culturally distinct from other Hutu in Rwanda (Lemarchand 1970, 99; Freedman 1975).

Diaries from the White Father mission at Rwaza in Ruhengeri, founded in 1906, indicate that Tutsi from the region of Mulera also saw themselves as distinct from Tutsi from the rest of the country. In their diary entries, the priests refer to local Tutsi as "Balera" or "people of Mulera," signifying their regional origins, and the Tutsi whom the royal court had recently dispatched to settle the region as "Batutsi" or "Tutsi people." Indeed, one of the earliest diary entries notes the lack of social status that outsider Tutsi had in the local community. The diarist notes that Tutsi from Nduga (the seat of the royal court) "have no authority. No one listens to them" (Diaire de Rwaza 1903–1910, 26 novembre 1903).[16] Decades later, the diarist explains the history of the rivalry between the two groups.

> In the territory of Ruhengeri, there are the old "Balera" Tutsi, like the family of Ruhanga and Kalinda. There are others who arrived in the country from Nduga only in the last few years. The latter do not like the Balera Tutsi for reasons that are not favorable to the Tutsi of Nduga. The most important

16. When referencing the White Father diaries, I use dates of the diary entry, not page numbers because the version I used was a typewritten transcription of the handwritten originals. All diaries are located in the Pères Blancs library on via Aurelia in Rome.

Balera chief is Donati Mulego, oldest son of Ruhanga. For several years, the
banyanduga [people of Nduga] have been doing everything they can so that
Donati is dispossessed. (Diaire de Rwaza 1923–1934, 14 février 1934)

The attempt at dispossession, to which the diarist refers, was tantamount to overthrow. As Des Forges (1986, 317) explains: "The northerners knew that whoever controlled the land controlled the people who
lived on it. Dispossession was a far more powerful sanction than raiding
and burning homes and crops, the usual methods of punishment in the
past." The conflict between the Nduga Tutsi and the local Balera (Tutsi)
chief was clearly a conflict over who would have control and, hence, authority in the region. In this case, the contest was between competing regional, not ethnic, groups.

Studies based on fieldwork conducted in the 1950s through the 1970s
confirmed the extent of regional variation in the meaning of the terms
Hutu and *Tutsi*. Catharine Newbury found, for example, during fieldwork
conducted in the southwest region of Kinyaga (known today as Cyangugu)
in the 1970s, that people living along the Rwandan border used the term
Tutsi, but in a way that did not accord with usage patterns in other regions.
On Ijwi Island in Lake Kivu (a thirty-minute canoe ride to the nearest
Rwandan peninsula in present-day Cyangugu), inhabitants referred to all
Rwandans as "Badusi," while identifying individual Rwandans by their clan
name. Moreover, the Ijwi Island inhabitants were unfamiliar with the term
Hutu despite their long-standing relations with Kinyagans and their inti-
mate knowledge of Rwandan society and practices (Newbury 1988, 11).

In areas where both terms (*Hutu* and *Tutsi*) were in common use, their
meaning tended toward status, wealth, or region of origin, and not ethnicity. Pierre Gravel (1968, 21), who conducted fieldwork in Remera in
southeast Rwanda in the 1950s, described the meaning of the terms this
way: "The origin of the terms Tutsi and Hutu is obscure, but, in fact,
'Tutsi' refers to a 'noble,' as 'Hutu' refers to a 'commoner' and not to different 'tribes.'" As demarcations of status, he goes on to explain, Hutu
and Tutsi were not immutable categories. Powerful Hutu lineages, for example, that had acquired respect and influence amongst neighbors and
the local administration might be "absorbed into the upper class" and its
Hutu origins "forgotten" (Gravel 1968, 170).

Historian J. K. Rennie adds that individual Hutu clients were also
adopted into Tutsi lineages, creating a self-reinforcing or "circular"
scheme. "Successful men (whatever their origin) tended to become Tutsi,
that is, to adopt their identity and way of life. Poor men, or politically un-
influential men, tended to become Hutu" (Rennie 1972, 33). Catharine

Newbury found the same circularity of meaning in Kinyaga. Kinyagans used the terms *Hutu* and *Tutsi* to indicate social and economic status. The use of "Tutsi" indicated a certain level of power and wealth (particularly in the form of cows) and was often associated with the powerful and wealthy who came from central Rwanda (the seat of the royal court).

Newbury points out further that both Alexis Kagame, the first Rwandan to produce written histories of the country, and Monsignor Léon Classe, a prominent White Father priest who served in Rwanda in the first half of the century, also recognized these meanings. As Kagame himself wrote: "According to pastoral law, whoever possesses many heads of cattle is called Tuutsi, even if he is not of the Hamitic race" (Kagame 1952, 96; quoted in Newbury 1988, 253–54n34). Classe made similar observations about the use of these terms.

> It should be noted that the term "Tuutsi" often refers not to origin (descent) but to social condition, or wealth, especially as regards cattle: whoever is a chief, or who is rich will often be referred to as Tuutsi. Frequently also, because of their manner and their language, . . . the inhabitants of the provinces of Central Rwanda, Nduga and Marangara, as well as those of Buganza are referred to as Tuutsi. (quoted in C. Newbury 1988, 12)

As these statements and studies show, *Hutu* and *Tutsi* were terms whose meanings varied by region and context. Those meanings, moreover, were social, not ethnic, in nature, referring to social origin, status, or place of birth.

Expansion of Power and Politicization of Terms. The terms *Hutu* and *Tutsi* began taking on more uniform meaning during the period of state expansion under *mwami* (king) Kigeri Rwabugiri (ca. 1876–95). Rwabugiri was intent on expanding the reach of the central court. His strategy for expansion was to project control outward from the political center by penetrating downward into the everyday lives of ordinary Rwandans, many of whom had never had any previous dealings with the court. To enact his plan, Rwabugiri began establishing a complex network of chiefdoms in formerly autonomous regions, appointing chiefs from the central region whose allegiances and obligations flowed to their superiors, not to the local people (Newbury 1988, 108). One group Rwabugiri was determined to crush was the Bakiga of the north, precisely because of their determination to remain autonomous from centralized forms of control (Turyahikayo-Rugyema 1974, 133).

The changes Rwabugiri enacted strained relations between chiefs and their populations. People started to associate the terms *Hutu* and *Tutsi* with levels of power. As Catharine Newbury (1988, 51; 1978, 21) argues in the case of Kinyaga, a region that had, until that time, remained independent of court influence: "Since the new chiefs were almost invariably of Tuutsi status, the category 'Tuutsi' assumed hierarchical overtones which heretofore in Kinyaga had been of minor significance. . . . Hutu [in turn] came to be associated with and eventually defined by inferior status." This is probably why, she goes on to explain, many of her Kinyagan respondents marked the arrival of the first Tutsi in their region to the time of Rwabugiri, even though Tutsi had migrated to the area a century before Rwabugiri's reign. As Newbury's analysis shows, state expansion changed the political and social context, and thus the meanings associated with the terms *Hutu* and *Tutsi*.

Rwabugiri's expansionist policies, however, were not intended to favor Tutsi as a group. They were developed according to a strict calculus of power and involved not only the appointment of Hutu to important commands but also, the elimination of Tutsi rivals, including Rwabugiri's own mother, wife, and uncle (Linden 1977, 20; Des Forges 1972, 13), whom he had assassinated for "knowing too much history" (Newbury and Newbury 2000, 856n58). Indeed, Rwabugiri was intent in quashing any and all threats to his power, including court ritualists and aristocratic elite (Newbury 2001, 309). Thus policies that did not seek to politicize the categories "Hutu" and "Tutsi" nevertheless had that effect. The arrival of European colonizers following Rwabugiri's death would result in even greater politicization of the terms and greater polarization of the two groups.

Colonial Transformations

German rule began in 1898, shortly after Rwabugiri died in 1895. The German presence was small, no more than five administrators for the entire country (Reyntjens (1994, 17), but with their superior military power, the new invader quickly became an important ally to new mwami, Yuhi Musinga, who ascended to the throne in a palace coup (D. Newbury 2001, 310–11). German firepower helped Musinga to consolidate his power by eliminating rivals and quelling rebellions. The Germans were content to go along with Musinga's wishes, for they, too, sought to standardize the level of state control across the country, which still varied greatly (Reyntjens 1985, 97).

Simultaneous to the Germans' arrival, a third elite entered the country—the Catholic Church. Like the Germans, the White Fathers also tried to establish good relations with the mwami, for their strategy was to convert the leaders so the population would follow in turn. Musinga, however, met their overtures with resistance and hostility. Only under German pressure did he consent to granting the Fathers land for their missions (Des Forges 1969, 178–80). More seriously, the mwami ordered people to shun Christianity. The Fathers' initial isolation resulted in the establishment of a largely Hutu church, since the first recruits were nearly all poor Hutu (Linden 1977, 52).

With Germany's defeat in World War I, the Belgians took control of Ruanda-Urundi, as the territory encompassing present-day Rwanda and Burundi was then known. Like the Germans, the Belgians were impressed by the highly ordered social structure they found, but unlike the Germans, the Belgians made heavy demands on the mwami from the start. Musinga vacillated in his response to his new colonial masters, at times appearing conciliatory and cooperative, at other times resistant and combative (Des Forges 1969, 188–90). The Belgians responded to Musinga's periods of intransigence by taking away more and more of his authority and finally removing him altogether. The Belgians then declared one of Musinga's own baptized sons, Rudahigwa, the new mwami in a ceremony the Belgians conducted in 1931 (Reyntjens 1985, 79–90).

Even before Musinga's deposition, most of the important chiefs had switched their allegiance to the Belgians, recognizing that the mwami was no longer "the top of the clientship chain" (Linden 1977, 157). The shift in alliances resulted in Tutsi nobles finally embracing the benefits of a Western education, so much so that by 1925, the Belgians were able to restrict enrollment at the main government school to Tutsi only. The Belgians' goal was to train the Tutsi elite who would form the nucleus of a colonially administered bureaucracy and the next generation of Rwandan rulers and chiefs. By the mid-1920s, Belgian support for Tutsi supremacy was in full flower.

The Belgians continued the project of state expansion by dismantling the existing system of customary rule and replacing it with their own version. The existing arrangement was a complex, tripartite system of chieftaincies that granted each chief authority over a single domain (cattle, land, or war). The new system replaced the three chiefs (many of whom were Hutu) with a single Tutsi chief (Lemarchand 1970, 72). Many of the newly appointed Tutsi chiefs had no ties to the region to which they were assigned. Indeed, the shortage of Tutsi in the northern kingdom of Mulera forced the administration to "import" Tutsi from the south (Reyntjens 1985, 98–99). The Tutsification of the system of customary rule caused resentment among local people. The new system introduced the concept of "ethnicity" where it had not existed before. In the new political hierarchy, being Tutsi was sufficient basis for claiming power.

Some of the newly appointed Tutsi chiefs wasted no time in exploiting their new position of power and authority vis-à-vis *le bas peuple*. Under the pretext of meeting the demands of the colonial state (which included the collection of head taxes and the provision of men for communal and wage labor), the new chiefs and their cronies used their power "to extract surplus from the common people, or forcibly to create a surplus where there was none" (Newbury 1988, 128). Colonial authorities were reluctant to rein in abuses, which were rife, not wanting to undermine supposedly traditional forms of authority.

One way in which Hutu sought protection from the arbitrary exactions meted out by the Belgian-appointed Tutsi chiefs was through *ubuhake*.[17] Before colonial rule, ubuhake was a way for individuals to seek protection, perhaps even prestige, from a more powerful patron. The symbol of this relationship was the patron's granting of a cow and usufruct rights to his client, who, in turn provided some form of labor (usually agricultural) to the patron. Under colonial rule, however, ubuhake became less of a voluntary relationship and more of a coercive arrangement that would-be clients could no longer avoid (Newbury 1988, 135). Ubuhake, in other words, became simply another form of exploitation.

The "most hated and humiliating" (Newbury 1988, 141) form of forced labor during this period, however, was not ubuhake, but *ubureetwa*, a particularly servile form of clientship that required a client to perform menial services for the local hill chief as payment for use of land (Newbury 1988, 111–12). Under colonial law, ubureetwa became required of all Hutu men except for the small number who had salaried jobs. Ubureetwa came to represent a system of Tutsi dominance and colonial extraction built on the backs of the poorest Hutu (Newbury 1988, 141).

Colonial rule under the Belgians thus resulted in more pronounced concentrations of power at the top which, in turn, created more intense forms of competition among elites, and more pervasive forms of exploitation and discrimination against Hutu as a group. Where before, the lines of difference were most clearly drawn between royalty and nonroyalty (and among nonroyalty, those from different regions), the lines drawn under colonial rule reinforced an "ethnic" basis for the widening gap between those with power and those with none.

Despite the strictures of the Belgian-Tutsi-controlled state, a small group of Hutu was able to pursue higher education through the church seminary, the only way Hutu could obtain a secondary education (Linden 1977, 209; Reyntjens 1985, 229). In this "purely Christian setting," the small group of Hutu seminarians became exposed to the ideals of equality

17. For more extensive treatment on the subject of ubuhake, see C. Newbury (1980; 1988) and Saucier (1974).

and social justice (Linden 1977, 198). On leaving the seminary, however, educated Hutu found themselves shut out from most avenues of social and economic advancement simply because of their "Hutuness." Being systematically denied opportunities to which they felt entitled bred a growing resentment and sense of injustice among this small elite (Linden 1977, 226; Lemarchand 1970, 139).

After World War II, Belgium continued to administer Ruanda-Urundi as a United Nations Trust Territory, but came under increasing pressure to introduce steps toward democratization. On 14 July 1952, the Belgians bowed to the changing times and issued a decree setting out the procedures for the formation of elective councils at the levels of subchieftaincy, chieftaincy, territory or province, and state (Lemarchand 1970, 79–81; Reyntjens 1985, 185–201). Their commitment to overturning the Tutsi oligarchy, however, remained lukewarm (Linden 1977, 230–31).

The battle over who would claim power in the newly independent state began as a contest of competing frames. Loyalists to the Tutsi monarchy began pushing for independence from colonial rule, utilizing the discourse of European discrimination of Africans as a whole. In their "Mise au Point" (Statement of Views), issued in February 1957, shortly before the arrival of a United Nations Visiting Mission to Rwanda, the mwami and the *conseil supérieur* refused to acknowledge systematic discrimination against Hutu (Newbury 1988, 191; Lemarchand 1970, 150). In their official response to the "Mise au Point," which became known as the "Bahutu Manifesto," the Hutu counterelite framed the issue quite differently, charging that this was not a classic independence struggle between Europeans and Africans, but a racial struggle between Tutsi and Hutu. The Hutu's oppressor, the authors claimed, was not the Europeans, but the Tutsi-Hamites. As the UN mission and Belgian authorities were debating whether to remove ethnic designations on identity cards, the authors of the Bahutu Manifesto called for retaining these categories, arguing that such information was necessary for monitoring actual progress in ending discrimination. In their response to the Bahutu Manifesto, the mwami and conservative Tutsi did not deny past injustices, but placed the source of that injustice on external actors—the Belgian colonizers (D'Hertefelt 1964, 229).

Political activity continued apace in the late 1950s with the formation of various political parties in anticipation of the country's first elections. Now, however, it was Hutu leaders, such as former seminarians Grégoire Kayibanda and Joseph Gitera, who began to dictate the content and pace of events. In 1957, Kayibanda formed the Mouvement Social Muhutu (MSM) to promote the objectives articulated in the Bahutu Manifesto (Newbury 1988, 192). Later that same year, Gitera formed l'Association pour la

Promotion Sociale de la Masse (APROSOMA) (Linden 1977, 251–52). While Gitera tried to appeal to all Rwandans, Kayibanda's appeal was mostly ethnic, stressing the need for the "liberation" of Hutu (Newbury 1988, 193).

The Hutu elite also found a new ally in the church, specifically the most recent generation of Flemish-speaking White Fathers who knew firsthand the experience of being treated as second-class citizens in their own country and who were eager to push their program of social Catholicism (Linden 1977, 256–57). The church's weekly publication, *Kinyamateka*, became the main vehicle for disseminating the Hutu elites' views and debating the prominent issues of the day (Linden 1977, 235). One of those issues was ubuhake, a practice which, to many, encapsulated a political system rife with de facto discrimination, even if it was no longer de jure. Though abolished in 1954, ubuhake still dominated the economic realities of the countryside since Hutu who had obtained cattle were still dependent on Tutsi chiefs to gain access to land for pasture (Newbury 1988, 146; 1980, 106; Reyntjens 1985, 207).

The first elections of 1952 and 1956 provided scarce time for campaigning, giving a huge advantage to the Tutsi candidates, who posted overwhelming victories. Shut out from political office, the Hutu elite became increasingly embittered at their inability to break through the Tutsi stranglehold on power (Linden 1977, 231; Lemarchand 1970, 83). The Hutu candidates' poor showing, however, was not just a reflection of Tutsi political advantage; it also revealed the extent to which the Hutu elite were not representative of most Hutu, either in outlook or circumstance. The majority of Hutu were rural peasants whose lives were as different from these educated Hutu as they were from Tutsi chiefs. Regional differences also produced different experiences amongst Hutu. Consequently, no extant corporate Hutu identity existed that could bridge the disparate socioeconomic realities between educated and rural Hutu or supplant regional identities, even as the country began to race toward independence. As René Lemarchand (1970, 93–94) points out,

> Of all the shibboleths that have gained currency about the Rwanda revolution, none has been more detrimental to sound analysis than the presumption of social and cultural homogeneity among Hutu "peasants." . . . On the eve of the revolution the term "Hutu" could no longer be used interchangeably with a single social category.

The real question, then, is how a narrowly based counterelite succeeded at turning majority oppression into majority rule.

Revolution or *Plus ça Change* . . .

The answer was not quick in coming. Different backgrounds and competing interests fragmented the revolutionaries. Northern Hutu leaders were not driven by democratic ideals but by their long-standing distrust of outsiders and a desire to return to a way of life unencumbered by any outside control or influence. Central and southern Hutu, by contrast, were driven by the yawning gap between rising expectations and sinking prospects (Lemarchand 1970, 103). For their part, some of the Hutu masses showed themselves resistant to change. For many, challenging the system of Tutsi rule was tantamount to overturning the natural order of things. Many Rwandans had internalized the precepts of Tutsi superiority. As one elderly respondent from Helen Codere's sample commented: "The Hutu ought to be dominated. The one who is the strongest and the most intelligent dominates" (Codere 1962, 72).

What helped to unify the masses and the Hutu leadership behind the common cause of revolution was the growing intransigence of the conservative Tutsi elite who, aware of the Belgians' newfound support of the nascent Hutu regime (an about-face from the Belgians' original position), began pushing for independence as a way to ensure the continuation of the monarchy and the privileges emanating therefrom. A statement issued in May 1958 by a group of elderly Tutsi in the mwami's court encapsulated the view of the most conservative and helped to galvanize anti-Tutsi sentiment. In their address, the authors claimed "there could be no basis for brotherhood between Hutu and Tutsi" because when Kigwa, the ancestor of the Banyiginya (the Tutsi clan that had ruled Rwanda for centuries), conquered the country, he had reduced the Hutu to a state of servitude (Lemarchand 1970, 154).

In 1959, political activity picked up pace. A Tutsi conservative named François Rukeba established a new party called Union Nationale Rwandaise (UNAR) to further the interests of those still loyal to a system based on the premise of Tutsi superiority. UNAR's message was clear: the king may be dead (Rudahigwa had died unexpectedly in July 1959) but the monarchy lived on. That same year, a well-respected, progressive Tutsi chief named Prosper Bwanakweri formed Rassemblement Démocratique Ruandais (RADER) as a moderate alternative to UNAR; but the party never gained much of a following. A month later, Kayibanda folded his original party, MSM, into a "more tightly knit organization" which he called Parti du Mouvement de l'Émancipation des Bahutu (PARMEHUTU) (Lemarchand 1970, 160). It was PARMEHUTU that would emerge victorious at the upcoming communal elections in the summer of 1960 and would lead the country to independence six months later.

Before PARMEHUTU's victory at the polls, however, came the riots of November 1959 or what Lemarchand (1970, 159) and Reyntjens (1985, 196, 235) call the *jacquerie*, evoking the parallel to the peasant revolts in fourteenth-century France. What sparked this modern-day revolt was news that a group of young UNAR militants (monarchists) had attacked and killed one of the few Hutu subchiefs in the country. While the attack was real, the victim's death was not. A group of Hutu in Gitarama acted on the erroneous news and went to the house of a local Tutsi subchief, known for his arrogance, and killed him along with two other Tutsi notables. The riot and violence spread across the country; the hardest hit areas were Gitarama, Ruhengeri, and Gisenyi. Perpetrators burned and looted thousands of Tutsi homes, though generally, spared people's lives (Reyntjens 1985, 260).

In the aftermath of the violence, resentment toward Tutsi chiefs reached such a pitch that many were forced to resign, particularly those in the northwest. Others were arrested and killed. The Belgians did little to restore the authority of the Tutsi chiefs; instead, Special Resident Logiest instructed local Belgian authorities to depose as many of the unpopular Tutsi chiefs as possible (Newbury 1988, 197). The administration then filled the vacancies with interim Hutu appointments, many of whom showed little to no aptitude for administrative leadership (Lemarchand 1970, 173–74). This did not deter Logiest, for the colonel was firmly committed to "accelerat[ing] the politicization of Ruanda." At a meeting of local officials in January 1960, Logiest made Hutu rule official policy (Reyntjens 1985, 278).

As the communal elections of June-July 1960 neared, violence became almost routine. Both sides engaged in rampant acts of arson as a way to discourage voting or to intimidate supporters of the other side (Lemarchand 1970, 179–80). The elections proceeded amidst vast irregularities and blatant fraud. PARMEHUTU emerged the clear winner, capturing 71 percent of the vote (Reyntjens 1985, 283).

Despite PARMEHUTU's overwhelming victory, Hutu state creation was no smooth affair. As a closer examination of the results showed, Hutu identities remained tied to tradition and did not extend much beyond the most immediate groupings, such as family and clan (Lemarchand 1970, 182). Part of the problem was that the party itself was highly fragmented; at the time of the elections, no less than fifteen PARMEHUTU splinter groups existed. Another problem was the situation created by Logiest's unconditional support of the newly installed authorities, who wielded almost total control over local affairs. Flush with their newfound authority, many of the new Hutu *bourgmestres* took it on themselves to manufacture revolutionary spirit where it was not already in place. The most common method was to intimidate Tutsi. In some areas, Tutsi were subject to arbitrary arrest and imprisonment. In other areas, the bourgmestres would create disturbances as a pretext for retaliations against Tutsi. Such tactics drove thousands of Tutsi to flee to neighboring countries or for less hostile regions in Rwanda. Each exodus proved profitable to the bourgmestres since it enabled them to dole out the abandoned property as gifts or keep it for themselves.

The use of anti-Tutsi violence to foment Hutu solidarity eventually backfired. The Hutu peasants themselves became resentful of the excesses of power exhibited by the Hutu bourgmestres, who were using the same exploitative tactics as their Tutsi predecessors, such as bribes and intimidation, to build loyal followings. The discontent many Hutu felt toward the Hutu bourgmestres resembled that which they had felt toward the abusive Tutsi chiefs. This was discontent over abuses of power, not the holders of power per se. It was only when the holders of power became synonymous with their abuses that dissatisfaction shifted to the group as a whole, be it Tutsi or Hutu. Thus, as support from below began to wane and factionalism above continued, PARMEHUTU leaders began to fear their revolutionary project would abort prematurely, even before they had achieved independence.

The Belgians, however, ensured a rapid transfer of power from the Tutsi monarchy to PARMEHUTU leaders, by facilitating "the coup of Gitarama." On 28 January 1961, 3,126 communal conseillers and bourgmestres assembled in the town of Gitarama to hear former seminarian Joseph Gitera declare the abolition of the monarchy and the birth of the newly independent Republic of Rwanda (Lemarchand 1970, 192–93). Fellow seminarian and PARMEHUTU leader, Grégoire Kayibanda, was named the country's first president. The elections of September 1961 made the declaration official and the United Nations granted Rwanda its formal independence on 1 July 1962.

While the coup appeared to consummate the upending of a highly entrenched and highly discriminatory social order, serious doubts remained as to the magnitude of change that had actually taken place. A UN report issued in March 1961 summed up the situation in prophetic terms:

> A racial dictatorship of one party has been set up in Rwanda, and the developments of the last eighteen months have consisted in the transition from one type of oppressive regime to another. Extremism is rewarded and there is a danger that the [Tutsi] minority may find itself defenseless in the face of abuses. . . . Taken as a whole, the political situation in Rwanda is distinctly disquieting. (quoted in Lemarchand 1970, 194–95)

Competition between elites continued. Almost immediately, the north-south rivalry reemerged in full force. Northerners were once again the Achilles heel of the southerner-run state. The most powerful interest group of the north, the *abakonde* (northern landowners), succeeded at retaining their traditional rights and privileges over their land. But abakonde political victories did not translate into a cohesive "northern political consciousness," for northern politics was also rent with numerous cleavages that ran along class and lineage lines (Lemarchand 1970, 233).

One development that did succeed at uniting all factions in the early days of independence were the *inyenzi*—literally "cockroach"—raids that began in 1961. Carried out by small bands of Tutsi exiles who remained committed to the restoration of the monarchy, the raids triggered violent reprisals against Tutsi living in Rwanda. The worst attack took place on 21 December 1963, when insurgents crossed the border from Burundi and came within twenty kilometers of Kigali. The government's reaction was swift. Authorities rounded up twenty Tutsi leaders affiliated with UNAR (the promonarchy party) and RADER (the more moderate alternative to UNAR) and executed them en masse. The government then granted emergency powers to ministers and local authorities to do whatever was necessary to counter attempts at "internal subversion." Local authorities formed civil defense units. In the southern province of Gikongoro, Hutu armed with clubs and spears killed approximately five thousand Tutsi. The killings spread quickly to other locales and when the rampage finally ended, some ten thousand to fourteen thousand Tutsi had lost their lives (Lemarchand 1970, 225).

The effect of the massacres on the new regime was salubrious. As one official admitted at the time: "Before the attacks of the inyenzi the government was on the point of collapse. We were faced with enormous dissensions among ourselves. Not only have we survived the attacks but the attacks made us survive our dissensions" (Lemarchand 1970, 227).

The unity was short lived. In an attempt to sustain cohesion, Kayibanda tried a mixture of intimidation and control. To eliminate the threat of rival parties, he pressured local authorities to switch their party affiliation from APROSOMA (the moderate party founded by Gitera) to PARMEHUTU (the exclusively Hutu party Kayibanda had founded) (Lemarchand 1970, 234), a tactic that various party leaders would use again in the early 1990s. In addition, Kayibanda expanded the party apparatus in an attempt to "mould the loyalties of the citizens" (Lemarchand 1970, 247). These efforts failed largely because they did not address the sources of dissatisfaction that led to dissension in the first place. Not only did the majority of Rwandans remain desperately poor after independence, but even the educated class, the ranks from which the first wave of revolutionaries came, remained shut out from prosperity. Indeed it was this group of students, teachers, and junior civil servants to whom the revolution had promised much but provided little. Their grievances were the standard fare of the disenfranchised: teacher salaries were abysmal, career opportunities nonexistent, and corruption at the top rife (Lemarchand 1970, 238–40).

The regime dealt with these grievances in the usual way, by redirecting them at Tutsi. Kayibanda had retained the Belgian system of identity cards that labeled each Rwandan "Hutu," "Tutsi," or "Twa." He also initiated a quota system that would restrict the percentage of spots in schools, the civil service, and private sector to 9 percent for Tutsi (to match the percentage of Tutsi in the population). The justification for the quota system (which Habyarimana eventually implemented) was most likely the continued dominance of Tutsi among the ranks of the educated. At secondary schools and universities, Tutsi often accounted for close to 50 percent of the teachers and students (Reyntjens 1985, 501); and at the Université Nationale du Rwanda in Butare, Tutsi accounted for 90 percent of the student body (Lemarchand 1970, 260). And because the church continued to maintain de facto control over the educational system (despite secularization in 1964), Tutsi attitudes of superiority prevailed, which reinforced the belief—held by Tutsi and Hutu alike—that Hutu students were destined to fail.

By 1973, corruption had eaten away the last thread of legitimacy for the Kayibanda regime. In May 1973, Kayibanda changed the constitution to allow him to continue in power (Gasana 1995, 213). Dissension within the northerner-controlled army, however, was growing. The timing seemed especially ripe for a "change" of leadership, for in the spring of 1972, the Tutsi-controlled army in Burundi responded to a Hutu-led insurgency in the south by killing an estimated 100,000 to 200,000 Hutu in a well-planned "selective" genocide (Lemarchand 1997, 323; 1998, 6). Hoping to capitalize on the resulting furor (stoked by thousands of Hutu refugees streaming into Rwanda from Burundi), Kayibanda created Public Safety Committees—essentially vigilante groups—to check up on businesses, schools, universities, and civil service to determine if they were violating "ethnic quotas" (Des Forges 1999, 40). Kayibanda's own military officers, however, allowed the violence to spread uncontrolled throughout the country. As the violence spread, people began going after the rich instead of Tutsi; those from the north went after those from the south, while others tried to exact payback from local authorities against whom they had grievances (Reyntjens 1985, 504). As with most episodes of violence, this, too, was planned. The chaos orchestrated by a small group of military officers provided the pretext for restoring order through a coup d'état (Gasana 2002, 21–22). Thus did the Kayibanda regime meet its end.

The Rise of the North

On 5 July 1973, Major General Juvénal Habyarimana, the senior-most officer in the northerner-controlled army, ousted Kayibanda in what was reported as a "bloodless" coup. The new power holders later killed fifty or so members of the deposed regime or left them to die in prison (Des Forges 1999, 41; Reyntjens 1985, 506; Gasana 2002, 21–27). Kayibanda himself was left to starve to death and was "buried discretely by some prisoners, like a common bandit" (Nsengiyaremye 1995, 241). Most Rwandans reacted to the coup with relief, including Tutsi, since Habyarimana restored order and put an end to the recent violence aimed at Tutsi, as he had promised to do when he seized power.

Order came at a price, however. On assuming power, Habyarimana banned political parties. Two years later, he created the Mouvement Révolutionnaire National pour le Développement (MRND), declaring every Rwandan a member at birth (Prunier 1995, 76; Des Forges 1999, 41). Habyarimana also extended the party structure down to the most local levels of government by appointing all officials and providing each with corresponding leadership positions in the MRND so that the state and party became an inescapable presence in people's everyday lives (Gasana 2002, 29).

The purpose of creating such an intensively administered state was mobilization and control. Under "Habyarimanism," the state monitored and controlled all movement. Residents were required to register with the local authorities who reported all births, deaths, and movement into and out of their communes on a quarterly and yearly basis (Prunier 1995, 77; Des Forges 1999, 42). The densely knit structure also facilitated mobilization for public works projects such as road repairs, ditch digging, or brush clearing. Under Habyarimana, people were required to perform communal labor, or *umuganda*, a practice reminiscent of the colonial past. Though supposedly voluntary and limited to four days per month, this requirement essentially amounted to forced labor, since authorities reported and fined anyone who did not show up for their assigned work duty (Prunier 1995, 79; Des Forges 1999, 42).

Another reason, however, for the hypercentralization of the state was to keep rivals in check—particularly those from the south who might seek to reassert their power. In this quest, Habyarimana's policy of *équilibre ethnique et régional* was particularly useful. For the real target of exclusion from government posts, the military, and especially the educational system was not Tutsi, but southern and central Hutu. Under this system, the number of openings in education and the public sector was capped according to regional quotas. This gave undue advantage to Hutu in the north, who were vastly overrepresented in secondary and tertiary education. Tutsi from the center and southern regions actually benefited from the system since they could be counted as southerners. Thus, Habyarimana could use the quota system to reward Tutsi from these regions while at the same time, keep potential Hutu rivals in check.

The system did not quash challengers, however. In April 1980, three of Habyarimana's most senior military officers, Théoneste Lizinde, Alexis Kanyarengwe, and Stanislas Biseruka, all of whom later joined the RPF, led an unsuccessful coup attempt (Gasana 2002, 32). The coup attempt did not unite the regime, but simply shifted the nexus of competition to the factions within the north. The system of political favoritism meant that those from Habyarimana's préfecture of Gisenyi were favored over those from Ruhengeri; and within Gisenyi, those from the Bushiru region over those from Bugoyi. The most favored of all were the abakonde, the powerful landowning class to which his wife's lineage belonged. Rather than work to enlarge his base regionally and ethnically, Habyarimana confined the spoils of power to a very small group, an inner circle referred to as the akazu. The akazu guarded its position jealously and would broach no compromise. Its ability to control the political and social landscape of the country remained absolute throughout the 1980s, until the twin pressures of structural adjustment and political reform threatened to unseat the group in the early 1990s.

Following the genocide in 1994, there was a tendency among journalists and other observers to read Rwandan history backward through the lens of the genocide—to view everything that came before as somehow building to the genocide (Newbury and Newbury 2000). Reading history backward creates a straight-line trajectory from past oppression to genocidal hatreds, from past Tutsi dominance to ever-present fears that Tutsi will try to reclaim the throne once again. It would be wrong, however, to view the genocide as the inevitable outcome of historical forces or cultural conditioning.

The historical record reveals little in the way of long simmering hatreds between Hutu and Tutsi as unified ethnic groups. What it reveals instead is a relentless and sometimes violent process of state-building in which rival elites jockeyed for greater power, control, and influence over the country. This process radically transformed local power relations and turned once fluid social categories into more rigidly ranked, "ethnic" terms. Even with the ethnicization of the terms *Hutu* and *Tutsi* under Belgian rule, regional divisions continued to fracture elite politics in the postindependence era. The north-south cleavage, active before the colonial period, remained salient throughout and into the postcolonial period.

Violence became a feature of Rwandan politics in the late 1950s (just before the country's first communal elections). The violence, however, was never spontaneous but always planned and led by political authorities. An ethnic hatred model would expect violence to explode or take on a life of its own. Yet, there is little evidence of wildfire forms of violence and much evidence that the violence was directed at specific targets for specific purposes. Moreover, in the instances where violence did become out of control, perpetrators failed to focus on ethnic targets, but began targeting others, such as the rich or people from rival regions. These patterns suggest yet again the intensely political nature of these episodes. When authorities promoted ethnic violence, their goal was to seize, gain, or consolidate power by making Tutsi the common enemy of the people. Ethnic violence was thus an elite tactic for diverting attention away from the real crises that threatened various leaders' legitimacy and power.

More recent events of the late 1980s and early 1990s also reveal little evidence that the most important cleavage among elites or the population was ethnic. The multiple crises that befell the county in this period created palpable insecurity and fear by widening the already pronounced gap between rich and poor. One observer on the scene even described "rich" and "poor" as the real "ethnicities" in place at this time (Gasana 2002, 51, 59–60). The invasion by the RPF on 1 October 1990 only heightened tensions. Despite these ongoing, multiple crises, the main axis of conflict continued to be political. Both Hutu and Tutsi rallied behind a handful of opposition parties, each promising to bring an end to the corruption and decay epitomized by the Habyarimana regime. Despite the war against the RPF, these opposition parties continued their calls for democratic reform. Eventually, these same parties would strike an alliance with the RPF. Had actors' goals been primarily ethnic, not political, such an alliance would have been unthinkable.

The real threat to Habyarimana was, therefore, not Tutsi or Tutsi political opponents, but the specter of multiparty politics, which would have brought an end to his one-party rule. To forestall its own demise, the regime tried repeatedly to reframe the most pressing issues of the day in ethnic terms. The RPF's strong-arm tactics on the battlefield and at the negotiating table played into the regime's strategy of turning political threats into ethnic demons. The assassination of the Burundian president reinforced an ethnic reading of events. When the RPF finally resorted to creating its own window of opportunity by shooting down the president's plane, it was simply tearing a page from the akazu's book. Victory on the battlefield, its leaders knew well, meant capturing power, not sharing it.

In sum, there is little evidence to support the most basic assumption of the ethnic hatred and ethnic fear theses—that in times of insecurity or threat, ethnicity will be the primary fault line that defines society and politics. In Rwanda, ethnicity was a strategy of politics, not its foundation.

3

Local Narratives and Explanations

> If someone who forces another out in the open and that person is
> killed by others, can't we say that the killer was the one who made
> that person leave his hiding place?
>
> —Émilie, Ngali

If the conflict that led to the genocide at the national level was political,
what factors led to violence at the local level? A tendency in the literature
on political violence is to privilege the center over the periphery (Kalyvas
2006, chap. 2).[1] An urban bias does more than simply ignore the periphery. It assumes that what goes on inside the capital is the same as what goes
on outside, that politics in the periphery will mirror or mimic politics in
the center. As numerous ethnographies and microlevel studies have
shown, however, politics and violence rarely flow from the center in unmitigated form. Mediating factors, such local power interests, almost always come into play. Rwanda was no exception.

Historically, regions differed in their political relationship to the center.
During the genocide, regions also varied in their response to the mass
killings that began in Kigali shortly after the plane crash that killed the
president on 6 April 1994. Within regions, different communities, groups,
and individuals also varied in their responses to the war and mass killings.
Indeed, it was precisely because of varying regional and local responses
that the interim government decided to bring the genocide to the people,
so to speak, by making personal appearances and bussing in professional
killers, whose job it was to jump-start and lead the killings in these locales.
Yet state intervention cannot guarantee uniform compliance. Thus we begin our investigation by asking how genocide unfolded in Kimanzi and
Ngali. How do people from the two communities narrate events from the
period of the civil war and genocide (1990–94) and how do they explain
what happened? Do they point to overwhelming hatreds or fears of Tutsi
or to other factors?

---

1. This critique has been made in other literatures as well; see, for example, Migdal (1988).

The data show that contrary to the expectations of the ethnic fear and ethnic hatred theses, people's explanation of events from the period of 1990 to 1994 do not focus on murderous hatreds or overwhelming fears. Instead, they point to situational factors and personal motives, such as greed and jealousy. These explanations do not necessarily rule out the existence of ethnic hatreds and fears; but neither do they rely on them for their explanatory power. What they point to are more precise pathways to mass violence than amorphous ethnic sentiment.

Narratives of Genocide at the Neighborhood Level

In this section, I present a narrative of what occurred in each community. Much of the data I use to piece together these chronologies were responses to a question I asked at every initial interview: "What do you remember from the period of 1990 to 1994?" I kept the wording of the question open-ended to allow respondents to define the period themselves.

Kimanzi (North)

The seminal event in Kimanzi was the RPF invasion of 1 October 1990 in Umutara, a region to the east of Kimanzi. The people of Kimanzi felt the repercussions of the war immediately. The most powerful local official was the bourgmestre of the commune where Kimanzi was located. Subordinate officials and former officials who had maintained their ties to the bourgmestre began harassing Tutsi, accusing them of being *ibyitso,* or "accomplices," of the RPF and imprisoning them. One elderly Tutsi man (b. 1922) was among the first to be imprisoned.

> In 1990, it was the start of the policy of threatening the Tutsi. They started to threaten us, saying we were the ibyitso of the Inkotanyi [RPF]. I was the first [to be accused] in 1990. The bourgmestre sent some police to my house and they put me in the jail. After two weeks, they took me to the central prison in Ruhengeri for three months. After three months, they released me because of the negotiations between the Rwandan state and the Inkotanyi.

The accusation of *icyitso* (or ibyitso, plural) also provided the pretext for searching Tutsi homes and making other sorts of accusations. A female survivor described these other techniques of intimidation.

> In the beginning, we heard that the war was in Umutara. The authorities kept us from assembling together, that is, they didn't want groups of people. After a few months, we heard the gunshots in the forest at [names location] and we fled. But before fleeing, people were threatening us a lot. They

started to come into our homes (the homes of Tutsi) saying that we have papers for the plans of the Inkotanyi [RPF]. They were even saying that the
Tutsi were giving money to support the Inkotanyi, and they said that they
were also looking for the accounting books.

Another female survivor gave an even more sweeping account of events
from this period, in which harassment quickly escalated to violence.

The war was starting in 1990 and in 1991, they were starting to speak of ethnicities and people were starting to kill people. That continued in 1992.
People were killed in 1993, too. The people would come during the night,
rape the women, pillage the belongings, kill the people with machetes, up
until 1994 when they committed the genocide.

What emerges from these accounts is a picture of daily life suddenly
transformed by civil war. The civil war presented legitimate dangers and
threats and, at the same time, opportunities for local power holders to
conduct any manner of activity under the guise of maintaining security.
While Tutsi were clearly the main targets, officials also imprisoned many
Hutu, accusing them of being ibyitso. The following man's testimony suggests that imprisonment of Hutu was widespread.

Q. What do you remember from the period of 1990 to 1994?
In 1990, October 1, 1990, there was the attack at Umutara. The 7th of October 1990, they imprisoned me saying I was an icyitso because there were
some young men I worked with. They were Tutsi. They were saying that they
[the Tutsi] were bringing guns in the water pipes and that I was helping
them hide the arms. It was the 7th when we were imprisoned at Ruhengeri.

Q. During this period, where were you living?
I was living in [names cellule]. They freed us on January 23rd, 1991 when
the Inkotanyi [RPF] opened the central prison in Ruhengeri.

Q. Who imprisoned you? Who had you imprisoned?
It was the police authority who arrested us and imprisoned us.

Q. How many people were imprisoned for being ibyitso?
We were 96 people.

Q. Was the entire group liberated in January 1991?
We were imprisoned individually. The Inkotanyi opened our cells and we
left with them. We were together for two days. When we got back to our
houses and arrived at home, the authority kept threatening us until he had
us imprisoned again, saying we had gotten out because of the Inkotanyi. At
that time, we were imprisoned at Rilima [Bugesera]. When the RPF were
saying on the state radio that there are people imprisoned for having done

nothing . . . and they exchanged prisoners. It was in 1991, the month of April when I left [the prison].

Q. After having been released the second time, what did you do?

I stayed at the house but there were policemen who wanted to shoot me but they didn't succeed. [302, #1/4][2]

The term *icyitso* was new to this man. That this word was literally unknown to the accused shows how war and violence can generate new identities (Kalyvas 2006, 80). Icyitso was a new category authorities were imposing on local residents. This man heard the word for the first time the day he was arrested, when he heard the court read the charges against him out loud. On hearing the allegations, the man had to ask one of the policemen to explain. The policeman told the man he had been accused of having plotted against the country. As this man's experience indicates, escalations in the war presented opportunities for local authorities to target Hutu and Tutsi alike. When the RPF scored a victory on the battlefield or at the negotiating table, authorities had the necessary pretext to target anyone in the community. Local discourse painted all Tutsi as accomplices of the RPF and made Hutu vulnerable to suspicion as well. This gave wide latitude to local authorities and those with the right connections to target at will.

Harassment and imprisonment escalated to killing Tutsi and some Hutu in late January 1991, after the RPF launched a "lightning strike" in the province of Ruhengeri (Des Forges 1999, 87). The RPF held the main town for one day and forced open the central prison, releasing all the prisoners. Attacks on Tutsi in Kimanzi and surrounding areas followed immediately. According to one Tutsi woman, the killings occurred under cover of darkness and killers went after Tutsi as they tried to flee.

> The people would arrive at midnight to kill us. We fled to the forest. Once we arrived in the forest, we ran into the forest guards. They hid us in their houses. The guards called almost the entire population and they [the guards] started to tie our arms behind our backs and they had the people stand back and some guards started to shoot. They killed all the men and the boys. They let us go saying that the time to kill us had not yet come. They put us in isolated houses. They threw rocks on the roof and they would scream, saying they were our god, that they were going to do whatever they wanted.

2. The nomenclature in brackets includes a 3–4 character unique identifier for the respondent followed by which interview, from the total number of interviews with that respondent, the quoted passage came. I have removed dates to help ensure anonymity.

Another female survivor referred to these killings as "the genocide of males."

By April 1994, most Tutsi from Kimanzi and surrounding areas had fled the area or had been killed. Some Tutsi remained, however, having gone into hiding. After the assassination of the president on 6 April 1994, killers ferreted out the remaining Tutsi and killed them. According to a former responsable who helped to rescue many Tutsi during this period, killers even expanded their range of targets.

> It was in 1994, the 6th of April, and the shooting down of President Habya-rimana's plane, the Interahamwe and the soldiers and nearly the entire pop-ulation were looking for Tutsi, Hutu who were married to Tutsi, the friends of Tutsi—at that time, were all killed. It was at that moment that I fled with the two Abagogwe [local Tutsi] women who had stayed because the others were killed.

For the most part, people's accounts of this period focus on what they themselves witnessed or experienced. Survivor accounts focus on the vio-lence targeted at them. By contrast, the accounts of those who were not targeted as Tutsi or Tutsi sympathizers include references to other forms of violence, such as the violence related to the civil war. For some resi-dents, it was war violence they remember most clearly. One Hutu man was a secondary school student at the time of the civil war and recalled how the RPF forced local people to work for the rebel army. According to this man, residents never saw these forced conscripts again and assumed the RPF had killed them.

> *Q. What do you remember from this period, between 1990 and 1994?*
> At that time, when I was at school, I heard that the war was at Umutara, by the Inkotanyi [RPF], supported by the Tutsi. The war was starting in Umutara; little by little, it came to [names cellule]. Certain people were killed, little by little, and belongings were stolen. People were saying that the death of these people and the stolen goods, that it was the Tutsi who were the instigators.
>
> *Q. Who were the people who were killed?*
> It was Hutu who were disappearing. These Hutu, who were taken by the Inkotanyi, would guard the cows and carry the goods that the Inkotanyi pil-laged. And they didn't return and after a certain time, people were saying to us that the Inkotanyi killed these Hutu people.
>
> . . . .
>
> *Q. When did the Inkotanyi take these people?*
> Between 1992 and 1993.

Q. What did you do when the Inkotanyi came here?

When the Inkotanyi were still infiltrators, there was the order to ensure security against the Inkotanyi. The men were doing the night patrols [*amarondo*]. At that time, there was one day when the Inkotanyi came to loot the medicine from the health center at [names cellule] and that made us really scared. They left pamphlets, papers that said that they wanted to return to the country. The papers were written in English. [312, #1/1]

As with most respondents, this man focused initially on the violence he himself witnessed. Only afterward did he mention the killing of Tutsi.

Q. What happened here in Kimanzi after the downing of the president's plane?

What started in Umutara, that continued in the whole country. It was in 1991 [sic], when they shot down the president's plane, the people were starting to kill others. We heard that in Kigali, people were being killed. Even in the whole country, there was killing.

Q. But what happened exactly in Kimanzi?

In Kimanzi, some people were going after Tutsi, but in my secteur, all the Tutsi who lived there were no longer alive; maybe our responsable was able to protect them. [312, #1/1]

In this man's description of events, the killing of Tutsi is but one piece of a larger picture. Such statements did not seem to reflect an anti-Tutsi bias on the part of this respondent, but rather acknowledgement that during the war, Hutu and Tutsi were both targeted. Another Hutu resident, for example, also stated that he saw people "from all ethnicities" killed during the period 1990–94. This man's best friend was a Tutsi so it seems unlikely this respondent hated Tutsi as a group. Another Hutu man also mentioned violence committed by "both sides" (the RPF and FAR soldiers). Whether these statements suggest anti-Tutsi sentiment is unclear. What these and other testimonies do underscore is how different forms of violence affected people in different ways. Indeed, the overall picture that emerges from these accounts is multiple vectors of violence occurring at the same time: RPF and FAR war crimes; RPF strikes; and violence targeted at Tutsi residents as well as a small, but not insignificant, number of Hutu.

After asking people what they saw during the period of 1990 to 1994, I then asked who committed the violence that was targeted at Tutsi civilians. People's initial responses were quite vague: "the people" or "the Hutu." A typical response came from one female survivor: "At that time, since 1990, when the war was starting, the Hutu were pursuing the Tutsi."

In response to these answers, I asked people whether it was all "people" or all "Hutu" who committed the killings and to this question, people said no. They would then go on to specify which Hutu did the killings by qualifying the type of Hutu who participated, pointing out that it was the "mean" Hutu or "bad" Hutu who committed these murders. Distinguishing the Hutu who participated from those who did not also prompted some survivors to note the Hutu who helped to save or rescue Tutsi. As one survivor pointed out: "No, there were some among them who did not attack us—to the contrary, they hid us. I can give you an example: the owner of this house. He, too, was attacked shortly after by these mean people."

For many survivors, the most salient fact was not that their pursuers were Hutu, but that they were their own neighbors, which may be why survivors as a group tended to identify the killers initially as "our neighbors," "our Hutu neighbors," or make reference to the local population as those who had perpetrated the killings. Other residents, by contrast, often identified other types of perpetrators, such as military soldiers, whom they referred to as "ex-FAR," or leaders. The former conseiller of Kimanzi, for example, insisted that it was not the people of his secteur who were killing Tutsi, but military soldiers. Pointing to soldiers as the main perpetrators of violence against Tutsi placed the bulk of responsibility on outsiders, not local residents. One survivor, however, drew a clear link between his neighbors and the military, explaining that "if the population did not kill someone, the ex-FAR would kill him."

People also identified killers who came from outside Kimanzi. According to one man whose brother was killed for being an icyitso, local leaders "changed" their strategy so that Interahamwe from one secteur would go to other secteurs to kill. A Tutsi survivor also mentioned the cleverness of authorities in sending people from one secteur to another to kill Tutsi. Another survivor explained the rationale behind this strategy: "Even the commune had them [lower-level authorities] send a group of killers to a place that was not theirs to prevent these people [the killers] from having pity on their neighbors." The strategy of sending killers outside their immediate community to kill suggests that leaders were cognizant of the ties Tutsi had to the rest of their communities, despite the small number of Tutsi in this region (less than 1 percent of the population). It suggests, too, that despite the war and repeated exhortations by government officials and MRND party elites (on the radio, at public meetings, in recorded speeches), leaders of the violence could not take for granted that the population would automatically obey or follow orders to kill their Tutsi neighbors. In fact, leaders' assumptions seemed to have been well founded, for not everyone saw their Tutsi neighbors in the fantastical descriptions circulating in rumors. As one Joiner explained: "They were telling us that the *Inyenzi* were the Tutsi who were in the forests.[3] For us, we had the impression that the Inyenzi did not look like us. We thought that they were not like our Tutsi neighbors." In sum, contrary to the expectations of the ethnic fear and ethnic hatred approaches, the leaders of the genocide could not be sure that hatreds or fears would be powerful enough to drive the general population to kill their Tutsi neighbors. As a result, they developed other strategies to ensure that people would comply with their orders to kill.

Ngali (Center-South)

In contrast to Kimanzi, the community of Ngali in the center-south préfecture of Gitarama felt few effects of the civil war. People from Ngali mentioned hearing about the war on the radio, but always added that the war was "far away" and that life remained "normal" or "calm" in their community until the president's plane crash on 6 April 1994.

Some people noted the tensions that arose when opposition parties began forming in the early 1990s. One survivor went so far as to say that "these political parties were the cause of the war and of the genocide." Nobody mentioned physical violence associated with these activities, in contrast to other parts of the country where *kubohoza,* or the practice of forcibly recruiting people into political parties, was widespread (Wagner 1998; Des Forges 1999). The lack of violence associated with political parties indicates that a single party was dominant in the area and therefore faced no opposition.

In the period before the president's plane crash, rumors spread, but the content of these rumors was quite different than those that had been spreading in Kimanzi. This difference was likely due to the geographic location of each research site. Where the most immediate threat to people in Kimanzi was the civil war and the RPF, the biggest threats to people in Ngali came from closer quarters. One early rumor was that people from Burundi were attacking the country. This may have been a reference to the Burundian refugees who were living in refugee camps in the southeast of the country. Nearly 200,000 Burundians had fled Burundi in October 1993 after the assassination of the country's first democratically elected

---

3. *Inyenzi* is a derogatory reference to the RPF. The word means "cockroach" and was originally used to refer to the cross-border raiders who attacked Rwanda after the monarchy was abolished in 1959–61 (see chapter 2). They were called inyenzi because they attacked at night.

Hutu president by his own Tutsi military officers.[4] These Burundian refugees were still encamped in Rwanda in April 1994 (UNHCR 2004, 241) and many became active killers during the genocide (Des Forges 1999, 277). One man said he heard the rumor about the attacking Burundians in January 1994, three months before the president's assassination. Another man enumerated events in greater detail.

> *Q. What do you remember from the period of the genocide?*
>
> Shortly before the genocide, people were saying that the Burundians are going to attack us. The people fled toward [the office of] the sous-préfecture but after a day, we returned to our homes and afterward, the war started.[5]
>
> *Q. Who was fleeing toward [the sous-préfecture]?*
>
> Everyone, Hutu, Tutsi, men, women, and children. It wasn't a question of separating by ethnicity. That changed at the time of the genocide because they would say that the Inkotanyi [RPF] were coming, that they were eating people, grinding up children, and at that moment, people were hunting Tutsi, and these Tutsi started to look for hiding places.
>
> *Q. The first flight toward [the sous-préfecture], was that before the shooting down of the president's plane?*
>
> The first time, it was through hearsay that the Burundians were going to attack us. At that time, it wasn't serious. It became serious right after the shooting down of President Habyarimana's plane. [121, #1/2]

To people in Ngali, located south of Kigali, "attacking Burundians"—the vast majority of whom would have been Hutu—posed a more credible threat than the Tutsi-dominated RPF in the period before Habyarimana's assassination. Ethnic solidarity, in other words, seems to have been absent. After the assassination, fantastical rumors of the RPF spread easily, just as they had in Kimanzi.

The event that finally launched actual violence in Ngali was the president's assassination on 6 April 1994. Tutsi were immediately frightened at what the assassination portended. For one survivor and her Hutu husband, the assassination meant a "bloody" war. For another survivor, it meant that all the Tutsi were going to die.

Change was swift. As one survivor stated, "I noticed the change in people toward me after the shooting down of the president's plane, that is to say that everyone changed their behavior toward the people hunted down the 7th of April 1994."

4. Newbury and Newbury (1999, 310) put the number at 400,000.

5. In addition to the main préfecture office, there were also sous-préfectures, an administrative division one step below the level of préfecture.

Unlike the multiple leaders in Kimanzi, all activities in Ngali after the president's assassination were centered around a single leader, Jude. Jude was a local resident, who, before the genocide, served as responsable for one of the cellules in Ngali. Following the president's assassination, political party leaders—most likely the "Power," or extremist wing, of the MDR which aligned with the MRND—named Jude the new conseiller of Ngali. Once in power, Jude wasted no time in organizing activities. He appointed new responsables for each of the cellules. He ordered people to conduct night patrols to protect the community against "outside" attackers. He gave orders to cut down the brush and banana trees "to prevent the arrival of the Inkotanyi [RPF]." He ordered people to join the MRND and threatened to kill them if they refused. He also began holding secret meetings and recruiting men into the killing groups.

Violence began with burning and pillaging of Tutsi homes. It escalated to killing Tutsi shortly thereafter, with one man pinning the date as 22 April 1994 [Paul, #4/4]. One tactic that Jude used was to lure Tutsi to a meeting by announcing that all Tutsi in hiding should attend; that they would be given safe passage and parcels of land in recompense for their destroyed homes and property. Those Tutsi who attended the meeting were killed on the spot. One survivor who did not attend because she was too ill watched from a distance. She recognized several elderly women who attended. After the meeting, killers continued to pursue those who had remained in hiding. The killings ended when the RPF arrived in the area in late May, driving out the killers and much of the general Hutu population, who fled westward toward then Zaïre.

When I asked people who had committed the killings of Tutsi, most spoke in the same vague terms as people from Kimanzi. As one survivor responded, "The Bahutu were killing the Tutsi." When pressed to be more specific, residents identified the killers using language that seemed to depersonalize the relationship of the killers to their communities. In contrast to survivors in Kimanzi, for example, survivors in Ngali make few references to "our neighbors" when identifying the killers. Instead, Ngali residents make frequent reference to "the Hutu" and "the people." I usually had to ask a second question to draw out the fact that "the Hutu" or "the people" were indeed people who came from Ngali.

Another way that people seemed to distance themselves from the killers was by referring to "attackers coming from afar." At first, I found this reference confusing because I assumed that "by afar," people meant killers who came from outside the secteur of Ngali. After further probing, however, I discovered that "attackers coming from afar" often referred to people who came from other cellules within Ngali—hardly outsiders to the community, particularly when there existed multiple channels for people of different cellules to interact and get to know one another, such as through association meetings, *umuganda* (communal work require-ment), and school. As Danielle de Lame (1996, 106) notes, however, Rwandans do not mark distance—or the relative categories of "near" and "far"—by administrative boundaries or units, but in the amount of time it takes to walk from one place to another. Given this understanding of dis-tance, "people from afar" could refer to people from the same secteur as one's own, but to a cellule that is more than an hour's walk away. In any case, there were very few references to killers who came from secteurs outside Ngali. Indeed, the paucity of such references suggests that the majority of killers did come from Ngali, though not necessarily from a "nearby" cellule.

People also made references to attackers from Bugesera, a region to the east of Ngali that has always had a high percentage of Tutsi inhabitants. According to one survivor, it was these outsiders who helped to "teach" the people of Ngali to follow their lead, and thus, it was these outsiders who were responsible for the killings in Ngali.

Q. What happened in April?

In April, after the shooting down of President Habyarimana's plane, the well-trained Interahamwe, they were starting to attack the Tutsi, even saying to the Hutu to help kill them.

Q. Among the Hutu, who helped with the killings?

There were some Hutu who agreed to help them and others refused. Before the killers coming from Bugesera arrived in our secteur, they would contact the founders and these founders would help them lead the residents toward the killing. President Habyarimana had these secret people in each place. Here, there was [names specific people] working for the state and it was these people from Gisenyi, even here below at Electrogaz [the electric com-pany], there was one; even at [the commune center], there was another. In the meantime, the people would receive MRND party clothes and hats. And when the Interahamwe would come from Bugesera and the Burundians, they would see these people in MRND clothes. The Burundians would set an example for the Rwandan Interahamwe to kill and show them how to kill someone because the people from here in Ngali were scared and ashamed of killing their neighbors, their friends. [120, #1/5]

Whoever was committing these initial attacks, residents from Ngali did try to put up an organized resistance. As the mother of one Joiner explained:

Q. What happened to cause the killings and the separations between people in 1994?

I don't know how to explain it because they were saying that there were people who were coming from afar toward our district. The men organized themselves to do night patrols against these people. The following days, we saw that our secteur had also been attacked.

Q. Who attacked your secteur?

People were saying later that it was some Interahamwe.

Q. The Interahamwe were the people who came from afar and attacked your secteur?

They came from far away. First, they would pillage the cows, they would sing in the road, the people were starting to flee, and a little while later, the Interahamwe started to kill people. [107, #1/1]

The reference both these respondents make to the Interahamwe requires clarification. Originally, the term *Interahamwe* referred to militia recruited and trained in Kigali by the president's MRND party. During the genocide, the self-appointed government would dispatch these militia to jumpstart killings in regions where local residents were reluctant to kill or where Tutsi (and Hutu) had put up resistance.[6] These militia epitomized Tilly's concept of "violence specialists" (Tilly 2003) in that they were specifically trained, armed, and deployed to kill Tutsi civilians. The usage and meaning of the term *Interahamwe* changed over time. In Ngali, people used the term to refer to bands of local killers. In these two interview passages, both meanings of the term might be implied. The man's reference to "well-trained Interahamwe" could refer to the militia recruited and trained in Kigali. The Joiners' mother's reference is more ambiguous. She may be referring to professional Interahamwe trained in Kigali, to local killers, or indeed, to both.

An older Hutu man (b. 1935), whom killers accused of being Tutsi, also referred to organized resistance by the people of Ngali to outside attackers.

Q. What do you remember from this period [1990–1994]?

Though I don't remember which years, I do remember that people were saying that there was a war at the border. When we would ask who was attacking, people would say that it was the Inkotanyi [RPF] that were attacking. That continued. We heard that in Kigali, they started to kill people. Another day, they would say that at Bugesera as well, they were killing the Tutsi and at [the commune center]. They would also say that the killers were heading toward the district [where Ngali is located]. We said that we were going to get together and

6. The largest mass resistance was at Bisesero in the western province of Kibuye. For survivor accounts of this resistance, see the African Rights' (nd) publication entitled *Resisting genocide: Bisesero, April–June 1994.*

fight against these people who were able to kill people. We would ask ourselves, "How could a person take a machete and kill another?" And we found
no answer. [Maurice, #1/4]

As this man's testimony indicates, there was confusion about who was doing what to whom. The sources of threat clearly came from outside Ngali
but in multiple directions—the war in the north, killers in the capital, and
killers coming from the region of Bugesera.

A final way that Ngali residents identified the perpetrators was to refer
to them as "the Pawa people." Pawa is the Kinyarwandan word for "power."
It became the rallying cry of the extremist wings of various political parties shortly after the assassination of the Burundian president in October
1993. The first utterance of "Hutu Power" occurred at an MDR meeting in
Gitarama, where Froduald Karamira, an MDR vice president, told the
crowd that the RPF—more specifically RPF leader, Paul Kagame—was behind the assassination of Ndadaye, the Hutu Burundian president. At the
end of his speech, Froduald called for all Hutu to stand together and ferret out the enemy within, which included any Hutu who worked against
Hutu solidarity (a clear reference to Hutu moderates within the MDR).
He ended his speech with a rousing chant of "Hutu Power!" followed by
variants for each party, such as "MRND Power!" and "MDR Power!" After
each cheer, the crowd shouted back "Power Power Power" (Des Forges
1999, 137–39; Bertrand 2000, 246).

The reference some Ngali residents made to "Pawa people" shows how
the violence was linked to the conflicts and splits among the various political parties. It suggests that those who participated in the violence in Ngali
were themselves supporters of the Power wing of the MDR (or possibly the
MRND) or were attempting to demonstrate their support for these extremist wings. In Kimanzi, by contrast, no one ever mentioned "Pawa" because the region was already dominated by the MRND.

As these data show, Ngali residents use a more ambiguous language
than their counterparts in Kimanzi when identifying the perpetrators of
the genocide in their community. This ambiguity is difficult to interpret
but one possible interpretation is that it was a way for residents to distance
themselves from those responsible for the killings, many of whom were
their own neighbors from Ngali.

Comparing Accounts

What emerges from these accounts is a clear difference in how genocide
unfolded in each community and the level of intimacy that characterized
the violence.

Violence against Tutsi in Kimanzi (in the north) was closely tied to the civil war, spiking and escalating at precise moments. The war's launch on 1 October 1990 in Umutara triggered a wave of imprisonment of Tutsi and Hutu carried out by local authorities under the auspices of the bourgmestre. This campaign of harassment escalated to mass killings of Tutsi in January 1991, after the RPF's strike in Ruhengeri. Violence against Tutsi spiked again after the downing of the president's plane in April 1994. Mass violence thus continued, off and on, over a period of three and a half years, much longer than in Ngali. Local residents and authorities were key participants in the violence, but "outsiders," such as FAR soldiers and killers dispatched from other secteurs, seemed to have been the main instigators and organizers of the violence. Actors from outside Kimanzi thus played a prominent role in the mass killings and genocidal violence that took place in Kimanzi.

In the center-south, by contrast, violence against Tutsi did not begin until after the president's assassination. Before that time, daily life remained relatively calm, despite tensions caused by the formation of political parties and rumors about Burundians or people from Bugesera attacking the country. Violence began shortly after the president's assassination. It began with the takeover of power by a new authority and the organization of local residents for purposes of violence, which began with the burning and looting of Tutsi homes, then escalated two weeks later to killing Tutsi. In Ngali, genocide seems to have been a more intimate affair than it was in Kimanzi, with people from Ngali both leading and perpetrating the violence.

Explanations of Violence

People's narration of events tells us little about how they make sense of what occurred in their communities. Both the ethnic hatred and ethnic fear theses would expect people to point to fears or hatreds of Tutsi driving the violence or, in the absence of such discourse, to point to strategies of ethnic solidarity to ensure their survival and security. Does the evidence support these expectations?

Situational Explanations

As the accounts above show, people often described the violence in ethnic terms. "Hutu were going after Tutsi" was a common refrain. People did not explain their neighbors' participation in ethnic terms, however. No one cited the cause of violence as emanating from a person's membership in a specific ethnic group. Instead, many people explained participation in situational terms. People's actions during the war and genocide were the result of circumstances, not identity. Circumstances compelled people to do what they did. People had no choice but to participate unless they were not afraid to die or unless they had the means to pay someone else to go in their place.

Even in cases where coercion was less prominent, the authorities wielded enormous power to mobilize people—to convince them to join the violence of their own accord. As one resident of Ngali explained: "It [was] the mobilization by authorities that made the war escalate between the people." Yet, even a sophisticated program of mass mobilization did not lead residents, including Tutsi, to believe that mass participation in genocide would follow. In fact, people expressed shock at the sudden transformation in their neighbors and family members when the moment for violence came. Until that time, relations with their Hutu neighbors had been amicable. Even those who did not consider themselves friends with their Hutu (or Tutsi) neighbors said there were no problems between them. As neighbors, they shared food, beer, and conversation, and helped each other when the need arose. So when I asked people if they could foresee the violence before it began, all said no. Typical was the response that Jude's wife, Thérèse, gave.

> *Q. WIn your opinion, was it possible to foresee the violence between neighbors during the genocide?*
> It was difficult to foresee the violence during the genocide among neighbors. Certainly there were times when you could see a neighbor who behaved badly; for example, there are boys who love to fight in the bars but that doesn't mean that would necessarily cause the violence during the war.
>
> *Q. Were you surprised by the change in people's behavior during the war?*
> That did surprise me and it made me really scared. [Thérèse, #7/7]

Émilie, a survivor from Ngali, echoed Thérèse's remarks. Émilie had the sense that the assassination of the president foretold a "bloody" war, but was nonetheless shocked to see the change in her longtime Hutu friends. She was especially shocked by her own brother-in-law who denounced her mother and brother's hiding place to the Interahamwe, who then killed them.

> *Q. Did you think that your Hutu friends were capable of killing you?*
> No, because we had been friends for a long time.

Q. Among your Hutu friends, were there certain ones who became killers?

Yes, even my brother-in-law and it was he who caused the death of my family.

. . . .

Q. Were you surprised when your brother-in-law showed himself to be a killer?

I was very surprised that my brother-in-law brought the attacks to our house rather than protecting us.

Q. When did your brother-in-law start to change his comportment?

He started to change after the shooting down of the plane, but I don't remember the date. It was in the month of April 1994. [Émilie, #3/5]

As Émilie's testimony suggests, survivors could have a general sense of foreboding after a crisis such as the downing of the president's plane, yet at the same time continue to believe that their long-time Hutu friends and neighbors would not turn on them. In other words, even if some people did believe that a level of rancor, animosity, or mass fear existed, they could also maintain a belief that the Hutu they knew would not act on those fears or animosities by turning on them.

Others, too, said it was not possible to foresee who would turn into a génocidaire. One resident remarked that the transformation could be instantaneous, as if it came out of nowhere. As this man explained: "For example, you were with someone, and the next second, you would see that they had become 'Pawa' in a minute."

The only exceptions respondents cited were people who had exhibited violent behavior before the genocide. An older man from Ngali, for example, told us about a neighbor who had killed another man before the genocide. The neighbor had rented land and when the landowner asked to be paid, the neighbor killed him. No one in Ngali was surprised when this same man took part in the genocide, since he had already shown himself to be capable of murder before the genocide. A survivor from Kimanzi made the same distinction. He expressed no surprise when his neighbors who had participated in previous episodes of violence (dating from 1961 and 1973) participated in the killing of his family in January 1991.

Just as people were not surprised when violent neighbors participated in killings of Tutsi, so, too, were they not surprised when Hutu who had blood pacts with Tutsi showed restraint and even helped to save these Tutsi. Blood pacts were a practice of an older generation of men—those born during the colonial period, before independence in 1959–61. Blood pacts were a ritual symbolizing close friendship between two people. In a blood pact, each person swears an oath of loyal friendship to the other, upon pain of death to the person's entire family. Blood pacts often came up in interviews with no prompting, as it did in my first interview with a rescuer in Kimanzi. This man had been a pastor at the time of the civil war and genocide and helped to save many Tutsi.

> *Q. When you were young, no one spoke to you about your ethnicity or your lineage?*
>
> At that age, I heard people talk about our lineage but it didn't mean anything to me. And when I became grown, I started to ask my father what that meant, our ethnicity and our lineages. I also heard about our lineages when the friend of my father made a blood pact with him [*kunywana*]; they would use lots of words containing lineage names after cutting under the navel with a razor blade and each drinking the blood of the other and at that moment, they became true friends who could never break their vow.
>
> *Q. How would people choose the people with whom they made a blood pact?*
>
> Because of the behavior of someone or someone who had done a good deed. You choose someone who could be your true friend.
>
> *Q. Were there people who broke the vow during the war or killings of 1959–63?*
>
> Since 1959, there were Hutu who made blood pacts with Tutsi and at the time of events, these people were scared of the vow to the extent that they did everything to protect their Tutsi friends and their belongings. I can give an example. My father had a Tutsi friend whom he had made a blood pact with and at the time of events, he hid him with his entire family and their belongings, including the cows. [325, #1/3]

Another older Hutu man (b. 1930) also maintained that Hutu with blood pacts with Tutsi did not participate in the genocide "because of this act." According to both men, blood pacts not only had a restraining effect on people (keeping them from perpetrating violence against their Tutsi friends with whom he had a pact), they also led people to try to save or rescue their Tutsi friends as well as their friends' belongings. These claims about blood pacts show the extent to which people believed that social ties not only could have, but should have, a powerful restraining effect, even or perhaps especially in violent situations.

If Hutu neighbors did indeed harbor an ingrained hatred of Tutsi as a group, it was not obvious to the Tutsi survivors in my two research sites. Indeed, survivors were quick to point out examples that demonstrated the persistence of friendship or neighborly ties, even amidst the chaos and commotion of violence, as if to underscore their commonsensical belief that neighbors and friends should help neighbors and friends, especially in times of crisis or need. As one survivor explained, "Not everyone killed. There was someone who could tell you where the killers were and that was my case, that there were people who didn't want to kill me." This survivor pointed out that the same person could be capable of killing others but at the same time, not want to kill him because of their prior friendship. A survivor from Ngali also remarked that it was a friend-turned-Interahamwe who came to alert him that the rest of the killers were on their way to kill him. When I asked this survivor why an Interahamwe would help him like that, he responded matter-of-factly because the man had been his friend.

As these data show, the norm was not to see people as Hutu or Tutsi first and neighbors second. The norm was to see neighbors who were Hutu or Tutsi. Murderous behavior toward people of a given ethnic group violated people's canonical expectations of what constituted normal behavior. Contrary to the assumptions of the ethnic hatred and ethnic fear theses, neither Tutsi nor Hutu expected their neighbors and friends to line up with their ethnic groups even under the pressures of war and mass violence. Instead, people expected their friends and neighbors to continue to play the role of friends and neighbors—that is, they expected their Hutu neighbors to protect, not hurt, them.

This expectation also seems to explain why people gave situational explanations for the violence committed by their neighbors. If the norm is that neighbors help neighbors in times of crisis, instead of hacking them to death, then the only explanation for the murderous transformation in some people was situational exigencies that were beyond anyone's control.

Legacies of Past Violence

If it was not possible to foresee the violence, then perhaps hatred lingered from past episodes of violence and lurked in the background, waiting to be resuscitated at the right moment. A few people did explain the genocide as a continuation or repetition of past political activity. These same people, however, also pointed out that normal or amicable relations were able to resume through state intervention. Maurice, an elderly man from Ngali who had been accused of being Tutsi during the genocide, offered one such explanation. Maurice tied conflicts between political parties in 1959 to the political conflict that presaged the genocidal violence of 1994.

Q. At the end of one of the interviews, you said that the events of 1959 formed the basis or the cause of the violence in 1990–94. Can you explain what you meant?

In 1959, it was the conflict between the two ethnicities. There was a revolt of one ethnicity against the other and in 1994, that was the continuation of this conflict of these ethnic groups.

Q. How did continuation of this conflict manifest itself between 1959 and 1994?

There was a similarity. In 1959, the Hutu were going after the Tutsi. In 1994, the Hutu were again going after the Tutsi and killing them. In 1959, they were saying that they wanted to get rid of the monarchy in order to have a president. The parents of Kagame [current president of Rwanda] fled when our president was still very small. His mother carried him on her back.

Q. Did the violence of 1959 create a permanent change in relations between neighbors?

That didn't change relations between neighbors because after the bad events of 1959, the people would give each other cows and the newly married like before these events. The difference between these two wars was that in 1959, when you hid someone or when you accompanied them, they wouldn't kill them and you wouldn't be threatened. But in 1994, you hid someone, you were killed with the person you hid. [Maurice, #4/4]

For Maurice, there was no unbroken line of ethnic hatred or animosity stretching from the past to the genocide; rather, the same kinds of factors—conflicts between political parties and by extension, ethnic groups—were the underlying cause for the violence that followed.[7] While people did see "resemblances" between past episodes of violence against Tutsi and the genocide, there was one salient difference they were careful to point out. In the past, people burned and pillaged Tutsi homes but there was no killing. Everyone stressed this difference. For example, when I asked one survivor from Kimanzi whether the violence of 1959 resembled the violence of 1990–91, he replied: "The war of 1959 resembled the war of 1990–91. The difference is the genocide." In other words, the difference between past episodes of violence and the genocide was not simply one of degree, but of kind. Past episodes did not include killing, whereas the genocide did. These data match what Straus found in his interviews with a nationwide sample of low-level perpetrators. As Straus (2006, 175) explains: "If they had heard of pre-1990 episodes of violence, respondents said that in the past Tutsi homes had been burned and Tutsis chased off their land but not killed in large numbers." This consistency with Straus's findings suggest that the views of people from Ngali and Kimanzi were not unique to the two research sites.

Another difference between past episodes and the genocide was that violence in the past did not create a permanent division between Hutu and Tutsi. This was due to the active role authorities played in reconciling communities after violence. One man from Kimanzi, for example, told

---

7. The most dominant political parties that formed in the late 1950s were ethnic in their appeal. The country's first president, Grégoire Kayibanda, founded a party called PARME-HUTU, which he fashioned as a Hutu party (see chapter 2).

the story of how the local authority tricked culprits into turning themselves in to the authorities. After one episode of violence targeted at Tutsi homes and property, the local authority assembled the community and asked those who had participated in the burning of Tutsi homes to step to one side to receive a "reward." "There were even innocent people who stepped to the side thinking they were going to receive something," the man recalled. The authority then took everyone who had stepped to the side to prison. A survivor from Kimanzi echoed this man's remarks: "At that time [1959], it wasn't serious. There was a difference between that period and what happened over the years 1990–94. After that war [of 1959], relations between the people continued normally." While people old enough to recall past episodes of violence were not surprised to see violence targeted at Tutsi start up again in 1990, these same people also noted the active role that authorities took in punishing the guilty and reconciling relations between Hutu and Tutsi after past episodes. Because of the actions authorities took in the past, normal relations were able to resume and permanent divisions were avoided.

Jealousy and Greed

Perhaps hatred did not exist at a mass level, but among a select few. Several people made reference to individuals who hated people of the other ethnicity. As one survivor from Kimanzi said about his neighbors who had participated in the mass killings in January 1991, they "simply did not like Tutsi without saying why." Sophie, an eighty-year-old woman who hid many Tutsi in her home during the genocide, echoed this man's remarks. She said she was not surprised by her neighbors' behavior because of their dislike of Tutsi.

Q. Did you know the Interahamwe that came here [to your house]?

Yes. I knew them all because they were my neighbors.

Q. Were you surprised when your neighbors became Interahamwe?

I wasn't surprised to see my neighbors become Interahamwe because before, they didn't like the Tutsi.

Q. How did you know that your neighbors didn't like the Tutsi?

There were some signs that indicated that the Tutsi didn't want the Hutu and the Hutu didn't want the Tutsi. I would see this especially at celebrations because there would not be a lot of guests from the other ethnicity.

Q. But before, your neighbors were never violent toward others?

No, there was only hypocrisy [*uburyarya*] in their relationships. [Sophie, #9/9]

Sophie was also quite clear that those who joined the Interahamwe were "bad" people or people with no conscience. Thus Sophie, too, invokes the commonsense logic that bad people will behave badly when given the chance.

Q. What is the difference between the people who joined the Interahamwe and the others who refused to support the Interahamwe?

The Interahamwe were bad people. They were very violent and mean. And the people who refused to join the Interahamwe were the people who had a good conscience, who didn't want to hurt others. [Sophie, #9/9]

Like the other respondents, Sophie was not surprised when people who were "bad" before the genocide acted badly during the genocide. What Sophie also mentions, however, is the tensions she observed between Tutsi and Hutu, a tension that seemed to go both ways. What was not clear from others' testimony, however, is whether these tensions were old or new and whether they amounted to the kinds of overarching hatreds that the ethnic hatred thesis posits can push one group to perpetrate genocidal violence against another. As Sophie herself notes, in spite of tensions she knew to exist between Hutu and Tutsi, there was no violence, only a certain amount of "hypocrisy." Hypocrisy suggests that people acted one way in front of others but differently behind their backs. It does not necessarily suggest hatred, though it does not rule it out either.

The hypocrisy that Sophie describes is consistent with the one motive that several people, including Sophie, identified as powerful enough to cause people to become violent. More frequently than group tensions or group animosities, people pointed to individual jealousy and greed as the cause of both conflict and violence. During an interview with Jude's wife, Thérèse, both topics came up as Thérèse was explaining how her neighbors suspected that my research assistant and I were working for the government's *gacaca* program, a local justice initiative that had begun in pilot form in June 2002. I asked her why people were afraid of participating in the anticipated *gacaca*, which had not yet begun in Ngali. Thérèse replied that people were afraid of being falsely accused and imprisoned as a result. Some innocent people had been imprisoned after the genocide, even by their own family members, she explained. I probed this logic further.

Q. Why would a family member have another member of his own family imprisoned if that person hadn't done anything?

It's the result of hatred between members of the same family.

Q. What causes a hatred so strong among members of the same family?

The one who has the other imprisoned thinks that they are going to kill [the imprisoned person] so that he can take over all of his [the imprisoned person's] belongings.

Q. It's just greed?

Yes.

Q. Do you think greed was a part of the genocide as well?

Yes, a lot of people were killed because the killers wanted to take their things.

Q. Do you think greed was a part of the imprisonment of people after the war?

Yes.

Q. Were there a lot of people imprisoned after the war just for their things?

The people of Ngali who were imprisoned after the war . . . but I don't know why each was imprisoned. Maybe they were imprisoned for different reasons. [Thérèse, #6/7]

As the hesitancy of her last response shows, Thérèse was always careful not to say too much about the period of the genocide. At first, I thought this reluctance was because she did not want to implicate herself, but through our many interviews, I came to believe her reluctance came from the same fear that others felt. She did not want to say anything that could be traced back to her, fearing repercussions from neighbors, officials, or both. Saying too much was dangerous.

Others besides Thérèse, however, also pointed to greed as an explanation for conflict and violence, both in the past and during the genocide. Typical is the response of Nicolas from Ngali, the best friend and neighbor of Maurice (the man who drew a link between political party conflict in the past and before the genocide). What is notable in this exchange about the causes of what Nicolas calls the "war" is where Nicolas locates hatred. For Nicolas, hatred is the result, not the cause, of war.

Q. In general, what can break up a friendship between two people?

In general, here in Rwanda, what I saw was that it was the war that broke up friendships between people. In earlier times, people liked each other, they shared everything, people would give cows to another person without distinguishing by ethnicity or other things. But the war caused hatred between the people.

Q. How did the war make friendships between people here break up?

It was during the war that there was what one would call greed. Lots of people wanted other people's things and they killed each other.

Q. Doesn't greed exist even when there is no war?

Yes, greed exists even when there's not a war. In any case, it's greed that causes all the misunderstandings between people. [Nicolas, #2/4]

According to Nicolas, greed is the source of misunderstandings and conflicts and is powerful enough to break up friendships. Sophie, too, cited greed as the cause of ruptures in friendships.

Q. In general, what can break up friendships?

It's greed because one person lacks what he wants to give his friend and the friend no longer wants to be friends with this person because of [the person's] poverty. Before, this is what kept me from having lots of friends. It was that almost everyone would ask me to drink beer or would ask me to give them beer even though I didn't have any. And my grandparents would say that it was bad to drink beer because the beer can change something in your memory. For example, you can tell a secret without realizing it because of the beer. [Sophie, #5/9]

The practice of sharing beer is an important form of socializing and expressing various modalities of everyday life, from status to gender roles (de Lame 1996, chap. 5). Thus it is not insignificant that Sophie refused to share or offer beers to others. Such behavior would have certainly made her unpopular. Sophie was not unaware of her marginal status in the community. At times, she seemed to resent it and other times, revel in it. Despite her marginal position, Sophie's views about greed were quite consistent with those of Nicolas and others. For Sophie, greed was the cause of violence from as long back as she could remember. "If someone had lots of things, they were killed," she said in response to a question about a war in the far past. Greed was therefore nothing new when the genocide began; it was rooted in everyday life.

Jealousy and greed provide the possibility for volitional participation in violence. As people from both communities explained, both greed and jealousy were sufficiently powerful to cause people to act badly toward others—including friends and neighbors—and even to commit violence against these people. The frequency with which people cited greed and jealousy as the cause of conflicts and violence stands in stark contrast to the lack of statements pointing to collective hatreds and animosities. Sophie is the only person who mentions general tensions and dislikes between Hutu and Tutsi; others point to specific people they knew who hated Tutsi for no apparent reason. Thus, while jealousy and greed seemed to have been part of daily life before the genocide, there is only scant evidence that collective hatreds were just as common. Instead, it seems to have been specific individuals who hated people of the other ethnicity.

Logic of Contamination

In addition to situational exigencies and personal motives, the third reason people cited for the transformation of their neighbors into genocidal killers was a theory that I call "the logic of contamination." According to this logic, people become like those around them through regular contact and interaction. Their beliefs, actions, and attitudes converge toward those in their immediate social environment. The process is natural and perhaps even inevitable.

Various stories people told illustrated this logic. One man explained the changes in how neighbors treated one another after the war as the result of people having been "infected" by their environment. By "environment," this man was referring to the different places to which people fled. As the war was ending, most Hutu fled to the Congo, while most Tutsi fled toward Uganda or RPF-controlled areas of Rwanda. Many of the refugee camps in the Eastern Congo were controlled by leaders of the genocide.[8] After returning to their homes in Kimanzi, this man explained, people no longer treated one another as they did before, as friends and neighbors, because of where they spent their time in exile.

Q. Did the war transform or change your friendships?

That changed because there were some people I used to work with before but who are no longer my friends because, before we were at the same level from the standpoint of wealth, but seeing that my means had diminished at home, they ended their friendships with me. But there are the others who continued to be my friends.

Q. How did the war affect friendships among the people of [your cellule]?

Because of the war, people fled toward different areas and because of the different atmosphere [in each locale], the people, infected by their environment, picked up a new way of behaving. When they returned, people no longer got along like before. [402, #2/2]

The idea of taking on new ways of behaving from one's environment expresses the logic clearly. A person's social environment is contaminating in the sense that it "infects" people with the prevailing or dominant outlook. In other words, people's social environment can change how they view and approach the world.

Another man used the same logic to explain why it was not good to be friends with a thief. When he was a little boy, the man knew another boy

8. For a firsthand account of conditions in the camps in the eastern Congo from the point-of-view of one aid worker, see Terry (2002). For a searing memoir by one refugee who fled Rwanda and spent time in the camps, see Umutesi (2000).

who habitually stole. This young thief continued to steal throughout his adult life, the man told us. When I asked the man if he had been friends with this thief when they were children, the man quickly responded, "No, it's bad to be friends with thieves." When I asked him why it was bad to be friends with thieves (thinking that as children, we make friends with all kinds of people without realizing who they really are or might turn out to be), he replied that by being friends with a thief, you, too, could become a thief. I was struck by this statement and pursued its logic in greater depth at a subsequent interview.

> *Q. During our second interview, we were talking about friendships and also about some children who stole when you were a child. If you have a friend who is a thief, how would you become a thief as well?*
>
> If you have a friend who is a thief, even if you are not a thief, it's normal that friends would share almost everything. Your friend who is a thief might give you something that he's stolen or he might ask you to try [taste] something he's stolen and you might be tempted yourself to go look for what your friend gave you and you absolutely become a thief. [306, #5/5]

The process of transformation this man describes occurs step by step and leads to an ineluctable end. Friendship helps the process along since it is normal for friends to share everything they have, even if that includes food or items that have been stolen. When the friend gets a taste (literally or metaphorically) of the stolen goods, he is on his way to becoming a thief himself, without even intending such an end. As this man's caution-ary tale points out, being around bad people will eventually turn a good person bad. This process occurs through normal, everyday forms of con-tact between neighbors and friends. In this sense, bad behavior can in-deed spread through social contact.

Accusations of icyitso, or "accomplice," waged against Hutu demon-strate another application of this logic. The basis for making this accusa-tion was that the accused had had some contact or relationship with a Tutsi. The underlying assumption is that a certain level of exposure to Tutsi makes people "like" Tutsi—in the sense of being similar to Tutsi or sympathetic toward them.

Three examples illustrate this causal logic. The first concerns a prisoner from Ngali who used to drive a truck for a living. The prisoner explained during one interview that whenever he drove north to Ruhengeri, people would accuse him of being icyitso. The basis of the accusation was the fact that the man had come from Gitarama, a préfecture known for its much higher percentage of Tutsi (as compared to Ruhengeri) and a high level of integration between Tutsi and Hutu. Having lived with so many Tutsi made the man a suspected accomplice of the RPF.

The second example concerns a Joiner from Kimanzi who had been imprisoned for being icyitso shortly after the start of the civil war. In the 1970s and 1980s, this Joiner had been living in Uganda. He returned to Rwanda by 1985–86. The basis for the accusation, then, was that living in Uganda made the Joiner familiar, and presumably sympathetic, with the RPF's plans.

The third example capitalizes on an actual friendship the accused shared with their Tutsi neighbors. The accused was a man from Kimanzi who said that Interahamwe from outside Kimanzi accused his brother and him of being ibyitso. The basis for the accusation was that he and his brother had exchanged cows with their Tutsi neighbors, a clear sign that the brothers were close friends with these Tutsi. Friendship with their Tutsi neighbors supposedly turned the two brothers into RPF accomplices.

The logic behind these accusations does not amount simply to guilt by association. Rather, it is a logic that assumes that no one person will—or indeed can—remain differentiated from those around her. It assumes that people are influenced by those around them and thus will inevitably take on the beliefs and attitudes of others. According to this logic, social environment is powerfully transformative. It can turn Hutu into Tutsi and RPF supporters. It can also turn some Hutu into génocidaires.

Proponents of the ethnic hatred and ethnic fear theses expect ordinary people to participate in campaigns of mass violence out of overwhelming fears or hatreds of the targeted group. In their descriptions and explanations of the violence that occurred in their communities, however, people from Ngali and Kimanzi do not always point to hatreds or fears, and when they do, their references are contextualized. People differentiate between those who hated Tutsi and those who did not, and those who participated out of fear for their lives and those who participated out of greed or jealousy.

Rather than point to collective hatreds or fears, people explain the violence in much more specific ways. First, they point to the exigencies of war in which authorities forced people to participate. Second, they point to greed and jealousy, timeless emotions so powerful they can cause friendships to rupture, family members to make false accusations against one another, and neighbors to turn on neighbors through violence. Third, people point to a logic of contamination. According to this logic, people adopt the same attitudes and behaviors of those around them through regular contact and exposure. In none of these explanations do collective hatreds or fears figure prominently. Rather, group-level hatreds and fears seem to be the product, not producer, of violence. They occur as a result of living in certain refugee camps or discovering that one's brother-in-law was greedy enough to have one's family killed.

The findings of this chapter beg the question: If ethnic hatreds and fears were the consequence and not cause of the violence, what role did ethnicity play during genocide?

4

The Enigma of Ethnicity

A Tutsi who has no cows is a Hutu.

—SOPHIE, elderly Hutu woman born Tutsi

In the previous chapter, ethnicity figured prominently in people's narration of events during the civil war and genocide. Yet, in their explanations, people highlight environmental factors and personal motives. This raises a puzzle: Where did ethnicity figure in the genocide? How exactly did it operate?

The literature on ethnic and mass violence locates the mobilizing power of ethnicity in the polarized categories that elites are able to construct and diffuse. Under conditions of threat or insecurity, elites will use ethnicity as a political tool to achieve more cynical ends. To polarize groups and radicalize group identities, they will create social (and sometimes physical) distance between a designated target and the rest of the population through the use of propaganda, decrees, speeches, and rallies. Such distance helps to harden identities and lock them in place as immutable categories. Elites then use these hardened identities to mobilize populations to participate in projects of mass violence.

The Rwandan genocide would seem to be a clear instance of an elite-led project. Before the genocide, extremists spewed a relentless discourse of racist hatred against Tutsi using incendiary speeches, vulgar political cartoons, and extremist radio programs (Chrétien et al. 1995; Article 19 1996; Chalk 1999; Des Forges 1999, 65–86). Stoked by these messages, Hutu, it would seem, began to see their Tutsi neighbors as the ultimate enemy that must be destroyed, lest they be destroyed themselves. This extreme view of Tutsi helped to incited Hutu peasants to join in the extermination of their Tutsi neighbors.[1]

Recent studies, however, challenge this account. Straus (2004b, chap. 6) shows that the majority of low-level perpetrators were not familiar with

---

1. Another version pins the construction of Hutu and Tutsi as racially distinct identities on colonial institutions (Mamdani 2001). The end result is the same, however. Identities, formed recently or historically, made people kill.

many of the extremist ideas that elites promulgated about Tutsi, such as the idea that Tutsi were foreigners to Rwanda and intent on taking over the country. As other scholars additionally point out, targeting did not always follow ethnic lines during the genocide. Outside Kigali, there was sometimes confusion about who was being targeted. Even after the genocide began, killers spared some Tutsi and some Tutsi joined the killers; some Hutu became targets and some tried to save Tutsi. Despite how clearly demarcated ethnic categories should have been under genocide, these categories, I will argue, remained multifaceted. Ethnicity continued to operate through multiple levels of meaning during the genocide, just as it operated in daily life before the violence.

The critical difference between genocide and daily life, however, was the diffusion of genocidal constructions of ethnic identity. When the ethnic hatred or ethnic fear models refer to ethnicity, they are referring to one particular set of meanings, which I call "state-sponsored ethnicity." State-sponsored ethnicity operated not as an external force that tapped into people's deep-seated attachments to their ethnic group, but rather, as a script or dramaturgical blueprint for violence. As a piece of theater, state-sponsored ethnicity depicted social life as radically threatened by the diabolical Tutsi threat. The dénouement was the extermination of Tutsi as a whole.

People did not have to believe the script to act it out. People did not have to reconstitute themselves inwardly to comply outwardly. People could kill with scripted ethnic claims, without believing those claims to be true or accurate, because as a script, ethnicity required certain performances, not beliefs. During genocide, ethnic claims came in the form of accusations that a person was Tutsi, looked Tutsi, or supported Tutsi. Actors deployed ethnic claims during the genocide to target at will, and, on rarer occasions, to save themselves or others. These claims were based on subjective determinations of categories that supposedly existed at an objective level. People did know the ethnicity of their neighbors. This was shared, common knowledge that enabled even those with no special status or power in the community to denounce others. Those with power, however, were able to make the ultimate determination as to whether a person's putative ethnicity mattered to her immediate fate. This power to "name" another's identity also derived from community sentiment toward a potential target. The ability to make such determinations was not only the most important form of power during the genocide, it was also the clearest expression of that power.

Ethnicity in Everyday Life

To understand how ethnicity became a resource for genocide, we must first understand how ethnicity operated in everyday life. How did people learn ethnicity? What did being Hutu or Tutsi mean to people? How did people navigate state-sponsored forms of ethnicity? Answers to these questions provide a baseline for how people deployed ethnic claims during the genocide.

Learning *Ubwoko*

The Kinyarwandan term for ethnicity is *ubwoko*, which means the type or kind of something. When referring to a person, the word used to refer to a person's clan. A person's clan, however, did not indicate the person's ethnicity, since all Rwandan clans include Tutsi, Hutu, and Twa members.[2] Eventually, the word *ubwoko* came to refer to a person's ethnicity. Indeed, by the time of my fieldwork in 2004, ubwoko had become so synonymous with ethnicity that to inquire about a person's clan, and not her ethnicity, required my interpreter to give a full explanation of the question, replete with examples. Making sure people knew we were asking about their clan, not their ethnicity, was very important since the government had prohibited any talk of ethnicity in an effort to erase ethnicity from social and political life. Appearing to violate that directive in an initial interview would have raised the suspicions of authorities and made people leery of talking with us.

All but one respondent knew her clan; a much smaller number knew their lineage (31 out of 36 in Kimanzi and 22 out of 44 in Ngali). Unlike clans, lineages are descent-based groups that trace back three to six generations to a common ancestor. When asking someone's lineage, my interpreter used the term *igisekuruza* (*ibisekuruza,* plural) and also provided examples in the same way she did when she asked a person her clan.

Clan knowledge was usually transmitted in the home, from parents or grandparents. It was generally fathers or grandfathers who passed this knowledge to children and grandchildren. In some cases, mothers or female family members played this role, usually because the father had died or left the family. Children would hear the parent or grandparent refer to the family's clan and lineage in a victory song or during a conversation with other adults. This would prompt the child to ask to what these names referred. From the answers adults gave, children would learn from which clan their family came or from which lineage head their family had descended.

2. On Rwandan clans, see D. Newbury (1980), Newbury (1988), and Vansina (2004).

Children often traded clan knowledge amongst themselves informally. Clan talk was a way for children to get to know one another, to find out who was in one's same clan, or who was in a clan that one's own clan was forbidden to marry. As one elderly Hutu man from Ngali, explained, "The girls loved to shout out their clan and the boys would find out the clan of the girls in order to get engaged." Another man from Ngali added: "We would wonder who had started the clans. How was it that some were Abasinga and others were Abagesera and so forth."

The method of transmitting ethnicity knowledge, however, followed a different path. In contrast to clan knowledge, knowledge of ethnicity was not transmitted in the home from one generation to the next. Rather, children would hear adults use these terms outside the home, without providing any explanation of their meaning. People recalled hearing the terms *Hutu, Tutsi,* or *Twa* for the first time when they were fairly young; most gave an age of seven to ten years old (although a few people said they were in their teens). This was about the same age when respondents first became curious about what clan references meant, or more generally, when they first remember becoming curious about who they were and who their ancestors were.

Generally, the child would overhear a relative, neighbor, or other adult make passing reference to someone's ubwoko, such as "that Tutsi family living over there." Yet, unlike clan names, there was no accompanying explanation for what the term *Tutsi* meant. When I asked people what the names *Hutu, Tutsi,* and *Twa* meant to them at a young age, all replied "nothing." Despite not knowing what the terms *Hutu, Tutsi,* and *Twa* meant, people nevertheless came to know the ethnicity of all their friends. Such information was common knowledge and accessible to any member of the community, even children. My exchange with Édouard, a Joiner from Kimanzi, was typical of the responses that people from both communities gave to my questions regarding familiarity with others' ethnicity.

Q. We were talking about lineages before. I would like to pose the same series of questions about ubwoko. When you were young, did you know the ubwoko of all your friends?

Yes, I knew the ubwoko of all my friends.

Q. How did you know them?

It would be my parents and even the neighbors saying that such and such child belonged to the family of a certain ubwoko.

Q. How old were you the first time you heard your parents or your neighbors saying that a certain child belonged to a family of a certain ubwoko?

It was at the age of fifteen.

Q. You were fifteen the first time your heard the names Hutu, Tutsi, and Twa?

I heard it when I was very young, but I was starting to really understand what ethnicity was when I was fifteen.

Q. At fifteen, what did these three categories mean to you?

I only knew that there was three ethnicities, Hutu, Twa, Tutsi but I knew that we were all created by God, because I had friends of every category and we shared everything, games, drinks, food . . .

Q. How old were you the first time you learned that you were one ubwoko and not the other?

When I was ten.

Q. Did you ever wish you were a particular ubwoko?

No, not at all. [Édouard, #5b/5]

Like most people to whom I posed this series of questions, Édouard learned as a child that Hutu, Tutsi, and Twa were terms for categorizing people even if he did not know what the basis for that categorization was or the implications of being one ethnicity and not the other.

Callixte, born in 1948, is a generation older than Édouard, but also came from Kimanzi. Callixte was a survivor of the massacres of Tutsi that took place in January 1991. Unlike Édouard who had no formal education, Callixte was highly educated. Like Édouard, Callixte, too, remembered hearing the terms *Hutu, Tutsi,* and *Twa* at a young age. He was eight years old when he first heard neighbors remarking that his father was Tutsi while they themselves were Hutu. When I asked Callixte what being Tutsi or Hutu meant to him as an eight year old, he replied: "It meant nothing to me because I knew that when someone would say that a given family was Tutsi, I knew that it was the father who was Tutsi or if a given family was Hutu, that it was the papa who was Hutu. And I didn't know that there were Hutu or Tutsi children." The inferences Callixte made as a child were quite accurate, for ethnicity does issue from the father in Rwandan culture, so references to a "Tutsi" family do indeed mean that the father is Tutsi. What Callixte had not yet learned was that children, mothers, and wives also have ethnic designations.

Residents of Ngali had similar memories of the first time they heard the terms *Hutu* and *Tutsi* and their attempts to make sense of the meaning of these labels.

Bernard, born in 1930 and thus a generation older than Callixte and two generations older than Édouard, said he was fifteen "when my father would talk to me about our ubwoko." As with Édouard and Callixte, the terms initially carried no meaning for him. Unlike Édouard and Callixte, however, Bernard came of age during the colonial period, when the Belgian-backed system of Tutsi hegemony would have been in full force. In addition, Bernard had grown up not far from the seat of the royal court in Nyanza, which gave him a different perspective on the link between "Tutsi" and "power" than that of Callixte and Édouard, who grew up in the north.

Q. When did it start to mean something to you, what it meant to be Hutu or Tutsi?

When people started to say that a given family was Tutsi among the Abanyiginya, the Tutsi among the Abega. I started to think of ubwoko when I would see the Hutu who were transporting the Tutsi chiefs toward the royal palace or when they would transport the king when he wanted to take a tour of his country. At that time, I started to feel that the Hutu were the servants and that the Tutsi were very powerful in the eyes of the Hutu.

Q. Were you thinking these things before Independence [1959–61]?

It was before Independence. [Bernard, #6/6]

As a young man coming of age during the period of "dual colonialism" under Tutsi-Belgian rule, Bernard observed firsthand the extent to which "Hutu" and "Tutsi" were power-laden terms.[3]

The generations that came of age in the postindependence era were more likely to learn about ethnicity in school. Learning about ethnicity occurred formally through school curricula and informally through peer and teacher pressure. Formally, children learned about ethnicity through Rwandan history lessons. As Émilie, a genocide survivor from Ngali born in 1972, explained: "They taught us the history of Rwanda, there were courses on ethnicity (abahutu, abatutsi, abatwa). They told us that the bahutu were the cultivators, the batutsi were the herders, and the batwa were the potters." Jean-Marie, a Hutu from Kimanzi born in 1965, told us he, too, learned about ubwoko through history lessons. Jean-Marie was sixteen when he first learned the history of Hutu, Tutsi, and Twa in a class of all Hutu students. The lessons, Jean-Marie explained, were meant to reinforce the idea that Hutu had been victims of Tutsi abuses throughout history. "What we heard, they wanted to show us how the Tutsi were bad. The teachers wanted to show us how the Tutsi mistreated the Hutu in years past," he explained.

Children not only learned difference through school lessons; they also learned to practice difference. As Émilie recalled, teachers routinely sepa-

---

3. The term *dual colonialism* comes from Newbury (1988).

rated children by ethnicity. Most children knew their ubwoko, but those who did not suffered the displeasure of their teachers and ridicule of their peers. As Émilie explained, when a child did not know his ubwoko, the other children "would mock him. They would say that he was like an idiot." History lessons reinforced these "bad" feelings. As Émilie went on to explain, learning about ubwoko "created a bad feeling in the hearts of some of the students." The Hutu children would remark that Tutsi had badly mistreated the Hutu for a long time. Through these experiences, children learned that "Tutsi" was associated with past abuses and "Hutu" with past oppression. They also learned the importance of knowing their own and others' ubwoko, whatever meaning the terms carried.

The lessons imparted in school did not constitute privileged knowledge. Even those with little or no schooling were familiar with the same version of Rwandan history that Émilie and Jean-Marie had learned. One man from Ngali who had never attended school, for example, said that he learned the same histories listening to old men talking over beers. The official and consensus history of Hutu and Tutsi was therefore widely known among Hutu and Tutsi, young and old, educated and uneducated alike. As such, it constituted a key component of state-sponsored ethnicity and formed a common discourse across all social strata.

In addition to learning about the history of "Hutu," "Tutsi," and "Twa," people also learned to identify themselves by their ethnicity in interactions with the state. School officials recorded the ubwoko of students. Courts required people to identify their ubwoko before resolving problems. The state required all Rwandans over the age of sixteen to carry an identity card, which listed, among other things, the card holder's ubwoko. Finally, a quota system capped enrollment in schools and issuance of government posts to 9 percent for Tutsi to match the official percentage of Tutsi in the population (in reality, however, those percentages were oftentimes much higher) (Prunier 1995, 75).

Many of the state institutions that sought to fix ethnicity had a long history, dating to the period of Belgian rule (1916–61). It was during this period that a statecentric history similar to what Jean-Marie and Émilie had learned in school and others had learned word of mouth became the "doxic" version of history—one that obviated the possibility of alternatives. The doxic version of Rwandan history was diffused through school curriculum, the press, and even scholarly work (Newbury and Newbury 2000, 848). Its goal was to make other possible histories unimaginable.

In addition to supporting the creation and diffusion of an ideologically driven history, the Belgians introduced a system of identify cards in the 1930s.[4] Both Kayibanda and Habyarimana continued the practice under the pretext of "equality"—supposedly to ensure that Hutu did not continue to face discrimination in the public and educational sectors.

A third institution that reinforced a fixed notion of ethnic membership was the census. In the postindependence era, the Rwanda government undertook two censuses, one in 1978 and the other in August 1991. One of the questions census takers asked each household head was the family's ubwoko.

Outwardly, these state institutions and practices reinforced the idea that ethnic categories were immutable and fixed. Beneath official forms of ethnicity, however, a more ambiguous system of categorization existed, shaped by people's strategic, not affective, approach to ethnicity. People changed their official ethnic identity by obtaining new identity cards. They also misrepresented themselves to census takers. The Rwandan government even acknowledged this latter practice, which it dated to the colonial era. The published findings from the 1991 census refer to this practice directly.

> The people of an ethnic group may declare themselves another ethnicity because of the socio-political climate prevailing at the time of data collection. In 1952, for example, a test conducted after the demographic survey showed that "more than a quarter of Rwandans counted as Tutsi were in reality rich Hutu." Since 1961, the end of the Tutsi monarchy, there is reason to believe that any false declarations would go in the other direction, Tutsi having a tendency to declare themselves Hutu. (République Rwanda 1994, 122)

As the government itself acknowledges, the practice of deliberate misrepresentation to census takers (in response to political conditions) occurred not only during the colonial period but continued through the present.

What is surprising, perhaps, is that there is no indication that the government ever attempted to stamp out this practice or adjust for it in the

---

4. I found no documents in the Belgian colonial archives that specified the precise date when the Belgians began the system. I did find two specimens of actual cards that date to the early 1930s, indicating the system was in place by that time. The use of identity cards was not unique to the colonies. The Germans introduced the identity card system in occupied Belgium during World War I. After the war, the Belgian government instituted its own system and extended this practice to its colonies. As Filip Reyntjens explains, so taken for granted were identity cards as standard administrative practice that "it would have been strange if the Belgians had not introduced identity cards in their colonies" (personal communication, November 2004).

census figures. According to its own published findings, the government forbade census takers from questioning or overriding the information people gave about their ethnic identity. As the final report (1994, 12) stated: "Taking into account the sensitivity of the subject, a census taker must accept the information given." There seemed to be no penalty or fine for misrepresentation. Thus, despite the fact that the state required people to declare their ethnic identity in all administrative transactions, the state nonetheless relied on a system of self-identification, which gave people space to define themselves according to current political conditions.

In sum, learning ubwoko started at a young age and took place through both formal and informal channels. People learned as children the importance of knowing their own and other's ethnicity. As adults, people learned how to deploy ethnicity strategically in their interactions with the state. Contrary to the expectations of ethnicity-based approaches, ethnicity was not one "thing," but many.

Deploying Stereotypes

Using ethnicity strategically requires extensive and intimate knowledge about what others know and what one can expect others to know. Unlike knowledge people gain through history lessons or administrative tasks, such knowledge is privileged. It is the domain of insiders—those living in the same immediate, face-to-face community and thus fluent in the same cultural forms. Such knowledge is beyond the reach of outsiders, for whom local distinctions are often undetectable.

To outsiders, the most accessible form of insider's knowledge is stereotypes. Outsiders often accept these stereotypes uncritically. As Russell Hardin (1995, 169) writes, for example, the distinction between Hutu and Tutsi is based on "visually compelling differences." The trope of "visually compelling difference" harkens back to early twentieth century European constructions of difference that were based on skewed samples and specious theories of race (see chapter 2). In reality, stereotypes in Rwanda, as elsewhere, are but crude indicators of ethnic identity. As such, they are often unreliable. They are unreliable precisely because of the extent of somatic variation within each group, which all respondents readily acknowledged. Rather than highlight the differences between "Tutsi" and "Hutu," stereotypes underscore the ambiguity of boundaries that mark off the two groups. Ambiguity, in turn, makes possible multiple ways to deploy stereotypes for strategic end.

All respondents were quite familiar with the physical stereotypes associated with each of the three groups. Tutsi were tall and had long noses;

Hutu were short; Twa even shorter. People were also quite familiar with the cultural stereotypes attached to each group. The most oft cited was that "Tutsi like cows." No one treated stereotypes as hard and fast rules, but as an indicator that a difference, however fuzzy, did indeed exist between Hutu and Tutsi. What people could not pinpoint was how they could tell that difference. As one man from Kimanzi explained in typically ambiguous fashion: "What distinguished Hutu or Tutsi, it would be that Tutsi really like cows. Hutu like to do other activities, including cows."

Not only are the criteria for distinguishing between Hutu and Tutsi ambiguous and subtle, there are also many exceptions to the rule, as people also pointed out. Not all Tutsi are tall. Not all Hutu are short. Not all herders are Tutsi, and not all Hutu are farmers. These exceptions did not render the categories any less valid; rather, they indicated the need to look beyond physical or cultural stereotypes to determine a person's "true" identity, since physical characteristics varied as much within groups as between them. Charles, a Joiner from Kimanzi, articulated well how physical characteristics could vary within ethnic groups, without changing any one person's ethnicity. The topic came up while discussing Charles's childhood. His mother had died shortly after giving birth to him. His father then remarried. Until the age of eight, Charles grew up in an orphanage run by a muzungu woman (most likely a European nun).

Q. During your childhood, did you know the ubwoko of the muzungu who raised you?

No, I only knew that she was a muzungu.

Q. Is "muzungu" a type of ubwoko or not?

I think that "muzungu" is a type of color like one might say "black" or "light" [*inzobe*].

Q. Explain to me the difference between the different colors of people and the different ubwoko of people.

There is a difference because the ubwoko does not change. If you are Tutsi or Hutu or Twa, that does not change but you can have people with light skin, black or between the two colors who are Tutsi, Twa and Hutu.

Q. Today, how do you understand the difference between the three ubwoko? How do the three differ?

Normally, I cannot see a difference between the three ethnicities. There is no physical distinction because you can find Tutsi, Twa, and Hutu with the same physical characteristics. I noticed only that there is a difference because the people of the same ethnicity like each other more than the others. For example, when a Tutsi authority can profit from whatever kind of position he has, he can give the job to all the people of the same ethnicity.

Q. In other words, people favor or have a tendency to favor people of the same ubwoko?
Yes. They favor the people of the same ethnicity. [Charles, #5/5]

Like others with whom I spoke, Charles readily acknowledged that physical characteristics are unreliable markers of difference because of the extent of variation that exists within each group. This variation means that it is necessary to use other criteria to tell Tutsi from Hutu. Charles pointed out one possibility—people's behavior toward others. Charles' logic, however, does not indicate how to distinguish Hutu from Tutsi since presumably both groups would tend to favor their own. Favoritism, in other words, could only arise after people's ethnic identities were known. What Charles's logic does point to is the impossibility of identifying a person simply from her appearance.

Stereotypes rely on cultural knowledge, which consists of knowing when and how to apply stereotypes. Thérèse, the wife of the Jude, the leader of the genocide in Ngali, demonstrated this facility during one interview. It was Thérèse who began this particular interview by mentioning lightheartedly that Rwandans knew bazungu (plural of muzungu), or foreigners, too, had different *amoko* (plural of ubwoko). Thérèse then went on to explain how Rwandan stereotypes map onto the different nationalities of foreigners. "They say that the Hutu are the Belgians, the Tutsi are the Ethiopians and Americans, and the Twa are the Chinese." We all laughed at this application of Rwandan stereotypes to other national groups. In the midst of this shared laughter, I probed how Thérèse thought about ethnicity in general—how ethnicity operates for all people, not just Rwandans.

Q. Why do they say that the Hutu are the Belgians?
They say that the Belgians are the Hutu because of their [the Belgians'] medium height. The Chinese are the Twa because they love to work. They are small in stature. The Ethiopians and the Americans are the Tutsi because of their tall size and in addition, they are nice looking.

Q. According to these criteria, I am Hutu?
No, because there are also Tutsi who are short.

Q. Why would I be Tutsi? because of my height or my nationality or what?
I can say that you are Tutsi because you are different from the Chinese and the Belgians. You, you are pretty. Your nose is long like those of the Tutsi.

Q. Neither the Chinese nor the Belgians are nice looking?
You can find some Chinese or some Belgians who are nice looking but not often.

Q. You have never seen an ugly American?

Never. Among the Americans I have seen, they are truly nice looking. Maybe there are some who are ugly but I have not seen them.

Q. Have you ever seen a real Ethiopian?

No, except for pictures of Ethiopians on television.[5]

Q. In these TV shows, you had seen real Ethiopians?

Yes.

Q. And you thought these Ethiopians were nice looking?

Yes. [Thérèse, #4/7]

While there was much levity in this exchange, Thérèse's mapping of Rwandan stereotypes onto non-Rwandans shows her facility with adapting these stereotypes to different settings. Like Charles, Thérèse knows which elements of the stereotype to disregard (height) and which to favor (nose and looks) in typing me as Tutsi instead of Hutu or Twa. It is also possible that Thérèse typed me as Tutsi because of my high social status as a foreign researcher. As Thérèse's adept use of stereotypes suggests, it is not that stereotypes can be wrong, but that one must apply them flexibly, because the combination of features—both physical and cultural—vary by individual.

As these data show, ethnicity does not reduce to official forms or commonly known stereotypes, as the ethnic fear and ethnic hatred models seem to assume. Rather, ethnicity is "contextually configured" (Newbury and Newbury 1999, 294). It is based on insiders' knowledge about how to tell difference and how to apply such knowledge in a given setting. People do not simply learn stereotypes; they also learn how to adapt, disregard, and refashion them depending on the situation and their goals.[6] In so doing, people reproduce certain meanings (e.g., Tutsi like cows) and practices (e.g., references to stereotypes); at the same time, they also reproduce the flexibility and ambiguity attached to these meanings and practices. Such flexibility is what enables strategic use of ethnicity in everyday, social settings as well as interactions with the state.

5. Thérèse said she saw the pictures of Ethiopians on television when she and her family were in the refugee camps in the Congo, following the end of the genocide and civil war. The significance of equating Tutsi to Ethiopians is that this was consistent with the Hamitic myth, which viewed Tutsi as closer to whites than black Africans, and originating from Ethiopia (see chapter 2).

6. I thank David Newbury for the latter insight.

Changing Ubwoko

In addition to shared awareness that exceptions were the rule, some people were also aware of the possibility that one's ubwoko can change. This awareness varied by region and age. Those who were familiar with such cases were all from Ngali and over fifty years of age. The people in Kimanzi I questioned on this topic, both young and old, were not familiar with this possibility, which is not surprising, perhaps, given the small number of Tutsi in this region. One older man from Kimanzi (b. 1935), for example, said it was not possible to change one's ubwoko when he was growing up and that even intermarriage was not possible before independence, because it would have been "shameful" for a Tutsi to have married a Hutu.

Those who were aware of the possibility of changing one's ubwoko mention two ways such change could take place. The first was through use of "status" rather than "hereditary" criteria for determining ethnicity. According to status criteria, a person's ethnicity depends on her socioeconomic level, viewed in terms of cow ownership. Those with lots of cows are Tutsi; those with few or no cows are Hutu regardless of their ethnicity at birth. If a person's socioeconomic circumstances change, her ethnicity changes accordingly. The second way a person's ethnicity could change was through strategic action. This involves obtaining a new identity card that specifies a different ubwoko. Both possibilities for changing one's ethnicity also rested in community acceptance of the change. People had to agree to the new identity.[7]

Those familiar with the first method were the oldest people in the sample. Sophie, for example, was more than eighty years old when we interviewed her in 2004.[8] She recalled how she first learned what made a person Hutu or Tutsi.

Q. How did you learn that you were one ethnicity and not the other?

I was playing with my grandfather. I would ask him a lot of questions concerning my family and my ethnicity. And it was at that moment that he told me my ubwoko.

Q. As a child, did you want to be one ethnicity and not the other?

I only wanted to know my ubwoko.

7. I thank Alison Des Forges for this point.
8. Sophie gave different years of birth at different interviews. Based on her age at marriage and the birth of her children, it likely that she was born in the early 1920s, making her between 80–84 years old in 2004.

Q. How did your grandfather explain to you your ubwoko?

He explained to me that we were Abasinga and he told me that those who possessed lots of cows, whether Hutu or Tutsi, were Tutsi and those who had nothing in the way of livestock were Hutu. [Sophie, #6/9]

Her grandfather's explanation of what makes a person Hutu or Tutsi draws on a status criterion for determining ethnic identity. A status criterion runs counter to the logic of a hereditary criterion, which assumes that people are simply born Hutu or Tutsi. (Ethnicity-based approaches tend to take for granted the latter basis for ethnic membership.) A status criterion implies, by contrast, that a person's ethnicity can change depending on her circumstances (though not that it will). Using a status criterion, Sophie recounted how her family's ethnicity changed from Tutsi to Hutu.

Q. And when you were young, did your family have lots of cows?

Yes, my family had lots of cows.

Q. Did your family ever lose their cows?

We lost them after the death of Rudahigwa, when people were saying that it wasn't necessary for the common people to have large livestock like the chiefs.[9] And the chiefs took our cows and the other cows were slaughtered.

Q. After losing their cows, did your family become Hutu?

Well, of course, because we became poor cultivators. [Sophie, #6/9]

Having no cows constituted Sophie and her family as Hutu, just as having lots of cows constituted them as Tutsi. Thus neither their "Tutsiness" nor "Hutuness" was fixed at birth because circumstances after birth changed.

Sophie was not the only person to talk about her family's ubwoko having changed. Another elderly respondent from Ngali, Bernard (b. 1930), also stated quite matter-of-factly that his family had been Tutsi at one time but became Hutu when it lost its cows.

Q. In the past, was it possible to change your ubwoko?

Yes, when a Hutu was rich, he would become Tutsi and when a Tutsi was poor, he would become Hutu right away.

9. Mwami Rudahigwa had traveled to Bujumbura, the capital of Burundi, on 24 July 1959 and while there, fell ill. He requested a shot of penicillin from his Belgian doctor and shortly thereafter died. Reyntjens (1985, 239–41) lays out the three main theories various observers have put forth to explain the king's unexpected death. Reyntjens concludes that the most plausible was that the king had had a bad reaction to the medicine.

Q. Did that happen often? when someone became rich or poor and as a result, changed his ubwoko?

Yes, that would happen often.

Q. Did your family change its ubwoko several times?

My wife changed her ubwoko one time. In the beginning we were Tutsi and when there was a decrease [in the number] of cows, we became Hutu.

Q. In what year did you lose your cows?

It was during the reign of Musinga.[10]

Q. Did you become rich again after losing your cows?

Since that time, we have been doing agriculture and we have been Hutu.

Q. Even though you were born Tutsi?

I was born Tutsi because of lots of cows that father possessed but after our cows suffered from disease, we became Hutu. [Bernard, #5/6]

Like Sophie, Bernard considers this change in ethnicity to be unremarkable. The change, moreover, is automatic and instantaneous. As Bernard points out, when a Tutsi became poor, he became Hutu "right away." Like Sophie, Bernard constructs ethnicity as a category demarcating socioeconomic status, not bloodline.

The ubwoko of Thérèse's father and grandparents also changed, but unlike Bernard and Sophie's families, Thérèse's family changed its ethnicity for political reasons. Thérèse's family members changed their ethnicity by obtaining new identity cards that said they were Hutu. Thérèse's family used the state's official system of ethnicity to affix a new identity.

Thérèse was in her fifties when we interviewed her and was therefore a generation younger than Bernard and Sophie. The news that Thérèse's father and grandparents had changed their ethnicity from Tutsi to Hutu came as a shock to me. I discovered this while asking general questions about her family and had no reason to believe Thérèse herself was anything but Hutu, that is, born of a Hutu father. So sure was I, based on my own stereotyping of Thérèse and the fact that she had been married to Jude, the leader of the genocide in Ngali, that I never even thought to probe this issue during our many interviews.[11]

10. This is likely an error on the part of Bernard or my interpreter. The Belgians deposed Musinga in 1931 and named one of his baptized sons as the new mwami that same year. Bernard is most likely referring to the new (Belgian-installed) mwami, Rudahigwa.

11. This was not the first time I and my interpreter were wrong in our assumptions about a person's ethnicity. In another case, we were equally sure that a man we had interviewed several times was Hutu, but he, too, turned out to be Tutsi. My interpreter and I generally had

During our last interview, however, I began asking general questions about Thérèse's family's background. Thérèse explained that her paternal grandparents had been rich. At one point, her grandparents did lose some of their cows, which forced her grandfather to work for his chief "to obtain cows again," but the family never became so poor as to be considered Hutu. During the transition to independence, however, when the newly installed (Hutu) authorities were targeting Tutsi for violence, her grandparents and parents obtained new identity cards that said they were Hutu. I asked Thérèse why her father had changed his ethnicity. She responded: "It was a question of protecting himself and saving his life. Even [today], if there is a change in government, lots of Rwandans would change to Hutu." Thérèse's remark that "even today" people would change their ethnicity to Hutu if the government were to change indicates a very strategic attitude toward ethnicity, not a deeply held, affective attachment, as ethnicity-based approaches assume.

The possibility that people can change their ethnicities creates a level of ambiguity about what it really means to be Hutu or Tutsi, for a Hutu today may have been a Tutsi before. This ambiguity played itself out in different ways during the genocide, at times creating targets (through accusations that a person was "really" Tutsi) and, at other times, providing the possibility for presenting oneself as Hutu.

Ethnicity during Genocide

Rigid views of ethnicity were not invented during the genocide. They were legacies of the colonial period, when Belgian administrators and European missionaries, drawing on the Hamitic myth, a specious theory of racial hierarchy, constructed Hutu and Tutsi as distinct races with distinct and uneven capabilities. My data show, however, that Tutsi continued to distinguish themselves from the RPF and did not automatically view the RPF as their "liberators." Some Tutsi, for example, expressed fear of the RPF and were alarmed by the rumors they were hearing that the RPF had big ears and tails. Hutu, meanwhile, did not automatically conflate Tutsi with the RPF either—rather other actors had to draw such links.

Hatreds and Fears among Joiners

If there was fertile ground for mass hatreds against Tutsi, we should find such evidence among the group of low-level participants whom I call

---

the same assumptions about people, which we usually did not discuss until after we learned that our assumptions had been wrong.

"Joiners." If either ethnic hatred or ethnic fears drove this group's participation in the violence in significant ways, we should find evidence of these hatreds and fears in their statements about that period. Moreover, the hatreds or fears we find should distinguish Joiners from the others I interviewed who did not join in the violence. For if hatreds and fears were constant across the spectrum of people I interviewed—if everyone felt the same fears and hatreds—then neither factor can explain why some joined while others did not or why after joining, Joiners did not always follow the genocidal plan.

The first question we must ask is whether Joiners constructed ethnicity differently than other people in their communities. Did they view Tutsi in more extreme or monolithic terms as the rest of the population? The answer is no. Joiners reified ethnicity the same way as everybody else. They also showed the same awareness that multiple meanings could adhere to either label. They demonstrated the same adeptness at navigating the grey zones of meaning.

Joiners did not claim any special authority on typing people. In fact, what enabled Joiners to locate and identify their Tutsi targets during the genocide was not any special ability to distinguish Tutsi from others, but local knowledge they had from having lived in the same face-to-face community as their victims. As one Joiner from Kimanzi remarked, it was easy to know who the Tutsi families were in one's own secteur. This was particularly true in the northern community of Kimanzi, where the number of Tutsi families was very small (approximately five families for the whole secteur).

There is also little evidence indicating Joiners harbored a special hatred toward Tutsi. Several Joiners, for example, said they participated in the massacres and genocide because they were forced to do so. Even the Joiners who said they participated willingly make no mention of pent-up hatreds they felt for Tutsi as a group. Indeed, both survivors and Joiners remarked just the opposite—that relations with their neighbors were fine before the violence began.

One might object that the reason the data do not reveal hatreds is because of the sensitive nature of the topic of ethnicity at the time of my field research. While the government had banned talk of ethnicity, it was not the case that people were unwilling to talk about ethnicity or ethnic relations. There were many topics people were unwilling to cover in any detail, and in these instances, people made it quite clear they preferred to talk about something else. No respondent, however, showed any reluctance to talk about ethnicity either in the context of the genocide or in daily life, though it is possible they felt reluctant to talk about ethnic divisions at the group level because of a recent government crackdown on people espousing genocidal ideology.

Despite these government restrictions, Joiners were willing to give their own explanations about why they and others participated in the genocide. The reasons they gave did not include collective hatreds of Tutsi. (These explanations are discussed in detail in chapter 6.)

Perhaps, however, it was not overwhelming hatred for Tutsi that Joiners felt but an overwhelming sense of fear. If the radio and authorities were telling the truth, and if the Tutsi were out to retake the country by force, then it would have been perfectly rational for the Hutu masses to line up behind their Hutu leaders to assure their own security against this overwhelming threat. The picture the ethnic fear thesis paints, however, is indeterminate. With which Hutu leaders were the Hutu masses supposed to align themselves? The MRND Hutu? The MDR Hutu? Northern Hutu? Southern Hutu? Moderate Hutu or extremist Hutu? Pro-RPF Hutu or anti-RPF Hutu?

Perhaps the answer became clear to people only as events unfolded. Perhaps internal distinctions became less important as the threat of civil war became more pronounced and as rumors of RPF war crimes and atrocities circulated more widely. Here, the data are mixed. There was a great deal of fear at key moments, such as the RPF attack on Ruhengeri, the assassination of the Burundian president, and the plane crash that killed the Rwandan president. All respondents, including Joiners, spoke of the fear they felt in these moments of crisis. The object of people's fears, however, was not always Tutsi or the RPF. Rather, the object of fear shifted according to the situation. The most immediate threat for Joiners who were forced to participate in the violence, for example, came from other Hutu leaders and Interahamwe. Refusing to go along with these men meant harassment and even being killed.

Some Joiners did participate willingly and did so, they explained, out of fear of the RPF and the possibility that their Tutsi neighbors were hiding accomplices as authorities were claiming. For these Joiners, fear of Tutsi was a primary factor in their joining the violence. As Édouard, the Joiner whose story began this book, explained, he did not want the people of Kimanzi to end up like the people of Umutara (where the RPF had invaded and held territory). Édouard was very clear about his motivation for participating in the violence. He wanted to protect his community from the RPF.

In sum, there is evidence that some Joiners, like Édouard, feared the RPF enough to join in the violence against their Tutsi neighbors. Other Joiners, however, were more fearful of other Hutu than Tutsi. There is also no evidence that any Joiner joined in the violence because of overwhelming hatreds he harbored for Tutsi as a group. Killers who hated Tutsi did indeed exist, as respondents mentioned in the previous chapter, but there did not seem to be such killers among the Joiners I interviewed.

Performing Violence

The lack of data indicating collective hatreds of Tutsi and only partial evidence showing collective fears does not mean that ethnicity did not matter during the genocide. What it means is that ethnicity did not matter in the way the ethnic fear and ethnic hatred models predict or assume—as a monolithic force that existed prior to, and distinct from, the process of violence itself. Contrary to the expectations of both approaches, Tutsi did not come "premade" as objects of extermination before the violence began, and Joiners did not necessarily view Tutsi as such during moments of violence. In fact, even in the midst of genocide, some Joiners continued to see their Tutsi neighbors and friends as neighbors and friends—as people to help, not hurt.

The mass hatreds and fears that standard approaches claim to observe were not evidence of people's affective attachments to their ethnic group, but a reflection of the deadly political contest that pitted powerful hardliners against both internal and external enemies (i.e., the opposition and RPF). Ethnicity, in other words, was not something people felt in their core being and then acted on; it was something people in power constructed in specific ways for specific ends. It had to be packaged for genocide, for its "natural" state was too ambiguous and fluid.

The most powerful technique for constructing ethnicity in radical terms was through violence. Political actors created a form of ethnicity that was constituted by violence. The creators of "state-sponsored ethnicity" were the hardliners in the Habyarimana regime who appointed themselves the new "interim government" after the president's assassination on 6 April 1994. Their project, however, started long before, when political pressures began to mount in the country in the early 1990s (see chapter 2).

What these hardliners produced was not just another officially sanctioned form of ethnicity—one that could be counted, assigned, and registered—or even a new ideology suitable for mass consumption. What they created was much more. It was a script for violence. The script was not intended to mirror or depict life as people knew it, but to conjure a new reality and social order out of existing and familiar elements. Performing the script meant instantiating this new order, one that ensured the hardliners' continued monopoly on power.

The creation process was highly adaptive. It involved presenting the conflict and civil war in strictly ethnic terms, because unlike any political conflict, an "ethnic war" could not be resolved through negotiation and bargaining. Creating the script also involved integrating key events, such as the invasion of the RPF and the assassination of the Burundian president, into the dramatic arc of the play. It involved creation of stock characters that were easily identifiable, such as the evil RPF, the diabolical Tutsi, the scheming Tutsi seductress, and even the ineffectual and hapless Habyarimana—all of whom were caricatures but appeared "real enough."[12]

Local leaders adapted the script to their own needs and goals. In Kimanzi in the north (as throughout the country), the most powerful local authority was the bourgmestre.[13] Working with select conseillers and responsables, the bourgmestre mobilized the population to go after Tutsi by telling them their Tutsi neighbors were supporting the RPF by giving money to the rebel army and harboring ibyitso (RPF accomplices) in their homes.[14] Kimanzi offered a particularly realistic backdrop for these claims since the war was literally on people's doorsteps. In Ngali, by contrast, the script was adapted to the new crisis at hand—the assassination of the president. In this version, all Tutsi had to be killed because it was the Tutsi/RPF that had just murdered the president.

Actual performances came down to the actors themselves and their enthusiasm and commitment to the roles they were assigned to play. Some Joiners remained faithful to their parts, while others followed the script only when they had no choice. Félix, for example, a Joiner from Ngali, accompanied a group of authorities to a nearby roadblock out of fear they would hurt him if he refused. There, he witnessed the murder of a local Tutsi boy. Moments later, Félix slipped away when leaders ordered everyone to bury the body, saying he was going home to "get his things."

Other Joiners followed the script when "onstage," that is, in the presence of other authorities or killers. Olivier, a particularly active Joiner from Ngali, participated in all genocidal activities, from pillaging Tutsi property to killing Tutsi. When he was alone, however, he passed up opportunities to

12. See Chrétien et al. (1995) for examples of the vulgar political cartoons published in *Kangura* and other extremist newspapers and the incendiary messages relayed over radio airwaves that featured these stock caricatures prominently.

13. Habyarimana appointed the bourgmestres himself and could remove them at will. This made the bourgmestre "clearly and directly the president's man out on the hills" (Des Forges 1999, 42).

14. It was never clear to me whether the conseiller of Kimanzi participated in the genocide. This man, imprisoned and sentenced to death by the time of my fieldwork, insisted he did not participate in the genocide. From residents' testimonies, the extent of the man's involvement remained unclear. Conseillers of other secteurs, however, seemed to have participated.

kill. Appearing to stay true to the script was an intentional strategy of some actors. Demonstrating their participation in the genocide helped to deflect suspicion away from their activities at home. In one telling example, local residents would show up for roadblock duty every day so that no one would suspect they were hiding Tutsi in their homes.[15] For most Joiners, participating or appearing to participate was important because failing to "perform" invited harassment, beatings, suspicions, and death threats.

The variability of performances arose because most Joiners knew better. They knew that the script was not an accurate representation of their lived experiences. In their lived experiences, neighbors generally played the role of neighbor, regardless of ethnic identity. Resentments, animosities, conflicts, and disputes were normal, everyday occurrences, but the basis for these antagonisms was generally personal, not ethnic. At the same time, Joiners also knew (as did the entire country) that the war, the tensions of multiparty politics, the perturbations of economic decline, and other crises had profoundly altered daily life. What the script offered Joiners was a ready-made way to navigate these profound changes, thereby obviating the need to figure out an appropriate response on their own. Thus when Stefan, a Joiner from Kimanzi, says that he did not think his close neighbor was an icyitso but nevertheless went to the man's house with a group of twelve to fifteen other men, what Stefan is saying is that circumstances being what they were, he could not be sure. He had heard the rumors. He had heard authorities' pronouncements that local Tutsi were helping the RPF. In the absence of other, clear options or responses, Stefan joined the "performance" because doing so made sense in the moment.

What did performing the script entail? It involved a variety of activities and roles (see chapter 6 for a fuller discussion), but at base, it entailed making claims about people's identity and then acting on those claims through violence. Claim-making was the purview of those with power—that is, leaders and their henchmen. Claims were accusations that a person was Tutsi, looked Tutsi, or supported Tutsi. Making these claims drew on shared knowledge about stereotypes about Tutsi being tall, being rich, or liking cows. By invoking different elements of the stereotype, power holders could accuse anybody of looking Tutsi. As Charles, the Joiner from Kimanzi (who explained the difference between skin color and ethnicity), pointed out, "Many people were killed because of their stature ["look"] during the period of the genocide." Claims based on stereotypes became

15. Alison Des Forges described this scenario during comments at the Rwanda I panel, African Studies Association annual meeting, Washington DC, 17 November 2005.

deadly precisely because everyone knew that exceptions were the rule. Known exceptions enabled those with power to enlarge or narrow the range of targets as they saw fit, to include certain Hutu or to exclude certain Tutsi. Their very flexibility made stereotypes an even deadlier resource than identity cards or other fixed forms of ethnicity, since stereotyping involves making subjective determinations. Indeed, it was these subjective determinations that enabled killers to ignore what was on some people's identity cards. With stereotypes, the ethnicity of a person is what those in power say it is.

Claim-making also entailed deciding when being Tutsi (or Hutu) did or did not matter to a person's fate. Determining the salience of identity in a given moment was the purview of leaders. Leaders were the ultimate arbiters of "Tutsiness" in their communities and the final arbiters of when being Tutsi mattered more than bribes or a person's identity card. In Ngali, for example, Jude, the leader of the genocide, targeted "all Tutsi and anyone who looked Tutsi," according to Jude's nephew, Paul. But as Paul himself added, Jude also had eleven Hutu killed for looking Tutsi, despite knowing the eleven victims were Hutu. Paradoxically, Jude also allowed a handful of Tutsi to join the Interahamwe and spared other Tutsi in exchange for money. What made these interpolations of the script possible was not ethnic relations, but power. National-level power holders created the script and gave their backing to local-level power holders who directed the script in their local communities. It was this hierarchy of power that linked local productions to center politics; local productions nevertheless reflected local interests and conditions.

In Ngali, what helped to reinforce Jude's power was shared knowledge among residents that people could and did change their ethnicity (by obtaining new identity cards or losing their cows). During the genocide, this knowledge gave rise to questions about the authenticity of some people's identity—who they really were. This uncertainty, in turn, made possible the accusation that a Hutu was really Tutsi. People had made such accusations during episodes of violence against Tutsi in the past. The likelihood that people would use them again during the genocide frightened some people. One woman from Ngali, for example, said she feared the attackers because years before, her family had been accused of being Tutsi because they owned a lot of cows. This woman feared such accusations despite being married to an alleged Interahamwe.[16]

---

16. She herself never stated what her husband did during the genocide, only that he was killed after the genocide and war. It was her neighbors who told me her husband had been an Interahamwe.

On rare occasions, counterclaims could thwart claims by Jude that a person was "really" Tutsi. Maurice was an older, long-time resident of Ngali. During the genocide, Jude and a group of killers came to Maurice's house, accusing him of being a Tutsi who had changed his ubwoko in 1959. The group threatened to kill Maurice, but Paul, the former conseiller of Ngali usurped by Jude, intervened. He told the killers that Maurice was an *umukiga*, or person from the north, and was therefore possibly related to the president's family. (Both Habyarimana and his wife came from Gisenyi, a préfecture in the north, as did most people in the couple's inner circle.) Paul's counterclaim saved Maurice's life. Jude and his group of killers left without harming Maurice, saying they would gather more information on him. The group never threatened Maurice again. In this example, Paul used one type of identity claim to counter another. Paul invoked the possibility that Maurice was an umukiga. In the context of Rwandan politics, a "northern" identity was not only assumed to be Hutu, but more important, was associated with the group of Hutu who were in power. The mere possibility that Maurice was related to those in power was sufficient to stop the killers from harming or harassing Maurice.

Paul's ability to intervene on Maurice's behalf and prevail also suggests that Paul with not entirely without power and authority despite Jude being named the new conseiller by the Gitarama authorities. Thus Maurice may have owed his life not to claims that he might be related to the president's family, but to his more immediate ties to Paul, the former conseiller who seemed able to assert his authority and influence at certain moments.

Maurice's situation was not the norm, however. Killers did kill many people for "looking" Tutsi, without anyone stepping in to save them. What Maurice's case suggests is that uncertainty could work both ways. The killers who threatened Maurice did not know if he was a northerner (umukiga) or not. This uncertainty stopped them from trying to kill Maurice. More often, however, uncertainty played to the advantage of leaders like Jude, who could capitalize on the uncertainty to target known Hutu under the pretext that they looked Tutsi.

Data from Kimanzi are consistent with findings from Ngali. Targeting followed a slightly different path, which was consistent with a different understanding of ethnicity in this region. The small number of Tutsi meant that it was easy for everyone to know who the Tutsi families were. More important, the lack of familiarity with the practice of changing one's ubwoko meant that accusing a local resident of being Tutsi had no basis. And indeed, there are no examples of people having made such accusations in Kimanzi. Instead, the basis for accusing someone of being Tutsi was regional stereotypes. The clearest example of this was a prisoner from

Ruhengeri who, when he drove his truck to Ruhengeri during the war, found himself called "Tutsi." The basis for this accusation, he explained, was that he came from Gitarama, a region known for having a high percentage of Tutsi.

Outward representations of ethnicity, such as identity cards, official histories, and stereotypes, appear to confirm the way the ethnic fear and hatred models conceptualize ethnicity—as a stable, objective category observable from the outside and assumed to be consistent with people's lived experiences. Both models, however, take a one-dimensional view of ethnicity, assuming that outward forms are all (or most of) what ethnicity is to people, and, more important, that they are accurate indicators of the level of attachment people have to their ethnic groups.

The data, however, do not support these assumptions of what ethnicity is or how it operates in crisis conditions. What the data show is not a surfeit of affective attachment to one's group, but a lack of such. People approach ethnicity as a fact of daily life—as something that is important to know and know about. They treat this social fact strategically and pragmatically. They learn at an early age their own ethnicity as well as that of others. They learn how to identify themselves in the manner that the state requires—as Hutu or Tutsi, but not a mixture of the two. At the same time, they also learn these labels can change if circumstances shift or can be changed, if the need arises. As Jude's wife, Thérèse, said, if the government were to change, people would find a way to change their identities accordingly. In other words, during crisis conditions, people do not cling instinctively to their own group; rather, some look for strategies that will enable them to camouflage their identities or change them outright.

During genocide, people continued to approach ethnicity strategically. For leaders, genocide was a means for consolidating power in their communities. By determining how the script for genocide would be interpreted and performed, leaders such as Jude, became the final arbiters of ethnicity in their communities. Deciding who was or was not really Tutsi was the clearest expression of leaders' power. In this way, the performance of genocide was ultimately about power, not putative identity.

Joiners, too, followed the script for violence with varying levels of fidelity and commitment. Variations in Joiners' performances arose because Joiners faced different pressures and incentives to follow the script at different moments. That their performances varied at all belies the most basic expectation of the ethnic fear and ethnic hatred theses—that in times of strife or insecurity, boundaries harden and crystallize providing no space for alliances across ethnic lines. There is certainly some truth to how dangerous ethnicity became. Tutsi were designated as targets, and people knew who their Tutsi neighbors were. Yet space for different types of actions did remain, which allowed Joiners to go along with the script at certain times, but deviate from or abandon it at others. Thus, while fixed at one level, ethnicity remained a term subject to interpretation and reinterpretation according to the shifting conditions of the war and genocide.

5

The Power of Local Ties

Q. Why was your uncle so important to you?
He was really important because every time my father wanted to hit
me, he would save me. And in the Rwandan culture, maternal uncles
love their nephews.
—HUSSEIN, Joiner from Kimanzi

If performances depend on the actors, how did leaders recruit for genocide? Straus (2006, 120) conjectures that recruitment was random but
notes the importance of face-to-face encounters for coercive recruitment
into the killing groups. Phillip Verwimp (2005) finds that perpetrator
households were generally represented by no more than one male member, such as the father or a son, as if the genocide was like *umuganda*,
whereby each household was responsible for sending one person to perform communal labor. What these studies do not tell us is why and how
some residents joined in the violence, while others did not.

Following Granovetter, I argue that genocide at neighbor level was so-
cially embedded in a set of dense ties. These ties did not reduce to objective categories of mother, brother, or conseiller. Rather, they were the sum
of shared knowledge and activities and regular, face-to-face interactions.
They were the product of talking, gossiping, greeting, visiting, sharing
beers, attending meetings, and participating in umuganda.

Different ties had different effects. Leaders and denouncers used family
ties to target family members for recruitment into the killing groups and
for eliminating unwanted rivals. Group ties had similarly pernicious effects. They created targets, making Joiners vulnerable to suspicions; they
also pulled reluctant or hesitant Joiners into the group. Ties of friendship
also remained important. Which ties became salient in a given moment
depended on context. In the presence of local leaders or other killers,
group ties prevailed, leading Joiners to go along with the group, no matter
how murderous its activities. Out of sight of leaders or other killers, Joiners
were able to act on ties of friendship, helping Tutsi they had known as

long-time friends or neighbors. I argue that it was social ties, not ethnic membership, that patterned processes of recruitment and targeting in Ngali and Kimanzi.

Disaggregating the Masses

Mapping how social ties linked people in Ngali and Kimanzi requires disaggregating the masses to identify key groups of actors.

At neighbor level, the most powerful actors were local leaders. Local leaders who had the backing of their bourgmestre or higher officials were responsible for organizing their communities for violence.[1] They began by enlisting dedicated lieutenants who helped to mobilize recruits and "demobilize" resisters (Gagnon 2004). Despite the extremist leanings of their patrons or backers, leaders were not necessarily true believers. Local leaders sought power. Connections to those more powerful were means, not ends. Genocide, too, was a means, not an end. Organizing their communities for genocide was both an expression of power and a means to consolidate that power in their communities.

Leaders benefited from the support of collaborators. Like leaders, collaborators sought to profit from the moment. They were often motivated by personal, not ideological, interests. One collaborator, for example, in the northern research site of Kimanzi, used his connections to the bourgmestre to have a local Hutu man imprisoned twice during the civil war as an RPF accomplice; after the war, he worked with the RPF authorities to have the same man imprisoned a third time as a génocidaire. Collaborators were not lackeys of leaders. Rather, collaborators used leaders' agendas to pursue their own private interests.

Beyond leaders and their collaborators were a diversity of actors. I focus on one specific group, which I call "Joiners." Joiners were the lowest-level participants in the genocide but were responsible for committing much of the violence directed at Tutsi in their communities.

Joiner Profiles

Who were these Joiners? Were they "loose molecules"—unemployed and disenchanted youth with no future and thus nothing to lose (Kaplan 1994)? Were they professional thugs who had no compunction about killing for profit or sport (Mueller 2000)? Or were they "violent specialists" (Tilly 2003) or "riot captains" (Brass 1997), that is, people whose

---

1. The head of a commune was called a bourgmestre. Under Habyarimana, bourgmestres wielded a great deal of power.

specific talent or job was to foment violence at specific moments? Joiners fit none of these categories. In both Kimanzi and Ngali, Joiners were, in every way, ordinary members of their communities. They were all married with children. Their average age was thirty-two, a figure consistent with other studies of low-level perpetrators (Verwimp 2005; Straus 2006). Most stated their occupation as cultivator (*umuhinzi*) or farmer.[2] Most were born in the same community in which they lived at the time of the genocide. In Ngali, for example, nine of eleven Joiners stated they were born in Ngali. Nearly all Joiners (from both communities) mentioned having Tutsi neighbors or friends. Many Joiners from Ngali also mentioned having a Tutsi parent or family members through marriage. None held positions of power with the state above the level of responsable before the genocide or civil war. None had any special training in killing or combat prior to the start of the genocide or massacres of Tutsi.

In addition to Joiners, the rest of the community included those who did not lead, collaborate, or join in the violence in any way. They include those who were the primary targets of violence (survivors); those who helped to save Tutsi or help them escape (rescuers); those able to avoid participating (by paying someone else to go in their place, for example) (evaders); those who tried neither to help nor hurt anyone (witnesses); and those who refused pressures to participate in the violence (resisters). I do not attempt to explain all these different responses to the genocide; rather, I use this range as context for understanding and explaining why Joiners joined in the violence.

One note about these categories: they are analytic tools for making distinctions among actors generally lumped together under the term *the masses*. They are not, however, indicators of a given person's range of actions. Rescuing, for example, was not the sole province of "rescuers." Leaders and Joiners also performed acts of rescue. And while all Joiners participated in the genocide, not all participated the same way. Some took active part in the physical murder of victims; others participated in less direct ways, such as tying up victims or taking victims to a particular site where others would kill them. Some Joiners raped victims before killing them, while others did not.[3] Some

---

2. Among the exceptions were a man who gave his profession as mason and another who gave his as driver and mechanic. It is common for many Rwandans to earn off-farm income through other means. See, for example, Jefremovas (2002) on how men and women make extra money working in brickyards and de Lame (1996) on how people make extra money brewing and selling beer.

3. References to rape during the genocide were scant. One Joiner told a story of seeing another killer take a female victim into a room of the victim's house supposedly to pray with her, but in actuality, to rape her. A survivor told of being threatened twice with rape but es-

pillaged victims' belongings, while others did not. The label "Joiner," therefore, does not imply anything about how the person participated or about the person's moral or legal culpability, only that the person did participate in the genocide in some way.

Community Ties

As Granovetter would lead us to expect, leaders, collaborators, and Joiners were linked to one another and to the rest of their communities through a dense set of social ties. In both communities, these ties were "multiplex" in that people were linked through overlapping roles (Boissevain 1974, 30–33). In multiplex relations, the same person could be another's geographic neighbor, in-law, and local official. Multiplex ties gave rise to multiple channels for contact and interaction. They served as conduits through which people expressed and maintained social order.

In both communities, ties crossed ethnic lines. Among the eight survivors whom I spoke with in Ngali, for example, half were married to Hutu spouses at the time of the genocide.[4] Many leaders, collaborators, and Joiners from Ngali also had Tutsi family members through marriage. In addition, Hutu and Tutsi from both communities shared longstanding friendships. In the northern research site of Kimanzi where the number of Tutsi was very small (approximately twenty-five Tutsi for the whole secteur as opposed to approximately three hundred Tutsi for Ngali), close friendships between Hutu and Tutsi were not uncommon. They were expressed through the ritual of a "blood pact," whereby two people swear lifelong loyalty to one another by cutting under their navels and drinking each other's blood. In both communities, Hutu and Tutsi also expressed close friendship through the exchange of cows.

Ties to Power

Not all ties were equal during genocide. The most important were those that emanated to and from those in power. Leaders constituted power centers in their communities. In Ngali, Jude stood as the single center of power. In Kimanzi, the involvement of outsiders created multiple centers. Let us examine these power relations in greater detail.

---

caping both times. The low reporting of sexual violence does not mean that these crimes did not occur; only that uncovering their occurrence would have required a different research strategy than the one I employed.

4. Because the selection strategy was purposive and not random, we cannot generalize these patterns to the community as a whole.

Center of Power in Ngali (Center-South)

Though Jude had died in 1997, there was no shortage of information that residents of Ngali were able to provide.[5] By all accounts, Jude wielded a monopoly on the means of coercion. Ngali residents variously describe Jude as "the head of the Interahamwe," "president of the Interahamwe," "the head of Pawa," "the head of the killers," and "our leader."

The seminal event in Ngali was the plane crash that killed President Habyarimana on 6 April 1994. Before that moment, daily life had remained fairly calm in Ngali, despite the civil war that had begun in the north of the country with the RPF invasion on 1 October 1990. Jude's actions in the aftermath of the assassination were swift. Powerful authorities—most likely the self-appointed interim government installed in Gitarama from 12 April 1994 onwards—named Jude the new conseiller, deposing Jude's own nephew, Paul. (Paul is the man we met in the previous chapter who saved Maurice by telling the killers Maurice might be related to the President's family.) As Paul explained:

> He named himself [conseiller] on 15 April 1994. He was coming to the J— center.[6] He told me that I was no longer conseiller because the Gitarama authorities had just appointed him, and that he was going to change all the responsables. The following day, as he was president of the MDR party, he called the AbaJDR (the youth wing of the MDR).[7] For each cellule, he named the responsables who belonged to his MDR party. [Paul, #2/4]

Jude's political party connections were crucial to his rapid rise to power. His backing by more powerful patrons, most likely the "Power," or extremist wing, of the MDR, or the interim government, with whom MDR-Power was aligned, guaranteed his takeover of power.

Jude's rise may have had a measure of support from below as well. Jude's wife, Thérèse, provides a more populist view of how Jude assumed leadership after the plane crash that killed the president.

> My husband was the responsable under the government of Habyarimana. When the war of 1994 started, everyone came to look for my husband to ask his

5. According to Jude's wife, Jude died shortly after he and his family returned from exile in the Congo in 1997. Jude was taken directly to the local jail (*cachot communal*) and died three days later. His wife never specified the cause of death. Others reported that Jude had been killed.

6. It was never clear to me what the J— center referred to. In 2004, the "center" was marked by no more than a small cabaret (local bar), with houses running along each side of the road.

7. MDR was the main opposition party to Habyarimana's MRND party (see chapter 2). The prefix "aba" signifies the plural for a person. "AbaJDR" thus means the "JDR people."

advice. Because of all his advice, my husband became the leader or conseiller of Ngali secteur. When people started to hunt down the Tutsi, they would pillage their belongings and they would bring all these pillaged goods to our house. After noticing that these Hutu were bringing all these Tutsi belongings to our house, my husband would ask them to take their looted things to their own homes. When they started to kill the people, I asked my husband: "Why are these people killing these Tutsi? What did they do?" My husband told me that it was the order coming from the high authorities. I was scared and I became ill. I put myself to bed until we fled toward the Congo. [Thérèse, #7/7]

This version of events emphasizes the leadership role that Jude already held in the community prior to the assassination of the president, and his ability to capitalize on that previous position. Indeed, as a skilled entrepreneur, Jude very likely cultivated both sets of connections—those to officials higher up in the MDR as well as to residents of his cellule (and, to a lesser extent, residents of the other cellules). According to numerous testimonies, Jude was adept at using force and terror to ensure compliance to his wishes, but as Thérèse's testimony also suggests, the relationship between Jude and residents may not have been based on coercion alone.

What is clear is Jude's power position vis-à-vis his nephew, Paul, whom he ousted as conseiller. People consistently describe Jude as all powerful and Paul as powerless. As one Joiner remarked, "At that time, Paul was incapable of making decisions. We saw that Jude had replaced Paul. It was Jude who was powerful." An older Hutu resident of Ngali went further: "He was a leader. He would say all the time that he was working with the authorities of the province of Gitarama. He would do whatever he wanted, no matter where, no matter when, at anyone he wanted."

I pressed Jude's nephew, Paul, for more information on their past relationship to glean a broader context for these events. Was Jude's move to become the new conseiller strictly political, or was there something more personal behind this action? Paul's response hints at both factors.

Q. How was your relationship with Jude before 1990?

Jude was first of all my maternal uncle. He was also responsable of one of the cellules of my secteur.

Q. Did you know Jude from childhood?

I knew him very well since I was a child.

Q. While you were growing up, did you see Jude often?

I was very young compared to him, but I saw him often because he got married when I was still a teenager. I would share a beer with him at the local bar and at the house. He would also come over to my house often.

Q. And his wife? Did you know her well, too?

I knew her well because she would come say hello to my wife each time.

Q. Did Jude's wife participate in his activities, too?

No, she was traumatized seeing what her husband had pillaged and filling the house [with] cows, goods of all kinds.

Q. After having been appointed conseiller, did Jude threaten you?

There was jealousy because he thought he should have been conseiller. After he was named conseiller, I would not give him the registry that helped me give Tutsi [a paper] so that they could go anywhere.

Q. When the killings started, did Jude target specific people?

Yes, all the Tutsi and their supporters (Hutu) and everyone who looked Tutsi.

Q. Among all Tutsi of Ngali, did he target specific people?

I am saying all Tutsi without distinction. [Paul, #2/4]

Becoming de facto leader of Ngali after the president's assassination meant that it was Jude who decided how the script for genocide would be performed in Ngali. And while Jude seemed to have followed a predictable path—going after Tutsi and anyone who looked Tutsi—his calculus, at times, seemed to have been shaped by his relationship with Paul. This relationship remained unclear to me, despite the fact that Paul had defied Jude's orders to kill Tutsi, and instead, helped many Tutsi escape by issuing them papers stamped with the official secteur seal (stamped documents carrying great weight in Rwanda). The document stated that the document-holder was Hutu and had lost his or her identity card. With this paper in hand, local Tutsi were able to flee the area. Jude threatened Paul on numerous occasions for his rescue operations, calling him an icyitso (accomplice). Jude also reported Paul's activities in his weekly reports to the communal authorities. There is no indication, however, that Jude ever roughed up or threatened to kill Paul. In fact, Jude and Paul's relationship appears to have wavered between rivals and collaborators, even during the genocide. One survivor, for example, explained how her husband approached Jude to protect her from a relative who had threatened to kill her: "My husband went to Jude. He gave him some beer and Jude asked Paul to give me a paper that said that I was Hutu." This woman's statement suggests how ambiguous the relationship between Jude and Paul remained even during the genocide. Though he openly defied Jude's orders for genocide, Paul's rescue activities may have served a useful purpose for Jude at times.

This woman's statement also indicates that Jude was no ideologue. In addition to sparing this woman's life in exchange for some beer, Jude also allowed several young Tutsi men to join the Interahamwe after the men paid Jude money. It is not clear what Jude's prior relations were to these four men. According to one of the four (Eugène, see below), the other three Tutsi came from outside Ngali but Jude knew them all well. Was it simply the case that Jude spared the life of any Tutsi who paid him money? It is not clear from the data. Suffice it to say that the calculus Jude used to determine who would live and who would die was, at times, neither strictly economic nor strictly ethnic. What the data indicate is that even with Jude, the undisputed leader of the genocide in Ngali, personal ties could make a difference in who lived and who died. This discretionary use of force underscored the absolute nature of Jude's power during the genocide.

The most pernicious form of social ties that Jude and his lieutenants used were ties of family. For these men, genocide started at home. Family ties served as avenues for targeting family members for recruitment into the killing groups. Jude went after male relatives, including cousins and nephews, and threatened to kill those who did not go along with his plans. One of Jude's chief lieutenants, a man whom one neighbor referred to as Jude's "advisor," also targeted family members for recruitment and for killing. This lieutenant killed the Tutsi children of his sister and then tried to kill the sister for having married a Tutsi man. He also forced his nephew to join the Interahamwe. A survivor, who had been friends with the nephew, explained the nephew's forcible recruitment:

Q. When you say that your friend became an Interahamwe because of his uncle, what do you mean? that his uncle forced him to join them?

He forced the child to be in the group of Interahamwe. Even my cow was killed by the [uncle's] group. My friend's father did nothing during the period of the genocide and there is another paternal uncle who did not participate in the genocide.

. . . .

Q. How did [the uncle] force your friend to join the Interahamwe?

[The uncle] was the head of Pawa. He was powerful and he told [my friend] to join the Interahamwe and if he did not join them, they were going to hurt him.

Q. If your friend refused to join the Interahamwe, would he [the uncle] have killed him?

He would have killed him. [201, #7/8]

As this man's testimony underscores, proximity to centers of power could be quite dangerous for those reluctant to participate in the genocide (and alternatively, quite convenient for those inclined to profit from it). Far from insulating those situated closest to the center of power, family ties made people ready targets for recruitment into the killing groups charged with carrying out the genocide.

Family ties also became a vehicle for turning people in to the authorities. Denouncers often acted on personal dislikes, jealousies, and resentments when going after family members. Denouncing was a convenient way of getting rid of unwanted rivals because it marked the accused as a legitimate target for killing. In Ngali, there were several instances of people denouncing family members. In one case, a man denounced his brother's Tutsi wife and her family who were in hiding. According to the wife, her brother-in-law wanted to claim her husband's house and belongings. In another case, a son denounced his father for hiding the children of the father's close Tutsi friend. (The Tutsi friend had died years before the genocide.) According to the father, the son denounced the father to claim his "inheritance." Inheritance in this case meant acquisition of land. Because inheritance continues to be the most common mode for acquiring land in Africa, relations between family members, particularly between fathers and sons, can be particularly volatile, creating lifelong resentments and animosities (André and Platteau 1998, 18). This man had always had a difficult relationship with his son, so the son may have been looking for an opportunity to act on his resentments.[8]

Family members could also target family members by accusing them of being ibyitso or accomplices of the RPF. One prisoner, for example, whom Jude had threatened, faced additional accusations from a cousin. As this prisoner explained: "[My cousin] also wanted me dead because of a disagreement between him and me, even though my father and his father are brothers." Family conflicts made family ties particularly threatening during genocide because of the personal motives underlying certain people's actions. Personal jealousies, resentments, and grievances provided powerful incentive for family members to go after those they felt had somehow wronged or bested them. In most of these instances, the motives were personal, not ethnic.

There were, to be sure, family members of Jude who did not participate, despite their close proximity to leaders or collaborators. In one notable case, Jude's wife, Thérèse, did not participate in or profit from her

8. We attempted to interview the son, who made an appointment with us but never showed for his interview and never made himself available for another appointment.

husband's activities despite being in a privileged position to do so. Such reluctance stands in stark contrast to accounts that emphasize the active role that wives played in stripping clothes and other belongings off the bodies of their husbands' recent victims (Hatzfeld 2000; 2003). Thérèse's proximity to Jude, however, did affect her. Being so closely situated to the center of power made it impossible for Thérèse not to know what was going on, particularly as the looted belongings of Tutsi victims piled up in her living room day after day. Thus, despite her attempt to retreat inward as so many others did during the genocide (Wagner 1998), Thérèse could not help but know what was happening, as her silence on the subject during our many interviews seemed to indicate.

For those less closely situated to Jude, by contrast, not knowing remained a viable option and one that many in Ngali seemed to have taken. Numerous people said they spent the period of the genocide staying at home or fleeing the area whenever necessary. A few people found ways to evade the Interahamwe and avoid being recruited into genocide. One man said he made sure to absent himself from his home at key moments to avoid being recruited. Those who stayed in their homes tried, as Thérèse had, not to know what was happening around them.

Those tied to Jude or his lieutenants through family, however, did not always have the option of evading or avoiding pressures to join his campaign of genocide. For these people, ties of family bound them to genocide in inescapable ways.

Multiple Centers in Kimanzi (North)

In Kimanzi, located in the northern province of Ruhengeri, there was no single center of power but multiple centers. This was due, in part, to the active role that nonresidents of Kimanzi played in the genocide. These outsiders included military, communal police, gendarmes, and other agents of the state. There was a conspicuous presence of military in Kimanzi because of RPF troops positioned in the mountains ringing Kimanzi. The deployment of Rwandan governmental forces (FAR) in this region provided FAR soldiers with opportunities to kill local Tutsi residents, rape Tutsi women, and pillage Tutsi property. As one witness remarked, soldiers used local Interahamwe to show them where the rich (Tutsi) families lived; the soldiers would then pillage the families' goods and rape the women and girls. They would then leave the women alive as they were only killing Tutsi men and boys at that point.

Other state agents also organized massacres of Tutsi. A Joiner related a mass killing led by an adjutant of the gendarmerie. Shortly after the president's plane crash, the adjutant brought a truckload of Hutu and Tutsi to a remote location in Kimanzi, telling residents that his captives were "RPF accomplices." He ordered the victims to carry rocks and then ordered local residents to dig holes. He then ordered the victims into the holes. He told residents to throw the rocks at the victims and then bury them. When I asked this Joiner who the victims were, he said they were RPF soldiers that included Tutsi as well as Hutu. All were killed that day.

The extent of outsiders' involvement in the killing of Tutsi obviated the need for local officials to organize the killings themselves. Local officials (conseillers and responsables) tended to act as collaborators rather than direct leaders of the violence, profiting from the opportunities that war presented to pursue their own interests. Local officials and those with connections to the bourgmestre were able to wield an inordinate amount of power. These people used their ties to the bourgmestre to intimidate, harass, and threaten local Tutsi and certain Hutu on an ongoing basis. Like the denouncers in Ngali, these local actors were also motivated by personal, rather than ethnic, animosities. In one notable case, the former conseiller of Kimanzi who had lost his post in 1989 because of secteur money that went missing under his watch, maintained his ties to the bourgmestre after losing his post. As one witness explained, this former official would "go to see the bourgmestre to give him nonwritten reports in order to threaten the people he wanted to get rid of."

Like denouncers in Ngali, people who maintained their ties to the bourgmestre were able to use the opportunity of war and mass killings to act on personal motive. After the start of the war in October 1990, for example, this same former official used his connections to the bourgmestre to imprison many Hutu and Tutsi. He had one man imprisoned on three different occasions. After hearing of his multiple imprisonments, I finally asked this man what his relationship to this former official was before 1990 (the start of the civil war). The man replied: "No other relationship. He just wanted to steal my wife, even before. By having me imprisoned, he thought that my wife was going to take him. Even after my imprisonment, he terrorized my wife quite a bit but to no end." As in Ngali, personal jealousies were powerful motivators for some, and those with ties to the bourgmestre could act on those jealousies with impunity.

Patterns of recruitment in Kimanzi, however, did not start at home as they did in Ngali. They started instead with those within close geographic proximity. Leaders of massacres often enlisted nearby responsables and the heads of ten households (*nyumbakumi*) to help with the disposal of bodies.

Other leaders ordered local residents to witness the killings of Tutsi or to take part in the killings more directly (as with the stoning incident related above). Because of the prominent role military and other state agents played in leading the violence, family ties to leaders seemed to have played a much smaller role in the recruitment of local people into genocide. Forcible recruitment did occur but not through that particular mechanism.

Ties to Friends

While family ties were powerful mechanisms for recruiting and denouncing, ties of friendship between Joiners and Tutsi also remained important. Stories from survivors from both communities attest to the importance of bonds of friendship in leading even the most active killers to save the lives of Tutsi friends, even as they continued to participate in the murder of other Tutsi.

How were ties of friendship constituted? A group interview with Paul, the former conseiller of Ngali ousted by Jude, and two Joiners named Eugène and Félix shed light on this question. The three were an unlikely trio, differing quite a bit in age, education, and demeanor. They presented themselves as a group of close friends so I chose to talk to them together for our first interview. Of the three, only Félix and Eugène had confessed to participating in the genocide. Paul maintained his innocence during the genocide and so had not confessed.

At fifty-two, Félix was the oldest of the three but seemed, by far, the most scared and nervous. With his slouched shoulders, bowed head, and eyes darting left to right to avoid eye contact, Félix gave the impression of a frightened boy steeling himself for a blow he knew was coming at any time. Félix's nervous demeanor contrasted with Eugène's detached air. Like Félix, Eugène did not volunteer any information but his silence seemed to come more from boredom than fear.

Eugène's aloofness and Félix's nervousness, in turn, contrasted even more sharply with the garrulousness of Paul. With his large physical stature and even larger personality, Paul quickly took over the interview. Paul seemed to welcome the opportunity to talk with a foreign researcher and to share what he knew about the genocide. He answered all my questions, while Eugène and Félix seemed content to remain silent. I cut the interview short when I saw it was not going to be a group interview, but an interview with Paul and two onlookers. What did come up during our brief exchange, however, was insight into the friendship the three shared before the genocide.

Q. Did you three know each other before the genocide? Since when?

[Paul]. Yes, we knew each other because we had been neighbors for a long time.

Q. You went to the same primary school?

[Paul]. No.

Q. Before the genocide, how much time did you spend together?

[Paul]. We were neighbors, we would share everything. Despite some being older than others, we were together a long time until the period of the genocide and the war.

Q. How did you become friends?

[Paul]. We lived in the same secteur, almost the same neighborhood. We would help each other. All that. It's that no one wished anything bad to come to anyone else.

Q. Can you give me an example where you needed help and the others helped you?

[Paul]. For example: Helping the other with work in the field, cultivating together. Another example: Helping each other at the time of a wedding where there was someone who would be receiving a cow. Another example: Helping each other take the sick to the hospital. [Groupe #1/1]

This description of what constituted friendship between the three is consistent with others' testimonies, Joiners and nonjoiners alike. Friendship was facilitated by physical proximity that enabled frequent and regular interaction. Friendships were constituted by shared activities and gestures of mutual aid and support.

Friendship did not lead the three to make the same choices during the genocide, however. This difference is not surprising given the trio's very different positions in the community when the genocide began. As conseiller, Paul had been in a position of authority and was even able to use the accoutrements of his former post to help Tutsi. His ability to help those in danger rested not only on his refusal to turn over the secteur stamp and registry to Jude, but also on his prior friendships and relationships to Tutsi of Ngali and those of surrounding secteurs.

Q. How did the registry aid you in helping the Tutsi at that time so that they could go anywhere?

To put it briefly, Jude demanded that I give him the secteur stamp from the very beginning and I refused. I gave papers to Tutsi that said that this Tutsi had lost his identity card and that he was going to obtain another one after the war. On this paper, I would write that the person was Hutu and with this paper, he could travel anywhere except that there were times when they would kill someone because of their physical characteristics.

Q. How many people did you give this paper to?

I don't remember very well. It was at least between thirty-five to forty people. I would even give these papers to people from other secteurs like the people of [names four secteurs] in the commune of [names commune].

Q. How did the people in Ngali find you?

They would send their friends to my house to ask me to write a paper for a certain Tutsi, but the others would come by during the night.

Q. How did the people from the other secteurs know that you were giving this paper to Tutsi?

I had friends in the other secteurs who were married to Tutsi who asked me for advice. And when I gave them a paper, they would go tell others what happened. [Paul, #4/4]

Despite being ousted as conseiller by Jude, Paul continued to use his prior position to help the Tutsi of Ngali as well as those from surrounding secteurs. Clearly, the genocide did not change how Paul saw Tutsi or how he related to them. What made Paul's rescuing efforts possible, however, was not just Paul's desire to help Tutsi, but also Jude's tacit acquiescence to his rescue activities.

Helping Tutsi friends also gave rise to forms of complicity. One person whom Paul helped, for example, was his friend, Eugène, who did not use the stamped paper to flee the area but to pursue a much different strategy of survival.

Eugène (Joiner, Ngali)

Eugène was a young man of twenty-five when the genocide began in 1994. He had married two years before and had one child. Like most people in Ngali, he experienced no problems when the civil war started in 1990. The war was far away and life remained calm. After the assassination of the president, however, people began to threaten and chase Eugène because he was among those "who had to be killed."

Eugène's prior relations with Hutu friends, Paul among them, shaped his range of options in clear ways. First, Eugène was able to obtain the stamped document from Paul, which allowed him to move about freely. Rather than use this document to flee, Eugène used it to join the Interahamwe in order, he said, to save himself. While at first glance, Eugène's strategy might seem irrational or even suicidal, on closer inspection, it was highly strategic. In joining the Interahamwe, Eugène was not placing himself in the hands of strangers, but a group of longtime friends.

Q. Why did you decide to confess?

It was because I saw the death of a lot of people.

Q. You confessed to having done what?

I was witness to everything I saw and by whom.

Q. You yourself killed no one?

Me, I didn't kill anyone.

Q. Even though you were among a group of Interahamwe?

Yes.

Q. What were you doing in this group if you didn't participate in the killings?

I was just an observer.

Q. What was your role, your job, as observer?

There were lots of us. These were the young men I had known for a long time. I was among the young people during the war and I saw everything that they did and I had no role. I was with them in order to save myself.

Q. The other young people in your group were your close friends?

Yes.

Q. No one in your group wanted you to participate in their activities?

Yes, there was one who gave me a person to kill but I refused to kill her. [Eugène, #3/4]

The extent of Eugène's actual participation may not have been only as an "observer." In his letter of confession to the prosecutor, Eugène details the killings of five victims and specifies his own participation as "handing over Tutsi to the group of Interahamwe and at the roadblock." There are reasons to be skeptical of both versions that Eugène gives. Prisoners wrote letters of confession with the express purpose of garnering favorable consideration from the prosecutor, who has the power to reduce the prisoner's sentence. Some prisoners even confessed falsely in an effort to get out of prison. Thus it is not surprising that in the letters, Joiners speak in a language of directness about the specific acts they themselves committed against specific people. In interviews, by contrast, Joiners tended to talk in terms that minimized their agency in the activities in which they admitted participating.

Regardless of the actual extent of Eugène's participation, what is clear is that Eugène deemed joining the Interahamwe his best strategy for survival. This choice Eugène admits freely. What made this option thinkable was Eugène's history of friendship with the others in the group he joined.

Q. How many people did your group kill? More than ten people?

It was a lot. More than ten people. It was my group that killed nearly everyone in our secteur.

Q. How did your group choose their victims?

The group killed Tutsi.

Q. Did you know all your group's victims?

Yes, they were our neighbors, because it was possible to know all the people in your secteur.

Q. And all the members of your group of killers were also from Ngali?

Yes, they were from Ngali secteur.

Q. Over how many days did your group kill?

I was with the group for a month. They went to the Congo, and as for me, I stayed in Ngali.

Q. When did your group form as a group?

Before the war, we were a group and we continued this group even during the war.

Q. A group of what? Friends? Killers? Bandits?

Before the war, we were friends. We were in business selling food and small livestock. [Eugène, #3/4]

Eugène's responses highlight the importance of prior connections among Joiners, and more specifically in Eugène's case, a prior history of friendship with several of the Interahamwe in the killing group he joined. This prior history of friendship shaped not only which options Eugène saw but also which options seemed optimal at the time. As Eugène remarked in a later interview: "For me, I followed the group because I knew the young men who made up the group really well." Knowing the young men in the group "really well" led Eugène to calculate that joining them as an Interahamwe would enable him to save his own life.

According to Eugène, he was not the only Tutsi to pursue this strategy. Three other Tutsi followed the same strategy, paying Jude money so he would allow them to join the Interahamwe just as Eugène had done. This strategy of joining the side of the killers not only defies the most basic assumptions of the ethnic fear and ethnic hatred approaches but also shows that ties of friendship could, in certain circumstances, trump the salience of a person's ethnic identity, thereby shaping and even generating new options during the genocide. In these moments, ties of friendship clearly mediated between the script for genocide and people's strategies and actions.

As with many Interahamwe, prior connections to Tutsi presented Joiners with stark moral dilemmas. Eugène had grown up with his mother and maternal grandparents because his father was often away. While growing up, Eugène's maternal uncle was a central figure in his life, doing everything for the young boy, including paying his school fees, a significant gesture in a country where many families cannot afford to pay the fees at all.

During the genocide, Eugène's uncle went into hiding. After joining the Interahamwe, Eugène tried to help his uncle by bringing him food in his hiding place. Eugène's efforts were ultimately in vain as a group of killers from an adjoining secteur found the man and killed him. When I asked Eugène how he heard the news of his uncle's death, he replied simply: "I was living in cellule M— and bad news didn't stay hidden for long. They told me that the people had just killed my uncle."

Despite his inability to save his uncle, Eugène was at least spared the ordeal of having to watch his own group kill the man or be forced to kill his uncle himself. When I asked Eugène what he would have done had Jude or one of Jude's lieutenants ordered him to kill his uncle himself, his answer was surprisingly frank. After hearing the question, Eugène paused for a moment, then said in an even, matter-of-fact tone: "It's hard to say. Maybe I would have killed him, to save my life." As Eugène's response suggests, joining in the genocide constituted a strategy of survival not only for many Hutu, but also for a few Tutsi.

Michel (Joiner, Ngali)

Eugène was not the only Joiner who tried to save Tutsi while going along with the mass murder of others. Michel was a Joiner who had been in prison since 1995. He had been in prison nearly ten years by the time of my fieldwork. He looked younger than his age. His demeanor was reserved, even shy. During our first interview, he avoided eye contact, and answered all my questions with a quiet earnestness.

At our second interview, I began by asking Michel about the Tutsi he mentioned saving during his first interview.

> *Q. The last time you told us that you saved four people. Tell us how you decided to hide these four people.*

I saw that the killing was terrible and I saw especially that our neighbors were suffering, that I had to do some good. I give you the example of the lady [names the woman]. Between her house and mine, there is a sister house. As we had shared everything before, I decided to save her.

Q. Did [this woman] ask you to save her?

She did not ask me to save her. She just came to our house and we agreed to hide her and to share with her what we had at the time until the end of the war.

Q. Who were you with at your house?

My sister [names his sister], my little brothers [names brothers]. Except that [one of the brothers] had his own house and we hid them together.

Q. Did you hesitate to hide this woman at first?

We did not hesitate to hide her except that each time the killers would come to search for people to kill. But we did everything possible to protect her. [Michel, #2/3]

Michel's rescue activities did not keep him from participating in the murder of another man. This victim was a stranger to Ngali and had stopped at Michel's house to ask for directions to a neighbor's house. Michel describes his involvement in this man's murder in ambiguous terms.

Q. What happened next at your house? after this man's arrival?

Once he got there, he asked me to show him the path that leads toward [a neighbor woman's] house. I kept him at my house a while and after a few minutes, a man named MG came to my house and asked him [the stranger] to follow him. This man followed MG to the roadblock where they were working.

Q. Who was this man named MG?

He was the leader of the roadblock.

Q. What did he want with this man?

He wanted to have him killed and he was killed at the roadblock.

Q. Were you able to see the killing of the man from your house?

No, because between the roadblock and my house, there is a forest.

Q. How did you know this man was killed at the roadblock?

The killers passed by near my house saying they had killed him.

Q. How did MG know that this man was at your house?

I don't know.

Q. Why did MG and the others want to kill the man who was at your house?

When MG arrived at my house, he started to ask him lots of questions and maybe he noticed that this man was among those people who they were supposed to bring to the roadblock.

Q. Did you know that MG was going to kill this man when he took him to the roadblock?

Yes, I thought about his being killed because there were some others who were killed like that except that there was nothing I could do for him.

Q. Did you try to keep MG from taking this man from your house?

Yes, I tried to stop him but he didn't listen to me. Afterwards, I ran into [the neighbor woman] who had me imprisoned and I told her that MG did not want to let this man go.

Q. What did you say to MG in trying to keep him from taking this man to the road-block?

After talking to this man, MG asked me what this man was doing at my house. I told him that he came to ask me the path that leads to [the neighbor woman's] family. He told me he was going to take him to the roadblock and I asked him to let him go to [the neighbor woman's] house before taking him to the roadblock. MG refused and asked the man to follow him.

Q. Was MG alone or was he with some others?

Yes, he was alone.

Q. Was he armed?

I don't remember if he was armed. [Michel, #3/3]

In his letter of confession, Michel paints a quite different picture of this incident. In the letter version, Michel not only helped escort the stranger to the roadblock, he also had a direct hand in killing him. Admitting to having played a direct role in the victim's murder was not uncommon in letters of confession, as mentioned above. In Michel's case, however, even his interview version denotes some complicity in the stranger's murder. Why else would Michel delay the man at his house if not to detain him long enough for MG to arrive and interrogate the man? That MG shows up a few moments later indicates that Michel expected, or perhaps feared, MG's arrival.

Michel's effort at preventing MG from taking the stranger to the road-block was hardly a sincere effort at trying to save the man since all Michel suggested was taking the man to the neighbor's house first (the house to which the stranger had originally asked directions) and then to the road-block, where the man would have been killed anyway. Whatever the extent of Michel's actual involvement in the man's death, the difference between the stranger and the four Tutsi Michel was hiding was that Michel knew the latter. It was his own neighbors Michel saw suffering when the genocide began. Michel had no such ties to the stranger. This lack of ties may have meant the difference between Michel trying harder to save the man, rather than go along, however reluctantly, with his murder.

Michel's response to the stranger also underscores the importance of immediate context in shaping people's actions. Michel not only faced a stranger at his door. He also faced the roadblock leader who had come to confront the stranger—and perhaps Michel as well—in Michel's own house. In the presence of authorities, Joiners like Michel tended to go along with the activities of genocide, usually because they did not see any other viable option (see chapter 6 for a full discussion of how Joiners saw themselves as powerless). As Michel himself says in this short passage, "There was nothing I could do for him" and "Yes, I tried to stop him but he didn't listen to me." In the presence of MG, the roadblock leader, Michel may have felt he had no other option but to go along with MG's plans to murder the stranger.

Despite Michel's ambiguous actions toward the stranger, what his story illustrates is that Joiners did not treat all Tutsi as targets. Ties of friendship continued to matter. Joiners acted on these ties when they could—when circumstances allowed. That ties of friendship led Joiners to save some Tutsi did not turn Joiners into rescuers or those willing to risk their lives to save others.[9] Unlike rescuers, who were willing to help friend and stranger alike, Joiners tended to help only those they knew.[10] At no time during his interview, for example, did Michel even indicate a desire to save the man from certain death at the roadblock, as if that possibility had never occurred to him. Helping Tutsi friends made Joiners ordinary members of their communities, with preexisting ties to some Tutsi, but not others. Such ties remained salient during genocide, contrary to the expectations of the ethnic hatred and ethnic fear models.

Ties to Groups

A third set of ties also became salient during the genocide. These were group ties that formed through group activities, such as night patrols, and group interactions. Like ties of family, group ties also served as avenues of recruitment and targeting. Indeed, as the case of Olivier shows, even Joiners could become targets through these ties.

Olivier (Joiner, Ngali)

Olivier was a small, wiry-built man when we met him in the prison in 2004. At the time, he had a job in one of the prison workshops and often sported a tape measure around his neck when he came to the interview. The combination of tape measure draped over blush pink uniform would have been an incongruous sight in any prison setting, but even more so in

---

9. This definition of rescuer comes from Monroe (2004).

10. Des Forges notes cases of just the opposite behavior—of people who opted to help strangers over friends or neighbors because it drew less suspicion to them (personal communication, 2 February 2008).

the courtyard of a rundown facility built in the 1930s, whose population was nearly all suspected génocidaires.

Olivier had been in prison since 1996. A rich neighbor had accused Olivier of killing his sister and mother, a charge that Olivier confirmed matter-of-factly: "Yes, I was in the group that killed these people. We killed them." Despite the seeming straightforwardness of this response, Olivier's demeanor during our interviews was wily; he often grinned and chuckled at questions I asked without giving any hint as to what he found so amusing. He generally gave only the briefest of answers, rarely divulging more than what the question minimally required, as if leaving it to me to come up with the right question that would elicit what I wanted to know.

There was one subject, however, where Olivier did not put up any guard. That subject was his wife. At our first interview, when I asked him how many children he had (one of a series of routine questions I asked at every first interview), Olivier hesitated, gave his answer, then reluctantly added that his wife had had other children by another man since Olivier's imprisonment. Olivier was clearly troubled by his wife having taken up with another man. At the very least, this meant that Olivier had one less person to visit him in prison and bring him extra provisions, a benefit on which all prisoners depended to ease the difficult conditions. Olivier never talked about his wife in cost-benefit terms, however, and this was yet another indication that his comments about her were sincere and not just based on strategic calculation.

In stark contrast to his demeanor toward the subject of his wife, Olivier's attitude toward confession appeared to be purely strategic. Olivier was the only prisoner we interviewed who admitted he would still have confessed even if he had not done anything because he found a definite sentence of three years preferable to languishing in prison indefinitely. (This was Olivier's understanding of the benefits of confessing.)

As to the killings in which he participated, Olivier's attitude was similarly matter-of-fact. He had been part of a large group of killers that included men from every cellule. There were more than thirty people at the group's first attack, which involved pillaging but no killing. Two days later, Olivier and his group engaged in their first killing. The family of the man whose house had been pillaged earlier had come out of hiding and returned to the family's house. The family included the man's wife, daughter, and three grandsons. Olivier's group let the wife and daughter go but killed the three grandsons by bludgeoning them with *massues* (nail-studded clubs). The wife and daughter were killed a week later, at the meeting at the secteur office that Jude had called to lure Tutsi out of hiding. Olivier's group continued their attacks throughout the rest of the secteur, until they had killed all the Tutsi in their community.

Q. How did you—you and your group—choose your victims?

At that time, we didn't make the choice. There was an order to kill all the Tutsi.

Q. Who gave this order?

Jude. Jude said that he came from a meeting where they ordered the killing of all Tutsi, who were the ibyitso [accomplices] of the Inyenzi-Inkotanyi [RPF].[11] So, all the Tutsi had to be killed.

. . . .

Q. Did Jude order you to kill the mother and sister of [the rich neighbor who had imprisoned Olivier] directly?

Yes. He gave this order when we were in the meeting. He didn't want to see them the next day, that is, this woman and her daughter had to be killed the same day as the meeting.

Q. Why exactly did Jude want this woman and her daughter killed?

It was because they were Tutsi and that the Tutsi at this time were ibyitso of the Inyenzi-Inkotanyi.

Q. But there were other Tutsi, weren't there? Did he give an order for each person he wanted killed?

Yes. There were lots of people who were killed long before. We killed them at the secteur [office] when they were at the meeting. The mother of [the rich neighbor] and her daughter were not at that meeting and that's why they asked us [to kill them].

Q. After having killed the mother and sister of [the rich neighbor], did you receive another order from Jude to kill other people?

No, because they were almost the last ones. [Olivier, #2/5]

By his own admission, Olivier was an extremely active and willing génocidaire. There is no hint that personal ties interfered with Olivier's ability to carry out Jude's orders to kill all the Tutsi in Ngali. The orders were clear about who were targets—all Tutsi living in Ngali. Yet, Olivier's active and sustained participation did not protect him from the suspicions of his fellow killers. Despite his active participation in the genocide, Olivier himself became the object of threats and accusations.

---

11. Inyenzi, or "cockroach," was a derogatory term for the RPF. Inkotanyi, or "those who fight valiantly," was a name the RPF had given itself. Many respondents would refer to the RPF by various combinations of these names, the most common being Inyenzi-Inkotanyi or RPF-Inkotanyi.

The first form of targeting Olivier experienced was the accusation that his wife was Tutsi. I came across this information unexpectedly when I was asking Olivier about whether he had engaged in any pillaging during the genocide. Olivier admitted he had, which was a rare admission for any of my respondents.[12] Given this admission, I was surprised when Olivier said his wife had not participated in the pillaging, particularly when other accounts of the genocide had highlighted the extent to which killers' wives engaged in pillaging the bodies of recent victims (Hatzfeld 2003). But the reason why Olivier's wife did not participate in the pillaging was even more unexpected.

Q. Did your wife also participate in the pillaging?
No.

Q. Why not?
She stayed at the house. She was being chased.

Q. Why was your wife being chased?
They suspected she was Tutsi.

Q. The killers in your group suspected she was Tutsi or who exactly [suspected that]?
It was some people in my group. My wife came from Bugesera and the leaders of the attack groups suspected she was Tutsi and it was why they wanted to get her.
. . . .

Q. Did [Jude] ever ask you to kill your wife?
No. Because after finding out there was a plan to kill my wife and some of my brothers who were tall, I fought back.

Q. Who made this plan?
It was [names two men]. They came to my house two times to look for my wife.

Q. What did they say each time?
One time, I wasn't there. The second time, they were saying to me that my wife was Tutsi. After uttering this word, I went to tell the whole group and the group stopped them from continuing to attack my house.

12. Throughout my fieldwork, I found people generally silent on two subjects: sexual violence and pillaging. The former did not surprise me as talk of rape and sexual violence is taboo in many societies. The latter, however, did surprise me, particularly since many had admitted to killing, a far more serious crime than pillaging. One Rwandan friend theorized that admitting to pillaging may have carried a worse social stigma than confessing to killing because pillaging showed that the pillager coveted or wanted something that someone else had. Another friend suggested that people did not want to admit to pillaging because such an admission would require them to pay restitution to the victim or victim's family. Both explanations may be valid.

Q. What did you say exactly to your group?

When I got to the side of the road where the group was, I told them that [the two men] wanted to kill my wife and I showed the group my wife's identity card to assure them she was not Tutsi.

Q. Were [the two men] your friends?

No. We weren't friends but I can say we weren't enemies either. [Olivier, #5/5]

Bugesera lies to the east of Ngali in a different préfecture. The first people to populate this region were Tutsi expelled from the north in the 1960s (Des Forges 1999, 39). Bugesera has since had a reputation for having a high number of Tutsi, which is probably why the killers cite "being from Bugesera" as an indicator that Olivier's wife must be Tutsi.

The second form of targeting was accusations that Olivier was hiding the Tutsi grandchildren of the victim (whose murder is described above). When I asked Olivier whether this accusation was true, he replied with a roll of the eyes, "It's a long story." He then hinted at the basis for the accusation. The victim's sister had been married to Olivier's paternal uncle. Because paternal uncles in Rwandan society are like fathers to their nephews, Olivier's link to the victim was significant.

Olivier's case stands in stark contrast to Eugène's and illustrates the perniciousness of group ties. Unlike Eugène, Olivier's relationship to his accusers was not based on prior ties of friendship, but rather, on group ties generated through the activities of genocide. He and his accusers had come together because of their participation in the killings, not because they had any prior bonds, as Eugène had with the members of his group. As Olivier himself said of his relationship with his two accusers: "We weren't friends but I can say we weren't enemies either." Unlike ties of friendship, group ties did not protect Olivier but instead made him the object of multiple accusations and suspicions. Group ties turned an active Interahamwe into a target for murder.

Stefan (Joiner, Kimanzi)

Group ties not only turned some Joiners into targets, they also helped to pull along reluctant Joiners by overriding doubts and hesitations, as the case of Stefan illustrates.

Stefan was a slight man when we met him at the prison in Ruhengeri in 2004. His face was hollow, with deep-set eyes and sunken cheeks that made him look much older than his age. In 1991, the year when he took part in the mass killings of Tutsi in Ruhengeri, he would have been twenty-seven years old, a married man with three children. He was a close neighbor of the victim, the sole Tutsi living in the area. As neighbors, the two had shared beers, conversation, and chores over the years. According to Stefan, they were friends in addition to being neighbors.

Like Michel, Stefan describes his involvement in his neighbor's murder in very ambiguous terms, wavering between having been mere witness to the killing and having taken direct part.

Q. Did you see the killings of your neighbors?

I saw the death of [the victim] and it was he we killed.

Q. How was he killed?

We were by the road, for example [names people in the group]. We were hearing that at [my neighbor's] house, there were ibyitso [accomplices] of the Tutsi. We arranged the day to go attack his house. Me and three others, we went there as well. When we got there, we searched for the ibyitso but there weren't any. It was [my neighbor's] son, [names him]. [One in my group] said to [my neighbor's son]: "It's you Tutsi who are causing all these problems." And he killed him with a machete. [Stefan, #1/5]

What emerges from Stefan's accounts of his neighbor's murder is the importance of Stefan's interactions with the group of other Joiners. Before going to the man's house, Stefan and his group discussed rumors they were hearing that Stefan's neighbor was hiding ibyitso. The rumors were that local Tutsi were hiding accomplices and spies for the RPF in their homes. Authorities urged the population to ferret out these spies. Interactions with the group helped to override Stefan's initial doubts that his neighbor was hiding accomplices as the rumors had claimed.

Q. At that time, how did the people distinguish between the Tutsi who were true ibyitso and those Tutsi who were not?

The community made no distinction between one kind of Tutsi and the other. At that time, all Tutsi were ibyitso.

Q. And that's what you believed at that time?

People differ from one another. For me, like my neighbor, I didn't think that he was an icyitso but the others had just come to tell me that he was an icyitso whatever that was. [Stefan, #2/5]

Despite Stefan's own, individual doubts that his neighbor and friend was really an icyitso, Stefan still acceded to the group's determination that the man must be icyitso. He then went along with the group to his neighbor's house and was present when the group killed the neighbor. Group interactions helped to transform Stefan's judgments. They made Stefan see the situation through the group's eyes and to go along with the group at each step, from discussing rumors and planning the attack to descending on the victim's house, then being a part of the group that ended up killing the victim. Despite the ambiguous way in which Stefan recounts this story, what seems clear is that Stefan did not set out with the intention of murdering anyone; rather, interactions with the group convinced Stefan to go along with the group, and by doing so, he ended up participating (either directly or indirectly) in the man's murder. Group ties pulled Stefan into an act of murder.

The people who participated in the genocide were not an undifferentiated body of executioners, but distinct sets of actors—leaders, collaborators, and Joiners—who led and participated in the genocide in different ways and for different reasons. What patterned recruitment and targeting were not ethnic allegiances but social and political ties that linked actors across ethnic lines and through multiple roles. These ties mediated between the script for genocide and people's performances in a given moment.

Leaders and denouncers used ties of family to target family members for recruitment into the killing groups. Group ties worked in similarly pernicious ways. These ties formed through group interactions and organized activities, such as night patrols and daytime attacks. Such ties made targets of some Joiners, such as Olivier, and helped to pull reluctant Joiners into the group, such as Stefan. Ties of friendship, however, also remained important. They helped to generate new and unexpected options, such as the strategy of joining the Interahamwe which Eugène adopted. They also led Joiners to help Tutsi they had known as longtime friends or neighbors when circumstances allowed.

If ethnic hatreds and fears were the main cause, ethnic identities should have prevailed over social ties. Yet, ethnic identities do not account for the specific patterns of recruitment and targeting that occurred in Ngali and Kimanzi. They do not explain the targeting of Hutu or the survival strategies certain Tutsi were able to adopt. Ethnicity cannot explain such patterns because it aggregates actors at too high a level. Social ties, by contrast, differentiate between those with power and those without and better explain participants' various responses to genocide.

6

The Logic of Groups

> People can be submitted to the dynamics of events independently
> of any self-reflective intention or act of reasoning to be so
> embroiled. They can become enmeshed in what may be called the
> logic of the situation, which has implications well-beyond any
> defined cultural orientation, for example, that might have been
> initially implicated.
>
> —Bruce Kapferer, *Legends of People, Myths of State*

So far we have seen how violence became a way for local leaders to express
and consolidate their power through performances of the genocidal script.
I have argued that it was social ties, not ethnic attachments, that patterned
these performances in both communities. Yet, structural factors such as social ties do not tell us much about the process by which people produced
and reproduced the violence over time. How did people come to commit
mass murder the first time? And why did they continue their participation
over time? The answers to these questions, I argue, lie in group dynamics.
Group dynamics were a powerful, homogenizing force. Through groups,
Joiners were able to make sense of a highly volatile and threatening situation. Through interacting in groups and acting as a group, Joiners came to
participate in the violence through a series of graduated steps. Each step
taken created momentum for the next. Once they joined in the violence,
Joiners continued their participation because "working" in groups conferred powerful group identity onto Joiners, who then reenacted the specific practices constitutive of the group's identity.[1] To adapt Charles Tilly's
(1985) phrase describing European state formation—that wars make
states—I argue that killing produced groups and groups produced killings.

To build this argument, I first look at how Joiners viewed their situation
at the time and the process that initially led them into violence. I then

---

1. "Work" was a euphemism that extremists used to mobilize people to kill, particularly
radio personalities on the extremist radio station, RTLM (Radio-télévision des mille
collines).

look at this process from the vantage point of what Joiners did—the acts and practices they engaged in while hunting and killing Tutsi.

Joiners' Explanations

In chapter 3, we examined how people from the community explained why their neighbors participated in the genocide. In this chapter, I examine how Joiners' explain their own actions. How did Joiners make sense of their situation at the time? Do they explain their involvement in the genocide differently than the rest of the community? Where and how do they locate agency in their explanations?

Motives and Constraints

Joiners gave a range of explanations for how they became involved in the violence. One Joiner from Kimanzi, Stefan, whom we met in the previous chapter, provided a three-part typology.

> *Q. How did you decide to participate?*
>
> I didn't make a decision to participate in the genocide killing. I was only in the group because that day, I was right next to the road and when the people were screaming, I went to see what happened and it was the killing of [names victim] by the group, which included me.
>
> *Q. How did the others decide to participate in the genocide?*
>
> First, there was the mobilization by the authorities. The others were forced. The others entered into participating without knowing it, that is, without deciding to do it.
>
> *Q. Which category fits you?*
>
> I was in the last category, and it was why I wanted to speak the whole truth and to speak out about everything I saw. [Stefan, #3/5]

Stefan's typology breaks down into three types of participants: those who were "forced"; those who joined "willingly," and those went along "unwittingly." This typology fits other Joiners' statements. Almost half the Joiners (six out of sixteen) said local leaders forced them to join; had they refused, the same leaders would have killed them. At the other end were those who participated willingly (four out of sixteen), out of a sincere belief that they had to protect their communities from the RPF threat. Édouard, the Joiner from Kimanzi, fits this category. He said he was not forced to join but did so because he really believed there were threats emanating from inside his community, as authorities had been claiming. As Édouard himself explained: "My motivation was to protect us from the

Inkotanyi [RPF], meaning the fight against the Inkotanyi." Finally, others like Michel, who helped to detain the stranger at his house who was later killed at the roadblock, and Stefan, whose group ended up killing his neighbor, seemed to have entered into the violence without any clear intention or conscious decision to do so.

All three categories bespeak situational exigencies, which others in the community emphasized as well (see chapter 3). A war was waging. Soldiers were shooting. People were fleeing. Some were getting shot and raped. Authorities were calling on residents to protect their community. Then the awful news: the RPF-Inkotanyi shoot the president's plane down from the sky—testimony to the rebel army's power and its ultimate goal of taking the country by force. Given these circumstances, even those who participated willingly did so under powerful external pressures.

Situational explanations, however, tend to rob actors of any agency. In situational explanations, actors become victims of circumstance, rather than masters of their own destiny. Was this truly the case for Joiners? Were they simply "victims" of circumstance?

The answer is clearly no. Joiners did make choices, even if they were not completely conscious of the calculus by which they were making them. By their own explanations, Joiners tend to straddle categories in Stefan's typology, rather than fitting neatly into one. For example, Eugène, the Tutsi Joiner who said he joined the Interahamwe to save himself, fits the category of "forced" participant since as a Tutsi, he had no choice but to try to save himself. Yet, given his precise circumstances when he joined the Interahamwe (the fact that he had a stamped document stating he was Hutu, not Tutsi), he also fits the category of a "willing" participant. With the stamped document he obtained from Paul, Eugène had another option. He could have tried to save himself by fleeing the area, as many other Tutsi did. But he did not take that option, which makes Eugène both a "forced" and "willing" participant.

Similarly, Stefan and Charles seem to fit Stefan's category of "unwitting" participants, those who did not make a conscious decision to join in the killings. That the two were unwitting participants does not rule out a willingness to go along with the group and its planned activities. Stefan talked about how he simply found himself with the group at the moment the group murdered his neighbor. Charles, too, spoke in similar terms about how he ended up in the same group as Stefan.

Q. You confessed to having done what?

I confessed that I had a part in the killing of my neighbor because we killed him before my eyes and I didn't lift a finger to save him.

Q. Who were you with when your neighbor was killed?

There were a lot of us, but I remember [names people in the group].

Q. Why were you with this group of killers?

The people who were coming from [names cellule] passed in front of our house and we followed them because they said that in our cellule, there was someone who was hiding ibyitso [accomplices]. That's how I ended up in the group.

Q. You wanted to hunt down the ibyitso?

Yes, me, I wanted to see these ibyitso and to chase them down.

Q. Were you certain that among your neighbors, there were ibyitso?

No, there were no ibyitso.

Q. If you didn't believe that there ibyitso, why did you go with the group?

He was my neighbor that they were saying was hiding the ibyitso and one in the group [names him] asked us to all go together to see if there was really some ibyitso and if not, we had to go explain to the authorities and we followed the others.

Q. If there had been people hidden in your neighbor's house, would you have killed him?

Yes, because that was our objective. [Charles, #3/5]

Both Charles and Stefan talk about their involvement as being unplanned, yet, both also express a readiness to act, a readiness created, in part, by authorities' appeals, but also by the momentum of the group at key moments. For Charles, that moment came when he heard the group whistling and screaming as it stopped in front of his house on its way to the victim's home. It was at that moment that Charles decided to "follow the others." For Stefan, the moment came when the group planned the time and day of its attack and later, when the group descended on the victim's house. In these moments, Charles and Stefan went along with the group not knowing what would happen but certainly knowing what the group was planning to do and, hence, what could happen. Thus, while Charles and Stefan fit the category of "unwitting" participant, they also fit the category of "willing" as well.

What the dynamics of Charles's and Stefan's experiences show is the power of group momentum to pull people along with the group and its activities. This momentum was critical to the process by which many Joiners became involved in violence for the first time, because group interactions not only created ties among group members, it also created momentum for acting as a group. This group momentum did not take away meaningful choices for Joiners, but they did enable Joiners to place the locus of agency—the responsibility to act—onto the group and away from themselves as individuals. By looking to the group to figure out what to do, Joiners gained control of their situation. Through interacting with the group and acting as a group, Joiners found their way. Through talking, exchanging information, passing on rumors, making plans, and coordinating efforts, the group became the site for Joiners to make sense—literally—of a highly volatile and threatening situation. The group offered a consensus perspective on what was happening and a consensus response to the situation. By "making sense," Joiners made order out of disorder and certainty out of uncertainty.

In Kimanzi, the war was immediate and real, not something taking place far away as it seemed to residents of Ngali in the central part of the country. In this context, it is not difficult to imagine how ordinary people could start to suspect a certain group of people, even if the group lived among them, particularly when authorities had labeled that group the enemies of the state. One need look no further than the United States' own record of rounding up citizens of certain ethnicities under the pretext of "security" to realize how easily such suspicions can arise in times of war. Thus it is not hard to imagine that Charles and Stefan, while knowing their Tutsi neighbor to have been a good neighbor and perhaps, even a friend, may have begun to wonder if the rumors about the man's loyalties were true, given the circumstances and the lack of any counterdiscourse that could have strengthened their doubts, instead of reinforcing their suspicions and fears. Indeed, silencing moderate voices was the strategy of extremists from the very beginning of the war. Violence was the most effective way of muting them. Whatever doubts Stefan and Charles may have had about the veracity of the rumors, group momentum helped to override these doubts and bring the two over to the group's side—perhaps unwittingly, but no less willingly.

In Ngali, group dynamics worked in a more coercive fashion. Coercion was direct and immediate. It took the form of face-to-face recruitment and intimidation. At the same time, situations were highly dynamic such that the level of coercion could change from one moment to the next, as the case of Félix illustrates. We met Félix in chapter 5. He was in the group interview with Paul and Eugène in which the subject of friendship arose.

Q. Why did you decide to confess?

I decided to confess because I had to give testimony about everything I saw, because I was in the group that killed a person despite being forced to be with the others at the barrier.

Q. Who forced you to go with the others to the barrier?

It was the authorities of Ngali secteur.

Q. It was who precisely? Which authorities?

There was Jude who was leading Ngali secteur. The other was [names one individual] who was a member of the cellule committee. And there was also [names another individual]. He was also a member of the cellule committee.

Q. How did these three people force you to be at the barrier with the others?

They ran into me at my coffee field where I was harvesting coffee. They asked me what I was doing since the others were at the barrier. They told me to go to the barrier and if I didn't, that they were going to hurt me. Without a lot of discussion, I went with them to the barrier and when I got there, they were killing someone in front of my eyes.

After the murder of the victim, Félix found a way to slip away from the scene undetected.

Q. After the killing of the boy, what happened?

After the death of the boy, they asked me to find a place where they could bury him.

Q. And then?

I put my hoe down on the ground and I told them that I was going to get my things. And I left without burying him. They killed him with massues.

Q. It was the first time that you had seen a killing?

Since the day I was born, it was the first time.

Q. And then you left? without burying the body?

Yes, I left without burying it.

Q. And no one prevented you from leaving?

No one knew that I left.

Q. If you had refused the three authorities who came to your coffee field, what would have happened?

They could have killed me.

Q. Did you know anyone who was killed for refusing orders?

I didn't know of anyone.

Q. Why did you think the authorities could have killed you?

It was because at the beginning of the war, they asked me to go to the barrier. They wanted to take the tiles from my house saying that I refused to go to the barrier even though my wife was seriously ill.

Q. Were you scared of these authorities?

Yes, I was scared of them.

Q. Did they order you to help them bury the body of the boy?

Yes, there were lots of us and when I left, the others stayed to bury the boy.

Q. Why were you not scared to leave the place right after the others had killed the boy?

I hid when I left the area and I never killed anyone. The proof is that I am still alive. I never hit anyone. [Félix, #3/4]

One moment, a group of authorities forces Félix to go to the barrier, where he witnesses the killing of a local Tutsi boy; another moment, he is able to slip away from the scene undetected. Félix's process of joining was typical of Joiners who said they were forced; none felt they could refuse to go when leaders or their henchmen confronted them in person. What is less typical, however, was that Félix found a way to leave the scene without anyone noticing and without incurring further harm to himself. The dynamics of the situation "forced" Félix to go with the others to the barrier, but they also enabled Félix to avoid participating any further. As Félix's case shows, the process of initiation into violence could be based on quickly shifting dynamics—opportunities and constraints that allowed for corresponding shifts in strategy and response.

The process of descent into violence was not only dynamic; it was also self-reinforcing. Each step taken created momentum for the next. In both communities, group activities began with conducting night patrols and manning roadblocks, then escalated to pillaging and burning Tutsi homes, and finally, to hunting down and killing Tutsi. Joiners began their involvement with the first of these activities and continued to go along even as activities escalated to more violent acts. Olivier, the Joiner from Ngali who was accused of having a Tutsi wife, described the first attacks his group conducted in orderly terms.

Q. Tell me about the attacks by your group. What was the first attack?

We did the first attack at SB's house. He was a neighbor. To get to his house took three minutes.

. . . .

Q. How many were you from Ngali? More than ten people?

There were a lot of us, more than thirty people. There were people from all the cellules of Ngali.

. . . .

Q. How did you kill this victim?

At my first attack, no one was killed. The people fled and the group of attackers pillaged. All the pillaged things were taken to Jude's house: the cows, the goats, the sheep, the chickens, the beds. . . . We transported everything to Jude's house, who was our leader.

Q. Was Jude present at this attack?

Yes, he was.

Q. Was he present at all the attacks.

Yes, he was.

Q. It took three minutes to pillage all the belongings of this person?

Impossible. That was the time it took to get to his house. There were a lot of things in his house. It took a few hours to finish looting these things. [Olivier, #5/5]

Olivier describes a very ordered and structured process. This was no frenzied mob, overcome with fear or hatred. Nor was it a free-for-all where each man was out for himself. This was highly organized activity, with a clear leader who set clear parameters for what the group was supposed to do and what it was not to do.

Eugène, the Tutsi who joined the Interahamwe to save himself, described his group's first attack in nearly identical terms. This first attack had a clear objective, which did not include killing.

Q. What was the first attack your group did?

The first time, my group attacked the man named [names the man].

. . . .

Q. How exactly did your group kill him?

My group didn't kill [the man]. It destroyed his house and pillaged all his things. After a few days, some people killed his two children. [The man] is still alive.

Q. Was it your objective to kill this man when you arrived at his house the first time?

For our first attack, we knew that we were supposed to destroy and burn the houses of Tutsi, not kill them.

Q. Who led this first attack?

He was called [names the person].

Q. Where was [the victim] during this first attack?

He was at the house.

Q. He was at home while you burned his house and pillaged all his belongings?

Yes, because we surprised him.

Q. This attack took how much time?
Almost forty minutes.

Q. What did you do with this man's pillaged things?
All the pillaged goods had to be taken to [names cellule], to Jude's house.

Q. Was Jude present at this attack?
No. [Eugène, #4/4]

By chance, we had also interviewed the victim of this particular attack. The victim's version is consistent with Eugène's, but adds details about the victim's experience of the attack that are missing in Eugène's retelling.

> *Q. What did you do when the killings started here in [your cellule]?*
> First, the team of killers arrived here. They told me to open up the house and to give them a gun and bullets [given to me] by the Inkotanyi [RPF]. They took my belongings, including the cows. They had massues, swords, axes, spears, hammers. They told me to sit down and look at the sun without moving. One of them wanted to hit me on the head with an axe, but the others stopped him. They asked me where the other cows, goats were. . . . They told me to leave the house because they also came to burn it down. I fled to the sorghum field. [122, #1/1]

Both Eugène's version and that of the victim highlight the disciplined nature of the attack. As Eugène remarks, "We knew that we were supposed to destroy and burn the houses of Tutsi, not kill them." Just as the group knew what it was supposed to do, it also knew what it was not supposed to do, which is why the group curbed the excessive behavior of one of its members by preventing him from striking the victim with an axe. As Eugène explained later in the same interview, "Everything was organized by Jude," implying that nothing occurred without Jude's direction or knowledge. Indeed, there is no evidence of entrepreneurial activities by any Joiner—of someone going off on his own to kill Tutsi. Did this ordered process make Joiners mere pawns of leaders with no choice but to go along with their orders and plans?

Power and Powerlessness

From Joiners' point of view, their actions were a matter of situational exigency, not choice. Whether willing, forced, or unwitting participants, Joiners felt they had to do what they did in order to protect themselves. As Eugène remarked about his own participation: "It was to protect myself so they couldn't kill me."

Part of the reason Joiners felt highly constrained lay in their sense of powerlessness. The most common refrain from Joiners when I asked them if they tried to resist or refuse orders was that they had no power or that no one would listen to them. One Joiner from Kimanzi illustrated this tendency most clearly. This Joiner said that he was with the same group of Interahamwe as Édouard, Stefan, and Charles but was not a member of the group. He thus refers to the killers in the third person and to himself as a witness unable to do anything but watch the group kill the victim before his eyes.

Q. Who was saying that the son of this woman was harboring people who were against the government?

It was the Interahamwe who called us and were attacking the house of [names the person].

Q. Who were the Interahamwe? These were your neighbors or people who came from far away or . . .

It was our neighbors. They had a group of Interahamwe who were supposed to go look for ibyitso.

Q. Why did you follow their orders to kill the son of this woman?

They were our neighbors. This group joined us in the vicinity, and they killed this person under our eyes. It was why people accused us of his death.

Q. How did the Interahamwe kill this man?

First off, he [the victim] struck one of the people [in the group of Interahamwe]. The others [then] struck him.

Q. With what weapons?

They used machetes.

Q. How many people participated in the killing of this man?

There were a lot. There were more than a dozen people.

Q. What did you do while he was being killed? Did you try to stop the Interahamwe, for example? Or did you try to run?

I did nothing. No power at that time. [407A, #2/2]

A Joiner from Ngali spoke in nearly identical terms. At the time of the genocide, this man was responsable for one of the cellules in Ngali and, hence, claimed some authority through his position. Yet, he, too, describes his situation as one where no one would listen to him.

Q. Who had you imprisoned?

In having me imprisoned, almost all the men of Ngali were imprisoned saying that we had killed the child of [names the parent]. They would ask us to accept what we had done, that is, our participation in the genocide. Normally, [this] child would arrive at my house when he [the child's parent] was in [a nearby town]. RT would bring the child to my house as [I was] responsable. The child would stay at my house like that. It was 3 pm when I would accompany RT. On the way back, I ran into [names two other men] [who were] at my house to kill the child. They left with the child and I followed them to see whether they would give me the child and they refused and they killed him in front of me. That's why I truly accepted that I took part in the death of the child.

Q. How old was this child?

Around thirteen or fourteen years old.

Q. Who is RT?

He is a mason and also a farmer.

Q. You said that normally, [the child] would arrive at your house when he [the child's parent] was in [the nearby town] but this time RT brought this child to your house?

Yes, that's right.

Q. How did these people kill this child?

They killed him with a small hoe.

Q. Why did these people kill this child?

Because he was Tutsi.

Q. Did you see other Tutsi being killed?

No.

Q. Were there other Tutsi who were killed?

Yes.

Q. What did you do after the killing of this child?

I did nothing because they weren't listening to me. After his death, we buried him. [206, #1/1]

Other Joiners spoke in similar terms when explaining the situations they faced. No one would listen to them or there was nothing they could do to stop others from killing someone. Even the former conseiller of Kimanzi, an extremely well-educated man, spoke in these same terms when I asked him if he tried to stop soldiers from taking people away to kill them. As this former official explained: "I had no power to stop them. They were military. I was a civilian. Having come from other secteurs, they were taking these people and were going to kill them somewhere else. What could I have done at that moment?"

These claims of powerlessness are, perhaps, too convenient to take seriously. Yet, at the same time, they are too numerous to discount out of hand.

There is certainly reason to be skeptical, but there is reason to be skeptical of all the data. The question is not whether Joiners were or were not telling the truth, but whether it is possible to detect the logic underlying what they do say, no matter the level of forthrightness of any individual.

One way to isolate this logic is to compare Joiners' actions to how others acted when faced with a similar set of circumstances and constraints. When we place Joiners' statements of powerlessness in these different contexts, the following points emerge.

First, Joiners were aware of the possibility of refusing. In fact, those who say they were powerless framed their statements in the context of having tried to refuse, resist, or stop others from killing a victim. Thus Joiners' insistence that they were powerless was not an indication that they believed they had no other choice, but rather that they did not believe they could affect the outcome in any way—no matter what they did. Insofar as any actor's agency lies in choices made, not outcomes obtained, Joiners' powerlessness—whether actual, imagined, or post hoc—did not obviate the possibility for agency in whatever actions they did take or failed to take.

Second, if coercion was the reason many Joiners joined in the violence initially, why is there not more evidence of people hiding, shirking, or finding ways out of participating when they could, as Félix did? If Félix, who by all appearances was quite easily intimidated, had the presence of mind to leave the scene and hide, why did others not look for the exit option when they could? To be sure, exit options were limited, but they did exist, for levels of coercion, as we saw above, could shift dramatically from one moment to the next. Plus, as all Joiners noted, the groups were large. The sheer size of the groups would have provided opportunities for other Joiners to slip away unnoticed as Félix did. Yet, with the exception of Félix, there is little evidence that Joiners tried to hide, evade, resist, or free-ride in any way once they joined in the violence. The absence of these types of behavior suggests a level of agency even among those Joiners who said they were forced to join in the violence.

(One caveat is in order, however. Joiners in Kimanzi, such as Stefan and Édouard, stated that after killing their Tutsi neighbor, they did not participate in any further killings. It is possible they are telling the truth. No other residents talked about their involvement in subsequent killings. Yet their decision to end their participation after this murder should not be taken as an act of defiance or evasion, because this particular episode of killings only lasted a few days in January 1991. It may be that Stefan and Édouard [and others] did decide not to participate in any other murders, and equally possible that they did not face further pressures to participate after January 1991. In other words, these data are inconclusive in terms of the argument. While they do not indicate participation over time, neither do they indicate evading or shirking.)

What the data show is not which moments Joiners had power over their situation and which moments they did not. Rather, the data indicate that Joiners' feelings of powerlessness were as much of their own making as they were an objective condition. Joiners' sense of powerlessness was as much a consequence of their actions as a cause. For going along with the group at each step, from conducting night patrols to killing Tutsi, shifted the responsibility to act, and act purposely, on the group. This shift empowered not only the group but also, Joiners in return, because it relieved Joiners of having to make sense of the situation on their own. Where an individual was powerless to affect any outcome, the group was powerful and could effect specific outcomes. The groups patrolled, set up roadblocks, burned homes, pillaged goods, transported those goods to a central location, and murdered Tutsi. The group, in other words, became a way for Joiners to make sense—literally and figuratively—of a highly dynamic situation. Acting in groups enabled Joiners to experience power in concrete ways.

The counterfactual only strengthens the argument. Going it alone would have required Joiners to step out of the group and face the same threatening and uncertain conditions on their own. Stepping outside the group would have required going against the momentum and power of the group. It would have led to possible repercussions in the form of threats, accusations, or physical harm. To understand the full import of this counterfactual, let us look at how two resisters responded to attempts to coerce their participation in genocidal activities.

Negative Cases: Frédéric and Gustave

Like the majority of respondents, Frédéric was born and raised in Ngali. He earned his living as a farmer and never went to school. He had married at a young age and shortly after his second child was born, problems between his wife and him began. His wife had become angry when Frédéric gave his sisters some land. So angry was she that she poisoned several of Frédéric's sisters in order to reclaim the land her husband had given them.[2]

By the time of the genocide, the two had been married for over ten years and had eight children. It would be safe to assume then, that by 1994, Frédéric was not unaccustomed to conflict and the use of violence

---

2. Poisoning is a common claim when people die mysteriously. It may be that Frédéric's wife did physically poison his sisters, but just as likely that their deaths were attributed to his wife's ill feelings toward them.

to solve one's problems. Indeed, one might go so far as to say he was re-signed to it, powerless to undo what his wife had done. But it would be wrong to assume that Frédéric took such an attitude when the problem of politics began to emerge. Even before the genocide began, Frédéric had run-ins with Jude who used both carrots and sticks to convince Frédéric to toe the line. While many in his community followed Jude's orders, Frédéric did not.

Q. Were there people who refused to follow this order [to join a specific political party] despite the threats?

For example, me. I refused to join the MRND party.[3] He [Jude] said that there was one party. I came to tell him that he shouldn't make my choice for me.

. . . .

Q. When you refused the order to join MRND, how did Jude react?

After having refused to join the party, there were tensions between him and me. When they started to do the patrols, I, too, would go and Jude would say among us is an icyitso, meaning me. I was able to go two days without going there [to do the patrols]. They would come looking for me and punch me. Another day, they were going to kill a cow of [a neighbor]. They came to ask me to take some of the meat. I refused again and they hit me, insulted me, saying that they didn't know my origin [i.e., ubwoko]. And they would block me saying that I had to stay by them to keep me from telling people what they had done.

Q. Why did you refuse each time?

Because it was wrong to eat someone else's cow. For me, I can accept dying instead of hurting others. [Frédéric, #2/5]

Frédéric's multiple refusals to go along with Jude's orders stand in stark contrast to the way in which Joiners responded to similar coercive tech-niques.

At a subsequent interview, I asked Frédéric about his relationship with Sophie, the elderly rescuer, who had helped raise Frédéric after his par-ents had died. Sophie had taught Frédéric that good behavior was show-ing obedience toward others. This understanding of what constituted good behavior came up regularly in interviews in which this topic arose. This valorization of obedience, however, did not translate into Frédéric obeying orders he knew to be wrong.

---

3. Frédéric's reference to the MRND is an indication that Jude was working closely with the MRND stalwarts in Gitarama.

Q. You said the last time that you refused to follow the orders of Jude. Did Jude ever threaten to kill you when you refused his orders?

Jude made threats to me after refusing to eat meat from the neighbors' cows. He sent a boy who beat me up and asked me to go do the patrols. The boy forced me to go. If not, they were going to kill me. When I got there, Jude told me that he didn't know my background [i.e., ethnicity] and right away, he asked me to pay him some money to save my life; if not, he was going to bust my head open. I gave him 7,000 [about fifty dollars] to save my life.[4]

Q. Why weren't you obedient at that time, with Jude and his group?

Because I saw that Jude and his group were harming others and well, everyone should have a right to his life. [Frédéric, #3/5]

Gustave, a resister from Kimanzi, gave a similar explanation as to why he refused to join any political activities. As Gustave explained:

The conseillers were giving the orders to the people to participate in the politics but some people accepted and the others refused to follow the orders because of their beliefs, which didn't accept participating in it, for example, the killing. And that was my also my case. My heart [conscience] did not allow me to participate in the politics.

Gustave's circumstances were different than those of Frédéric. Gustave did not face the same level of coercion to join in what he called "the politics." I understood Gustave's use of the term *politics* to be a euphemism for targeted killing of Tutsi. Whether he used the term *politics* in a narrow sense (to refer to violence only) or broad sense (to include non-violent forms of politics), Gustave refused to participate. Unlike Frédéric, no one ever tried to force Gustave to change his mind, though he did admit that others in Kimanzi were threatened for refusing.

Like Frédéric, Gustave predicated all his actions on what he thought was the right thing to do. The people he chose to be friends with also reflected these same beliefs about right and wrong. He explained his views of friendship while telling us about his best friend, a Tutsi who had joined the army in 1980 and died while fighting in Kigali in 1993.

Q. Why was MW your best friend?

MW was my best friend because we were in the same class. Our parents were also close friends. He would come visit me and I would go visit him.

4. The official exchange rate in December 1993 through third quarter 1994 was 144 Rwandan francs (Frw) to 1 U.S. dollar (Central Intelligence Agency 1994). In the informal market, the exchange rate was 182Frw to the dollar (Prunier 1995, 130n7). At these rates, 7,000Frw would have been equal to about $40–50, a tidy sum by rural standards.

Q. What is the difference between true friends and acquaintances?

The difference is that a true friend is someone who gives you good advice. It's someone you trust in everything without hiding anything from him and vice versa.

Q. Can you give an example of bad advice?

For example, someone might recognize you and might ask you to help kill someone or to go steal the belongings of others, saying you'll be rich.

Q. Was there ever someone who asked you to help kill someone or steal another's things?

No one did, because when I notice that someone has bad ways, I cannot go near them. Even today, I cannot be friends with people who think like that.

. . . .

Q. In general, how do people show they are true friends to one another?

True friends must have the same ideas, that is, good ideas. They have to help one another in everything. Each has to steer the other in the right direction. [Gustave, #5/6]

For Gustave, friendships must be based on shared values about what is right or wrong. Absent these shared values, there can be no real friendship—indeed, there can be no relationship at all. As Gustave explained, he stays away from bad people. In addition to shared values, friends also have an obligation to keep one another on the right track and to correct the other if he or she goes astray. In other words, friendship is about making sure each lives by their shared values.

What makes Gustave and Frédéric different from the Joiners in their communities? The key difference seems to be that, in stark contrast to Joiners, Gustave and Frédéric drew firm lines between what they were willing to do and what they were not willing to do. Both had a clear sense of what was right or wrong under any circumstances and both abided by that sense of right and wrong even under threat of harm. For these two men, situational exigencies did not override their own personal, moral compass. During the war and genocide, they refused to engage in activities they believed were wrong. Gustave refused to get involved in any killing and whatever else he meant by the term *politics*. Frédéric remained firm in his refusal to join Jude's political party or to partake of stolen meat.

Joiners, by contrast, never mentioned the rightness or wrongness of their actions when they explained or described what they did during the genocide. This does not mean that Joiners did not know that what they were doing was wrong, only that in the moment of committing violence, this sense of right or wrong was overridden by the group's objectives and plans. Like the theory of social contamination that the elderly man from Kimanzi described in chapter 3, Joiners did indeed become like those around them through regular contact and exposure. They adopted the same attitudes, beliefs, and understanding of what was appropriate to do during war and mass murder. Resisters, by contrast, never went along with the group without considering the rightness or wrongness of their actions. They never looked to any group to make sense of the situation they faced. Instead, they looked to their own consciences or "hearts."

Becoming Interahamwe

It is one thing to join in the violence initially and quite another to continue that participation over time. Joiners in Ngali continued their participation over the duration of the genocide, which lasted from late April until the RPF took the area in late May 1994.[5] Why? Why did Joiners not find ways to avoid further participation, particularly those Joiners who said leaders or authorities forced them to join initially?

To explore these questions, I move away from Joiners words and look more closely at their deeds.

Most analyses of mass violence in political science eschew examinations of what some dismiss as "the particular," assuming details that are not relevant to the goals of violence—its instrumentality—are not relevant to explanations of why the violence occurs. Yet, I argue that the question of how people carry out violence is not necessarily separable from the question of why they commit that violence. Investigating how people carry out violence can tell us quite a bit about why they do so in the first place. By "how," I do not mean the structural opportunities necessary for committing violence, but the specific way that actors perform the violence—who does what, when, where, to whom, and with what sorts of violation to the victims and their bodies.

For some types of violence, form is what makes the act what it is. By definition, riots need crowds and lynchings, an audience. The public and dramatic nature of these acts is what gives them their power as a form of political protest or method of social control. To ignore the public nature of these events—the element of crowd involvement; the timing and choice

---

5. Joiners in Kimanzi maintained that they ceased their participation after the one killing in which they participated. Because the pattern of killings in Kimanzi occurred at precise moments and did not continue uninterrupted over a long period, it is quite possible that these men were telling the truth.

of sites; and in the case of lynchings, the ritualized hanging, burning, and mutilation of victims' bodies—would be to overlook the most obvious clues as to why people participate in these acts in the first place.[6]

Genocide, too, takes specific form in specific settings. Where the Holocaust was mechanized and bureaucratic, mass killings in Cambodia and Bosnia involved face-to-face executions performed with guns, grenades, and more mundane instruments of torture and destruction. These differences in form underscore the limitations of a strictly instrumental approach to genocide. Understanding actors' goals for genocide (or any type of violence) tells us little about why that violence would take one form but not another. Investigating the form that genocidal violence took in Rwanda helps us to understand why Joiners continued their participation over time and space.

Form of Killing

In Ngali and Kimanzi and throughout the country, genocide took consistent form. Joiners killed in groups, not individually.[7] These groups were large, oftentimes far larger than what was physically required to kill the victims at hand, who were usually unarmed and unable to flee.[8] Joiners estimated their groups to include ten to fifty (or more) people.[9] The sheer size of the groups meant that many members watched as a handful performed the physical murder of the victim(s).[10] In the killing in which Édouard, Stefan, and Charles participated, for example, Joiners estimated the group's size to have been between ten and fifteen people with only one among the group responsible for the actual murder of the victim.

6. Not all lynchings were public events. As William Brundage (1993, 18) notes, "for all of [its] common traits, the term *lynching* embraces a wide variety of mob actions and murders, some of which conform to a model of communal rituals but some of which emphatically do not."

7. This finding is consistent with Straus (2004b, 171). Of his random, national sample of 210 mid-level perpetrators, only one mentioned killing as an individual. Charles Mironko (2004, 202) also confirms that killings were conducted in groups: "None of my one hundred and ten respondents talked about participating in the genocide in any way other than as part of an *igitero* [attack group]." Des Forges concurs but cautions that, as with everything, there were exceptions (personal communication, 2 February 2008).

8. The one exception was mass killings that took place at sites to which thousands had sought refuge, such as churches, schools, and stadiums. In these sites, the number of killers was likely much smaller than the number of potential victims. In Ngali and Kimanzi, however, there were no mass killings at schools or churches, and no stadium in either locale.

9. My data on group size are also consistent with Straus (2004b, chap. 5).

10. Mironko's research also confirms this. Mironko (2004, 193–202) discusses the historical-institutional basis for *igitero*, or organized attacks.

Second, the vast majority of killings were public acts. They took place in broad daylight, in full view of onlookers. For example, Charles noted the time of his group's attack as roughly four o'clock in the afternoon. Even killings in remote areas, such as the killings that took place in the forests around Kimanzi, were conducted in full view of the local population, who were ordered to witness the murder of the victims.

Third, killings were physically intimate. Killers killed up close and face-to-face. The instruments of mass murder included clubs, hoes, axes, massues (nail-studded clubs), hammers, spears, swords, and machetes. These weapons were common farming tools that Joiners already owned. Killers bludgeoned victims with blunt instruments or struck them with edged weapons. They also threw people into holes and latrines. (In Kimanzi, only soldiers or elites had guns, but even those with guns did not always shoot their victims.)

Fourth, killings featured theatrical elements. In Ngali, when killers spotted a victim, they would chant "Pawa, pawa, pawa" or "MDR Pawa" to announce that they were about to kill someone. Killers also banged on empty jerricans and whistled and shouted. Some dressed in costume or "disguise." One survivor recalls having seen a neighbor dressed in what she described as "a suit of knives."

Once the killers spotted a victim, other types of activities ensued. Killers sometimes raped women and girls before killing them. They also, at times, tortured victims.[11] Another survivor from Ngali reported that killers forced her father-in-law to dig a hole where the killers intended to bury her mother and brother after killing them. Forcing relatives to witness, and even to take part in, the murders of family members was a regular feature of the killings. Finally, killers often "announced" a killing they had just committed or were about to commit by stopping in front of specific people's houses. Sometimes, these announcements were meant to recruit others to join the group; at other times, they were intended as warnings or threats to the people inside the house.

Once the killing was completed, another set of activities ensued. These activities might involve burying the bodies or ordering residents not to bury the bodies.[12] In some cases, killers mutilated the bodies. One lieutenant of Jude, for example, reputedly cut the heads off victims "to show how Tutsi looked like each other." In another example, a Joiner noted in

11. For more extensive accounts of atrocities, see Hatzfeld (2000); Taylor (2002); African Rights (1995); Des Forges (1999); Physicians for Human Rights (UK) (nd); and Landesman (2002).

12. Before the order came to hide the killings from the international community, killers left dead bodies out in the open and forbade people from burying them (Des Forges, personal communication, 2 February 2008).

his letter of confession that after killing its victim, the group dismembered the body, cutting the limbs off the trunk. (None of the other four letters that concern this same murder refer to this act of mutilation, however.) Mention of atrocities was not frequent and came up only when respondents brought up the subject themselves, as I asked no direct questions about atrocities myself.

The repertoire of killing practices in the two communities included the following acts. This list may not be exhaustive but it does reflect the testimonies of the Joiners and residents with whom I spoke. Some of the practices listed were instrumental to the goal of exterminating Tutsi, while others were more performative in nature. Both types of practices were consistent features of the violence. (The practices that were specific to one research site are noted in parentheses.)

- accusing people of being Tutsi or ibyitso
- stopping in front of a house to recruit additional people
- stopping in front of a house to announce a killing
- stopping in front of a house to threaten inhabitants
- encircling a victim's home
- throwing rocks onto the roof to scare the people inside (Kimanzi)
- standing watch
- watching others kill
- forcing others (e.g., family members) to watch the murder of the victim
- forcing others to take part in the murder
- extorting money
- pillaging Tutsi property
- burning Tutsi homes
- digging holes (for burial or killing or both)
- throwing or forcing victims into holes
- forcing the population to dig holes
- wearing costumes or special dress
- chanting political party slogans (Ngali)
- banging on empty jerricans (Ngali)
- whistling
- shouting
- tying victims' arms behind their back[13]

13. This act comes from the testimony of one Joiner who said that the local *responsable* ordered him to tie the hands behind the backs of four people who were to be killed. According to Des Forges, tying hands behind the back was standard practice for the RPF but was not part of the repertoire of genocidal killers. This might suggest that the responsable and hence, this Joiner, were actually doing the bidding of the RPF. More data would be needed to confirm this.

- torturing victims
- raping women and girls
- mutilating the dead bodies of victims

All these acts were performed by groups during the course of killing a victim. No one reported seeing anyone perform any of these acts outside the context of killing. No one reported performing any of these acts on his own or in private. Indeed, the exception proves the rule. A rapist who wanted to claim a victim all to himself would take the victim to a private area to rape her;[14] such a rape took place during the course of killing victims, indicating that rapes were part of the practices of killing, and not the act of individuals going off on their own.

Constitutive Power of Groups

Why did killings take this specific form? Mironko (2004, 200) offers a functional explanation.

> The result of involving everyone in the killings, whether directly or indirectly, was that all of them were made to feel equally complicit. Those who blew the whistles, those who attacked with clubs, hoes, machetes, as well as those forced to bury the dead, or contribute their agricultural implements, became part of the carnage.

Mironko's argument, echoed elsewhere (African Rights 1995, 993), explains why leaders of the genocide, even at the local level, tried to implicate as many people as possible in the killings. If all were guilty, none could be absolved later should the political winds turn.

For Joiners, however, the instrumentality of their continued involvement is much less clear. Joiners did not have much more to gain (individually or as a group) by continuing their participation in the genocide. They did not profit the same way as leaders and with each act, they implicated themselves further, thereby incurring greater risks should the political tide turn. This raises several questions. Did those who were forced to participate ever try to shirk or evade participation? Or did mass hatreds and fears grow—spurred on by the violence—and reveal themselves more clearly over time? Once again, there is little evidence of increased shirking, evading, or free-riding over time. Indeed, one of the remarkable facets of the genocide is the continuity of the groups' participation—the fact that the groups stayed intact over weeks and sometimes months of

14. Brent Beardsley reported that this occurred in Kigali (Biennial meeting of the International Association of Genocide Scholars, Boca Raton, Florida, June 2005).

killing. Why? What accounts for such consistent and sustained participation in the killing?

I argue that it was not increasing fears and hatreds that propelled Joiners to continue their participation over time, but the constitutive power of killing in groups. In group contexts, Joiners engaged in specific acts of killing (enumerated above); these acts constituted the group as a particular kind of social actor with a particular identity, what I call an Interahamwe identity. To be a real Interahamwe meant engaging in these acts, but not others, in the specific context of killing victims—that is, in a "group" context.[15] Once constituted, the group engaged in those acts that were constitutive of its identity, thereby reproducing the violence over time.

While some acts were more instrumental to the mass murder of victims than others (such as tying victims' arms behind their back), no act was more or less vital to the constitution of the group's identity. It was the combination of acts that mattered. Thus, "watching" or "observing" formed an integral part of the violence. Just as players sitting on the bench play an important role in supporting their fellow teammates on the court, so, too, did fellow Interahamwe play an important role watching as a select few clubbed or hacked the victims to death. Watching or observing enhanced the performance of genocide and, thus, its expressive power as a form of complete domination over victims, Tutsi as well as Hutu. Watching, in other words, was not a way to stand apart from the killings (as Joiners maintain), but formed an integral part of the performance of violence.

The Interahamwe identity adhered to groups, not to individuals, and only in the context of killing or hunting Tutsi. Outside the group, an individual was no longer an Interahamwe. The maintenance of the identity thus depended on both context and activity. Group members had to engage in certain practices in specific contexts, but not others. Anyone who deviated from those practices in the group context threatened the very basis on which the group was able to make and remake itself. Deviant or prohibited practices, such as saving a particular Tutsi instead of killing her, mandated the severest form of punishment, because such practices threatened the very groupness of the group—its raison d'être. This is why, as Olivier explained, it was impossible for Joiners to save someone, because if anyone even suggested saving a Tutsi, the group would make that person kill the victim himself.

15. By this definition, those who participated by denouncing others were not "true" Interahamwe. As Émilie, a survivor from Ngali, pointed out, for example, her brother-in-law who denounced her and her family was a "simple" Interahamwe because he did not participate in the killings himself, but only informed those who did.

This concept of group as social actor has quotidian analogies. In the U.S. military, a soldier is not an individual, but a member of a collective actor called "the army." As part of this actor called army, the soldier must engage in certain practices and not others, and in specific contexts and not others. Firing weapons in the right context constitutes the group as an army. Firing weapons outside prescribed contexts would, on the other hand, constitute the same group as a band of renegades or worse, mass murderers, as the case of Lieutenant Calley at My Lai exemplifies. Such behavior would also invite the severest forms of sanction and punishment and would very likely culminate in the dismissal of offending individuals from the army.

We could also cite a sports team analogy. What constitutes a dozen men (or women) in baggy shorts as a social actor called "basketball team" is a set of specific practices performed in specific contexts. These practices include not only the physical components of the game itself, such as passing, dribbling, and shooting, but also a host of accompanying acts, many of which are social in nature. They include cheering, arguing, shouting, huddling, and sitting on the bench. The social actor "basketball team" exists only so long as its members engage in these practices, and not others, and in specific team contexts, such as games or practices.[16] In this way, a player in uniform who sits through a whole game on the bench does not undermine the "teamness" of the team, because bench-sitting is a practice constitutive of the team. The same person who sits on a gym bench for two hours outside a game or practice, however, would be viewed very differently. She or he might be seen, for example, as a student in detention or a person waiting for friends to arrive. In other words, outside a team context, the same act has very different meaning.

Similarly, a group of men carrying machetes, clubs, and hoes constitutes Interahamwe, and not a farmer's cooperative or a group of residents engaged in umuganda (communal work duty), so long as the men are engaged in Interahamwe activities—that is, hunting and killing Tutsi and other legitimate targets. Only through these practices is the group's identity generated and sustained. Once generated, the group identity takes precedence over individual identities, including ethnic identities. The predominance of group over individual identities explains why it did not matter if a member or two (or any number) in a group of Interahamwe

---

16. And, indeed, coaches usually fine or reprimand players who engage in proscribed practices, such as sitting on the floor instead of the bench and taking off one's shoes during a game, as Dennis Rodman was wont to do when he played for the San Antonio Spurs in the 1990s. The basis for these reprimands was that Rodman's behavior undermined the cohesion or "teamness" of the team.

were Tutsi like Eugène. What mattered was not the ethnicity of individual members, but the combination of acts performed by the group as a whole. What mattered was that Joiners, whatever their ethnicity, engaged in the practices constitutive of the group's identity.

The nature of the Interahamwe identity also explains why Joiners acted one way in a group, but quite another outside the group. In groups, Joiners killed or went along with killing; alone Joiners made other choices. If this were not true, if Joiners saw themselves as Interahamwe even when they were outside the group, then we should see cases where individual Joiners killed Tutsi when they had the chance. At the very least, we should see opportunistic or entrepreneurial Joiners who, when finding themselves alone (outside the group), took the same initiative to kill Tutsi as they did when with their group. Yet, there are no examples in my two research sites of individual killers or killings during the genocide. Indeed, there are examples of just the opposite behavior—of individual Joiners saving or helping Tutsi when they were not with their group.

A case in point is Olivier. Olivier was the Joiner whom fellow killers accused of having a Tutsi wife and Tutsi brothers and of harboring the Tutsi grandchildren of a victim. By his own admission, Olivier took part in nearly every killing in Ngali. Yet, when I asked Olivier if it was possible to save anyone, he replied that it was impossible because if someone even mentioned saving someone, that person would be forced to kill that victim himself. Olivier then went on to give an example to illustrate his point. One day, he explains, he ran into a Tutsi boy fleeing. Rather than kill the boy, ignore him, or alert his group, Olivier directed the boy to take another path to avoid the killers. The boy took Olivier's advice and survived the genocide. I asked Olivier if he had some special tie to the boy. Olivier said he had no special connection to the boy; he only knew the boy from the neighborhood. He helped the boy, he said, because he could— because he was alone. Being alone meant he did not risk punishment or sanction by the group if he helped the boy and, just as important, the Interahamwe identity—and the pressures to perform that identity—no longer applied. Not being Interahamwe provided Olivier with options he would not otherwise have had. It enabled Olivier to drop the script for genocide and act as a neighbor instead.

There is additional evidence that the production of the Interahamwe identity also depended on the size of the group. A survivor from Ngali recounts that she ran into a group of two young killers while fleeing. One told her to sit on the ground so he could rape her; the other stopped the would-be rapist by taunting him: "You're going to rape this old woman? You don't have young girls?" The two men spared the woman and she was able to escape. She then ran into another small group of killers who had spotted her. They, too, let her go and she was able to escape being raped and killed once again. I asked this woman why the killers let her go each time, and she theorized that they did so because they knew another group would get her. But why would Interahamwe pass up the opportunity to rape and kill a Tutsi woman whom they encounter while she is trying to flee? One possibility is that very small groups provided a context that was qualitatively different than when there were ten, twenty, or thirty people present. In very small groups, the constitutive power of killing or raping in groups correspondingly diminished. Very small groups of two or three did not produce a very powerful Interahamwe identity; accordingly, people felt much less pressure to kill or rape.

Finally, that the Interahamwe identity adhered only to groups and not to individuals also explains why some Joiners did not gain privileged status for killing—why even a particularly active Joiner like Olivier could become a target himself. Far from reaping extra rewards or status for killing, Olivier had to defend himself against accusations that came from other Interahamwe in his own group. Olivier's vulnerability stands in stark contrast to the privileges that killers enjoyed during the Holocaust, for example. Even the Sonderkommando, those groups of Jewish inmates selected for crematorium duty, received special privileges during the short term of their duty; these privileges included decent living quarters and ample food, unheard of luxuries in the context of the camps (Nyiszli 1960). Browning's (1992, 61, 68–69, 100) ordinary men also received extra compensation in the form of whiskey intended to mollify the effects of their gruesome duty of shooting Jewish civilians in the back of the neck day in and day out. As these examples demonstrate, authorities in other genocides construed mass killing as a type of hardship duty that merited extra compensation or privileges. With Rwandan killers, however, privileges were not always forthcoming because once outside the group context, individuals were no longer Interahamwe. They reverted back to being ordinary residents of their communities, with ties to Tutsi friends, neighbors, and family members.

The proposition that people entered into the mass murder of their Tutsi neighbors and continued their murderous campaign out of collective hatreds or fears of Tutsi is not borne out by the evidence. Instead, the evidence shows that powerful group dynamics helped to pull certain Joiners into violence initially and led Joiners to continue their participation over time. For Joiners, groups became sites of sense making. Through interacting with their group and killing in groups, Joiners were able to create order out of disorder, certainty out of uncertainty, and power out of powerlessness. In groups, Joiners knew who to be and thus how to act. Killing in groups generated new identities and new forms of power. The constitutive power of killing in groups turned loose collections of friends and neighbors into tightly bound, social actors called Interahamwe.

Conclusion

> All forms of radical politics make their appearance at moments of
> rapid and decisive change, moments when customary status is in
> doubt and character (or "identity") is itself a problem. Before
> Puritans, Jacobins, or Bolsheviks attempt the creation of a new
> order, they must create new men.
>
> —MICHAEL WALZER, *The Revolution of the Saints*

When I began this project, I had little understanding of what anthropologists meant by the term *local* and the importance they placed on "local knowledge" in shaping both large- and small-scale processes. From my macrolevel vantage point, I had little grasp of how "the local" could figure into a project as all encompassing as genocide. I assumed instead that whenever leaders had the means, motive, and opportunity to pursue a strategy of genocide, they would proceed by turning flexible identities into rigid and polarized categories. This process of polarization would precede the violence and generate the necessary force to drive even ordinary people to commit mass violence.[1] It turns out I was wrong.

Genocide, I came to realize, implicates ethnic identity by definition, not theoretical axiom. By definition, genocide requires a target group, often but not always constructed in ethnic terms. This definitional requirement, however, does not necessarily make ethnicity a cause of genocide. It makes ethnicity an organizing principle. How and why people join in such violence is a question for empirical investigation. For while leaders and politicians can frame any conflict in ethnic terms, "the actual purpose of the violence may lie elsewhere" (Gagnon 2004, 11).

Revisiting the Ethnic Hatred Thesis

How is this possible? How is it possible that ethnicity does not drive violence in some fundamental way? Were not Hutu killing Tutsi to the last

1. For a statement of this thinking, see Fujii (2004).

person? Did people not describe what happened in their communities as "Hutu killing Tutsi?" Some have argued the answer lies in powerful ethnic hatreds that have simmered over time. When the opportunity arises, people will go after the hated group with violence.

The data from the two research sites, however, offer only faint support of these expectations. In Kimanzi and Ngali, there were certainly people who did not like one another. Several respondents recounted stories of ill treatment, jealousy, and resentment they suffered at the hands of another. Frédéric, for example, the resister from Ngali, told us how his wife had poisoned his sisters to reclaim the land he had given them. A Tutsi man told us how his own brother had him imprisoned as a génocidaire after the genocide; this act, he insisted, was motivated solely by his brother's long-standing resentment over their father's favorable treatment of the imprisoned brother. As these examples show, conflicts were very real and very serious, and could even lead to violent outcomes, but their bases were more personal than ethnic.

Perhaps, however, only a segment of the population shared this hatred, and it was these actors who participated in the genocide. People did indeed make references to specific people who hated Tutsi and evinced little surprise when these Tutsi-haters participated in the genocide. The data on Joiners, however, do not reveal a preponderance of these types of individuals. In fact, there is little evidence that Joiners hated Tutsi as a group before the genocide.

One might object that the reason there are no such data is because of political conditions that prohibited certain narratives and sanctioned others, cultural norms that kept people from talking openly to a stranger, and basic human nature, which inclined people to present themselves in the best possible light. The political conditions in Rwanda in 2004 do raise serious questions about whether people would have talked about group-level hatreds had they felt them. During the period of my fieldwork, the government had begun going after anyone who it believed was promoting a genocidal ideology, charging these people with "divisionisme." The government's pursuit of divisionistes may well have silenced any talk of Hutu-Tutsi divides that existed in the past or present.

Yet, despite these constraints, there are still several reasons to trust the data.

First, while political conditions were repressive at the time of my fieldwork, people did not always adhere to prescribed narratives or avoid proscribed subjects. People did bring up RPF abuses and war crimes, which was also (and no doubt continues to be) a very sensitive subject for the government.[2] In fact, several people who suffered violence at the hands of RPF soldiers or ex-FAR infiltrators (launching cross-border raids from the Congo after the RPF's victory) refused to acknowledge that any violence against Tutsi had even occurred, as if to wrest attention back to their own experiences of victimization. More tellingly, perhaps, people also made references to the divisions that currently existed between Hutu and Tutsi as a result of the war and genocide. These references were perhaps the clearest indication that the government's campaign to stamp out divisionisme did not completely silence people on this subject. This is not to say that people did not couch their views in the most general terms possible, particularly at initial interviews. It is to say that over time, the level of prevarication and dissimulation generally diminished, indicating that whatever walls of silence existed, they were not entirely impenetrable.

Second, people did not always give self-serving or self-aggrandizing statements. People did not paint their actions in heroic terms. And while many Joiners minimized their agency when recounting what they did during the genocide, more than one Joiner admitted to murders beyond those they specified in their formal letters of confession. People also made self-implicating statements. A man from Ngali, for example, admitted that he pillaged crops from his neighbor who had been in hiding at the time. Olivier, too, admitted pillaging. These were clear admissions of wrongdoing that both respondents did not have to make.

Third, people did not always take the opportunity to point the finger at others. In fact, people passed up such opportunities on numerous occasions. After Frédéric told us the story of how his wife had poisoned his sisters, I asked him whether she had participated in the genocide. Despite having no reason to protect her and every reason to point the finger at her, Frédéric said no. I asked another man from Kimanzi whether his friend who had accused him of participating in the genocide (which landed this man in prison for seven years) had participated in the genocide. This man, too, said no. I asked a Joiner from Kimanzi whether the gendarme he saw kill a truckload of people pillaged the victims' bodies. The Joiner said not only did the gendarme not pillage, he even threw back any money he found. As these examples indicate, people did not take any and all opportunities to implicate others.

Fourth, people did not refrain from saying negative things about others. Many people talked openly about jealousies, conflicts, or resentments

---

2. The RPF's strategy of targeting civilians for abuses, including atrocities and rape, mass killing, and mass displacement are chronicled in Des Forges (1999, 701–35), Ruzibiza (2005), Dallaire (2004), Umutesi (2000), and Gasana (2002).

they had with others, just as they made clear references to the divisions that existed between Hutu and Tutsi at the time of the field research.

These metadata convinced me that people were being honest and forthcoming in their interviews—within differing bounds. They suggested that people were not simply trying to minimize their own or others' involvement in the genocide or refrain from talking about officially banned topics. So while there are reasons to be skeptical of the data, there are just as many reasons to trust them.

What the data indicate is that preexisting hatreds tended to be personal and individual, not collectively aimed at an entire ethnic group. These personal hatreds were rooted in specific grievances, such as jealousy over parental favoritism toward another sibling, rivalries with family members over property, resentments over another's better fortune, or the coveting of another man's wife. Given these existing conflicts, Tutsi survivors still expressed shock and surprise when their neighbors, friends, or family members turned on them. Many people (Hutu and Tutsi) remarked that they did not see the change coming; for some, the transformation of their neighbors into Interahamwe seemed to have been instantaneous. Conversely, no Tutsi was surprised when a Hutu friend—even friends who had joined in the killings—helped to save them, indicating that their expectation up until the moment of violence was that their neighbors, friends, and family would protect, not hurt them, or at the very least, do them no harm.

A final area where the evidence does not support the ethnic hatred thesis is in the link people drew between past episodes of violence and the genocide. Some people did note similarities, pointing out that the conflicts underlying past violence and the genocide were the same—it was conflict between political parties, and by extension, between ethnic groups (since most political parties had both an ethnic and regional cast). Yet, at the same time, people noted that there was one big difference between past episodes of violence and the genocide. As people from both communities said time and again, there was violence in the past targeted at Tutsi, but past violence did not involve any killing. For residents of Ngali and Kimanzi, killing made the genocide qualitatively different from past episodes of violence they lived through or witnessed. This difference led to contrasting reconciliation processes. In the past, people were able to resume amicable relations under the stewardship of local authorities. In the aftermath of genocide, by contrast, both Tutsi and Hutu noted that relations between the two groups were not the same as before. What the data show most clearly, in other words, is that ethnic hatreds seemed to have been a consequence of the genocide, not a cause.

Revisiting the Ethnic Fear Thesis

Perhaps, however, elites were able to construct identities in such a way that highlighted and amplified people's fears, not their hatreds. Once people became fearful, they instinctively lined up with their own, knowing that aligning themselves with their own ethnic groups was the best way to ensure their security and survival against the Tutsi threat.

Here again microlevel evidence does not fully support this expectation. There was fear, which everyone in both communities, and indeed across the country, shared. The source of people's fears, however, varied across time and space. In the north, people's fears were tied to the war. Hutu were afraid of the RPF; these fears were not based solely on propaganda but on the conduct of the RPF that locals witnessed firsthand, such as the RPF's practice of raiding and pillaging supplies and forcing local residents to transport their looted goods. Alongside fears of the RPF, however, were also fears of certain local elites and authorities during the genocide, particularly those who had ties to the bourgmestre. Through such ties, local elites had the power to intimidate, harass, imprison, and kill Tutsi as well as Hutu. For this reason, local leaders sometimes posed a more immediate threat to residents than the RPF.

In Ngali, people were initially afraid of attackers from Bugesera and Burundi, not Tutsi. Such fears caused both Hutu and Tutsi to organize patrols to safeguard the community from attacks and at certain moments to flee their homes. Only when it became clear that it was Tutsi whom attackers were targeting did people's fears shift. Tutsi obviously feared Hutu killers, but at the same time, sought protection in Hutu homes or with Hutu friends and relatives. Thus Tutsi had to make calculations that differentiated between Hutu they could trust and Hutu they could not trust.

Among Hutu in Ngali, sources of fear varied as well. One fear was of the RPF/Tutsi threat, but until the assassination of the president, that threat remained distant, like the war itself. After the plane crash, the RPF threat became much more real and immediate to people in Ngali. An even more immediate threat, however, came from other Hutu—that is, Hutu leaders such as Jude who did not countenance resistance, defection, or refusal of his orders. For Joiners, then, the source of fear was local authorities with power, not local Tutsi with none.

In sum, there is much evidence that fear shaped Joiners' actions, but the data also show that the object of this fear was not exclusively, or even primarily, Tutsi as a group. Rather, the data show that the object of fear shifted to different groups at different moments. Whatever the object, it did not make Hutu, including Joiners, line up with their own. This was because some of "their own" were sometimes the most immediate source of danger and threat. Neither did fear make Hutu, including Joiners, view or treat Tutsi as a monolithic group, despite the rumors, pressures, and uncertainty. The fact that people did continue to make distinctions even during the violence makes the genocide a truly intimate affair. For it indicates that people were not just going after an abstract category of people, but actual neighbors they knew and some they knew well.

The Counterargument

If not ethnic hatreds or ethnic fears, then what drove so many ordinary people to participate in the genocide? I argue that a "social interaction" thesis better explains ordinary people's participation in mass violence than an ethnic hatred or ethnic fear model. According to a social interaction argument, Joiners did not kill because they hated or feared Tutsi as a group; rather, Joiners killed because of more immediate, and less abstract, reasons. The mechanisms that were critical to the process were local ties and group dynamics, which exerted powerful pressures on Joiners to join in the violence and powerful new identities for continuing.

In this alternative view, people did not kill over ethnicity, they killed with scripted ethnic claims. Scripted ethnic claims were accusations and statements people made about another person's ethnic identity. The most common was that the accused was Tutsi, looked Tutsi, or supported Tutsi. Any one of these claims made the accused a legitimate target for killing. Counterclaims could sometimes succeed at thwarting or overcoming the charge, allowing the accused to go unharmed or in a handful of cases, enabling Tutsi to join the Interahamwe as a way to save themselves. These cases seemed to have been rare, however. Most of the time, the targeted person was whatever those in power said she was. It was leaders' subjective interpretations of who was Tutsi and their determinations of when ethnicity mattered that shaped how the genocide was performed.

Joiners, too, made decisions about how faithful they would be to the script during a given performance. In coercive situations, they spoke their lines and followed the stage directions carefully. In less coercive or less public moments, they were able to deviate from the script or drop it completely. Even the most active Joiners, like Olivier, did not act the same "off-stage" as "on." When contexts changed, so, too, did Joiners' actions.

What mediated between the script for violence and people's performances were social ties and powerful group dynamics. Local ties helped to generate targets and recruits by spotlighting those in closest proximity— both geographic and social—to leaders or their henchmen. Leaders used family ties as avenues of recruitment, while collaborators used family ties to denounce family members. Group ties also generated targets and recruits. These ties formed through group interactions and activities. They helped to pull along reluctant Joiners by overriding individual doubts or hesitations. Group ties also turned some Joiners into targets, such as Olivier who, despite actively participating in the genocide, became a target of suspicions and accusations from fellow Interahamwe. Ties of friendship continued to matter but Joiners acted on these only in certain contexts. In the presence of authority figures or other killers, group ties prevailed, pushing Joiners to go along with the group in its genocidal activities. Outside the presence of authorities or groups, Joiners did not kill or commit violence on their own. Instead they made other choices, sometimes going as far as hiding or helping Tutsi.

The process by which Joiners first joined in the violence was shaped by group dynamics; these dynamics generated group ties, and group ties, in turn, strengthened these dynamics. Group actions and interactions pulled Joiners toward the group, trumping their prior ties to victims. Through groups, Joiners were able to make sense of highly volatile and uncertain situations by talking, planning, exchanging information, and finally, by acting as a collective unit. Each step taken created momentum for the next. When activities escalated to killing Tutsi, Joiners continued to go along because to do otherwise, would have required them to step outside the group, oppose the group's momentum, and most serious of all, manage the situation on their own.

Once Joiners joined in the violence, they continued their participation over time because of the constitutive power of killing in groups. In large group contexts, Joiners engaged in specific acts and practices of killing, which constituted the group as a social actor with its own identity, what I have called an Interahamwe identity. Once constituted, the Interahamwe actor engaged in those practices consistent with its identity, thereby reproducing the violence over time. Put simply, killing produced groups and groups produced killings.

Situating the Findings in the Literature

Placed in the context of other work on the Rwandan genocide, the findings of this study appear robust and not confined to the two small secteurs that served as my research sites. Most notably, the findings are consistent with Straus's study of the genocide, which used very different methods and approaches. Much of the agreement concerns negative findings. Consistent with the present study, Straus finds, for example, little evidence that perpetrators were driven by anti-Tutsi ideology, extremist propaganda, preexisting or accumulating hatreds of Tutsi, or obedience, an alleged cultural trait of Rwandans.[3]

Where this study complements Straus as well as work on other genocides is by magnifying the lens and focusing it on a smaller field of observation. While Straus looks at the social and political dynamics within communes, this study examines the dynamics at the secteur level, a much smaller administrative unit and a closer approximation to the geographic and social spaces that rural people occupied in their daily lives. By training the lens at people's interactions before and during the genocide, this study adds a level of complexity to Straus's argument in two ways. First, it allows for a more multilayered treatment of ethnicity. While Straus argues that a "collective ethnic categorization" became activated at crisis moments, this study cautions against assumptions that state-sponsored forms of ethnicity automatically overtake or deactivate all other forms of identity. As Straus and I both found, despite the best efforts of determined elites, state-sponsored ethnicity took hold unevenly throughout the country. This finding alone points to other, more immediate factors that led ordinary people to join in the genocide.

Second, the more granular approach this book takes helps to reveal the mechanisms that pushed and pulled some to join in the violence while others did not. The mechanisms that I have identified—social ties and group dynamics—illuminate this process of joining and point to the forms of agency that Joiners exhibited.

The finding that social ties and group dynamics played a key role in leading ordinary people to join in the violence is also consistent with one of the most seminal works on the Holocaust, that of Christopher Browning. To explain how the most ordinary of men became mass killers, Browning points not to ideology, anti-Semitism, or obedience to authority, but to the obligation the men felt toward their fellow soldiers—their unwillingness to leave the "dirty work" to others. Powerful disincentives also discouraged men from breaking ranks. Even though the majority of men found killing duty to be gruesome and abhorrent, they also felt pressure to go along with their group, no matter how violent the assigned task, just like Joiners in Kimanzi and Ngali. As Browning (1992, 184) writes: "To break ranks and step out, to adopt overtly noncomformist behavior, was simply beyond most of the men."

The insight that group contexts can lead people to do things they would not otherwise do underscores the importance of endogenous factors in

---

3. The most noteworthy proponent of the obedience thesis is Gérard Prunier (1995).

pushing and pulling ordinary people to kill. Focusing on endogenously generated dynamics does not rob actors of agency; rather, it points to how people help to reproduce the very contexts they initially confront. People do so not through blind obedience or deference to authority, but through actions taken, such as going along, and actions not taken, such as refusing to go along. Engaging in violent acts is a constitutive process that not only generates new identities but also transforms old ones.

Next Steps

Where do we go from here? Is it possible to map out an alternative theory of mass violence to those that currently dominate the study of political violence? Such a theory should start with the assumption that ethnicity (or any type of identity) is not an objective thing out there, easily observed and analyzed from outside, but a shared and complex set of understandings that become reconstructed and deconstructed through processes of violence. From this starting point, we would expect violence to refashion identities, not only the identities of victims or targets, but just as important, the identities of those who commit the violence.

We would also expect the identities that are formed through violence to be critical to the reproduction or maintenance of violence over time. A constructivist theory, in short, would expect violence and identity to be co-constituted, rather than existing separately, one prior to the other. Rather than drawing a straight line from ethnicity as a precondition to violence as outcome, we would draw a double arrow that would show how performing violence reconstitutes the identities of the performers. Reconstituting the identities of the performers is perhaps key to campaigns of mass violence that stretch across time and space and require committed participants. We should therefore start to look at violence as a creative, not just destructive, process—one that is capable of making "new men," not just destroying old enemies.

Generating a constructivist theory will require more local-level analyses that can trace the processes of violence that unfold in other parts of the world or during other time periods. It will also require focused comparisons at this level. Focused comparisons will enable scholars to identify how local processes of violence differ across settings, and whether differences in time and place generate alternative pathways to mass violence.

All such studies will take time and extensive fieldwork, archival research, and close reading of the existing literatures. The obstacles are numerous, but the potential rewards are equally so. These rewards are not limited to scholarly contributions but include insights that can help policymakers find more effective ways of stopping or preventing genocide and mass killing. All knowledge is partial but some views are less partial than others. If we know mass killers are made, not born, and that large-scale processes of violence hew to local, not just national, dynamics, then we can begin to look for more effective approaches that can disrupt local processes, and by doing so, help to avert bloody outcomes. If this book contributes in any way to this effort, it will have done its job.

Dramatis personae

Kimanzi (northern préfecture of Ruhengeri)

RESIDENTS

CALLIXTE (b. 1948), survived the massacres of Tutsi that took place in January 1991 with the help of friends who had joined in the killings; as a boy understood that "being Tutsi" meant the father of the household was Tutsi

GUSTAVE (b. 1962), refused to join in any "politics"; best friend was a Tutsi who was a member of the FAR

JEAN-PIERRE (b. 1965), learned in school how Tutsi had mistreated Hutu

JOINERS

CHARLES (b. 1970), explained difference between skin color and ubwoko (ethnicity); participated in the killing of a Tutsi neighbor in January 1991

ÉDOUARD (b. 1963), joined in the violence to protect his community; participated in the killing of a Tutsi neighbor in January 1991

HUSSEIN (b. 1967), imprisoned as an icyitso because he had lived in Uganda for nine years and was therefore (supposedly) familiar with RPF plans; participated in the killing of four people under the direction of a local responsable

STEFAN (b. 1964), provided three-part typology of how people came to participate in the genocide; participated in the killing of a Tutsi neighbor in January 1991 (along with Charles, Édouard, and others)

Ngali (center-south préfecture of Gitarama)

RESIDENTS

BERNARD (b. 1930), denounced by son for hiding two Tutsi children; family became Hutu when it lost its cows

ÉMILIE (b. 1972), mother and brother denounced by her husband's brother; saved herself by paying off the killers

FRÉDÉRIC (b. 1957), refused to share stolen meat or join Jude's political party; wife had poisoned his sisters to reclaim land he had given them

JUDE (died in 1997), led and organized the genocide; married to Thérèse; uncle of Paul

MAURICE (b. 1935), accused of being Tutsi during genocide; saved by Paul who told killers that he was an umukiga (person from the north) and possibly related to the president

NICOLAS (b. 1940), neighbor and best friend of Maurice; explained that greed causes war and war causes hatred

SOPHIE (b. 1925), rescued many Tutsi during the genocide; family became Hutu when it lost its cows

THÉRÈSE (b. 1950), wife of Jude; father and grandparents were Tutsi who changed their identity cards in 1959 to read Hutu

JOINERS

EUGÈNE (b. 1969), Tutsi who joined the Interahamwe to "save" himself; friend of Paul and Félix

FÉLIX (b. 1952), friend of Paul and Eugène who was forced to go to the roadblock but slipped away after witnessing murder of a local Tutsi boy

MICHEL (b. 1964), saved Tutsi neighbors but detained a stranger at his house who was later killed at the nearby roadblock

OLIVIER (b. 1956), participated in nearly every killing in Ngali; accused by fellow Interahamwe of having a Tutsi wife, Tutsi brothers, and hiding Tutsi grandchildren of one victim; helped Tutsi boy escape the killers

OTHER PRISONERS

PAUL (b. 1957), former conseiller deposed by his uncle, Jude, after plane crash that killed the president; issued stamped documents to Tutsi that said the document holder was a Hutu who had lost his or her identity card

Glossary of Kinyarwanda Terms

abakonde	powerful landowners
abiru	official (court) interpreters of rituals and customs
akazu	little house (nickname for powerful inner circle centered around Mme Habyarimana)
amarondo	night patrols
gacaca	community-based conflict resolution mechanism
icyitso (*ibyitso*, pl.)	accomplice
ibiteekerezo	historical tales
igisekuruza	lineage
igitero	attack group
inyenzi	cockroach (derogatory term for the RPF)
inzobe	fair or light-colored complexion
umuganda	communal work duty
Imana	God
Impuzamugambi	those with a single goal (youth militia of the CDR)
Inkotanyi	those who fight valiantly (self-chosen sobriquet of the RPF)
intambara	war
Interahamwe	those who work together (used to refer to youth militia of the MRND and to local killing groups)
kubohoze	to free or liberate (practice of forcible recruitment into a political party)
kunywana	to make a blood pact
mwami	king
nyumbakumi	head of ten households

ubwoko (*amoko*, pl.)	ethnicity (formerly, clan)
ubuhake	form of voluntary vassalage
ubureetwa	form of involuntary vassalage
uburyarya	hypocrisy, shrewdness, cunning
umuhutu (*abahutu*, pl.)	Hutu
umututsi (*abatutsi*, pl.)	Tutsi
umukiga	person from Kiga
umunyarwanda	Rwandan
umutwa (*abatwa*, pl.)	Twa
umuzungu (*abazungu*, pl.)	foreigner (usually, but not always, Western foreigner)

References

Abdelal, Rawi, Yoshiko M. Herrera, Alastair Iain Johnston, and Terry Martin. 2001. "Treating identity as a variable: Measuring the content, intensity, and contestation of identity." Paper read at the Annual Conference of the American Political Science Association, 30 August–2 September, at San Francisco, CA.

African Rights. 1995. *Death, despair, and defiance*. London: African Rights.

———. nd. "Resisting genocide: Bisesero," April–June 1994.

Alvarez, Alex. 2001. *Governments, citizens, and genocide: A comparative and interdisciplinary approach*. Bloomington: Indiana University Press.

André, Catherine, and Jean-Philippe Platteau. 1998. "Land relations under unbearable stress: Rwanda caught in the Malthusian trap." *Journal of Economic Behaviour and Organization* 34: 1–47.

Article 19. 1996. *Broadcasting genocide*. London: Article 19.

Barnett, Michael N. 2002. *Eyewitness to a genocide*. Ithaca: Cornell University Press.

Bax, Mart. 1995. *Medjugorje: Religion, politics, and violence in rural Bosnia*. Amsterdam: VU Uitgeverij.

Bertrand, Jordane. 2000. *Rwanda: Le piège de l'histoire*. Paris: Karthala.

Boissevain, Jeremy. 1974. *Friends of friends: Networks, manipulators, and coalitions*. New York: St. Martin's Press.

Braeckman, Colette. 1994. *L'histoire d'un génocide*. Paris: Fayard.

Brass, Paul R. 1997. *Theft of an idol: Text and context in the representation of collective violence*. Princeton: Princeton University Press.

Bringa, Tone. 1995. *Being Muslim the Bosnian way: Identity and community in a central Bosnian village*. Princeton: Princeton University Press.

Browning, Christopher R. 1992. *Ordinary men: Reserve Police Battalion 101 and the final solution in Poland*. New York: HarperCollins.

Brubaker, Rogers, and David D. Laitin. 1998. "Ethnic and nationalist violence." *Annual Review of Sociology* 24: 423–52.

Brundage, W. Fitzhugh. 1993. *Lynching in the New South: Georgia and Virginia, 1880–1930*. Urbana: University of Illinois Press.

Central Intelligence Agency. 1994. *The World Factbook: Rwanda*. Washington, DC: CIA.

Chalk, Frank. 1999. "Hate radio in Rwanda." In *The path of a genocide: The Rwandan crisis from Uganda to Zaire*, edited by Howard Adelman and Astri Suhrke. New Brunswick: Transaction.

Chandler, David. 1999. *Voices from S-21: Terror and history in Pol Pot's secret prison*. Berkeley: University of California Press.

Chrétien, Jean-Pierre. 1997. *Le défi de l'ethnisme*. Paris: Karthala.

Chrétien, Jean Pierre, Jean-François Dupaquier, Marcel Kabanda, and Joseph Ngarambe. 1995. *Rwanda: Les médias du génocide*. Paris: Karthala.

Codere, Helen. 1962. "Power in Ruanda." *Anthropologica* 4 (1):45–85.

Coleman, James S. 1988. "Social capital in the creation of human capital." *American Journal of Sociology* 94 (Supplement): S95–S120.

Colletta, Nat J., and Michelle L. Cullen. 2000. "The nexus between violent conflict, social capital, and social cohesion: Case studies from Cambodia and Rwanda." In *Social capital initiative*. Washington DC: The World Bank.

Dallaire, Roméo. 2004. *Shake hands with the devil*. New York: Carroll and Graf.

Dean, Martin. 2004. "Microcosm: Collaboration and resistance during the Holocaust in the Mir Rayon of Belarus, 1941–1944." In *Collaboration and resistance during the Holocaust*, edited by Pau A. Levine, David Gaunt, and Laura Palosuo. Bern: Peter Lang.

de Figueiredo, Jr., Rui J.P., and Barry R. Weingast. 1999. "The rationality of fear: Political opportunism and ethnic conflict." In *Civil wars, insecurity, and intervention*, edited by Barbara F. Walter and Jack Snyder. New York: Columbia University Press.

de Lame, Danielle. 1996. *Une colline entre mille ou le calme avant la tempête: Transformations et blocages du Rwanda rural*. Tervuren: Musée royal de l'Afrique centrale.

Des Forges, Alison. 1969. "Kings without crowns: The White Fathers in Ruanda." In *Eastern African history*, edited by Daniel F. McCall, Norman R. Bennett, and Jeffrey Butler. New York: Praeger.

——. 1972. "Defeat is the only bad news: Rwanda under Musinga (1896–1931)." Ph.D. diss., Yale University.

——. 1986. "The drum is greater than the shout: The 1912 rebellion in northern Rwanda." In *Banditry, Rebellion and Social Protest in Africa*, edited by Donald Crummey. London: James Currey.

——. 1995. "The ideology of genocide." *Issue: A Journal of Opinion* 23 (2): 44–47.

——. 1999. *Leave none to tell the story*. New York: Human Rights Watch and Fédération internationale des ligues des droits de l'homme.

D'Hertefelt, Marcel. 1964. "Mythes et idéologies dans le Rwanda ancien et contemporain." In *The historian in tropical Africa*, edited by J. Vansina, R. Mauny, and L. V. Thomas. London: Oxford University Press.

Ellis, Stephen. 1995. "Liberia 1989–1994: A study of ethnic and spiritual violence." *African Affairs* 94 (375): 165–97.

Fearon, James D., and David D. Laitin. 2000. "Violence and the social construction of ethnic identity." *International Organization* 54 (4): 845–77.

Fédération Internationale des Droits de l'Homme. 1993. *Rapport de la commission internationale d'enquête sur les violations des droits de l'homme au Rwanda depuis le 1er octobre 1990*. Paris: FIDH, Africa Watch, Union Interafricaine des droits de l'homme et des peuples (UIDH), Centre international des droits de la personne et du développement démocratique (CIDPDD/ICHRDD).

Fein, Helen. 1979. *Accounting for genocide: National responses and Jewish victimization during the Holocaust*. New York: Free Press.

——. 1993. *Genocide: A sociological perspective*. London: Sage Publications.

Feldman, Allen. 1991. *Formations of violence.* Chicago: University of Chicago Press.

Freedman, James M. 1975. "Principles of relationship in Rwandan Kiga society." Ph.D. diss., Princeton University.

Fujii, Lee Ann. 2004. "Transforming the moral landscape: The diffusion of a genocidal norm in Rwanda." *Journal of Genocide Research* 6 (1): 99–114.

——. Forthcoming. "Shades of truth and lies: Evaluating testimonies of war and genocide." *Journal of Peace Research.*

Gagnon, Jr., V. P. 2004. *The myth of ethnic war: Serbia and Croatia in the 1990s.* Ithaca: Cornell University Press.

Gasana, James K. 1995. "La guerre, la paix et la démocratie au Rwanda." In *Les crises politiques au Burundi et au Rwanda (1993–1994),* edited by André Guichaoua. Paris: Karthala.

——. 2002. *Rwanda: Du parti-état à l'état-garnison.* Paris: L'Harmattan.

Gioia, Dennis A., and Peter P. Poole. 1984. "Scripts in organizational behavior." *The Academy of Management Review* 9 (3): 449–59.

Goffman, Erving. 1959. *The presentation of self in everyday life.* Garden City, NY: Doubleday Anchor Books.

Goldhagen, Daniel Joshua. 1996. *Hitler's willing executioners: Ordinary Germans and the Holocaust.* New York: Knopf.

Granovetter, Mark. 1985. "Economic action and social structure: The problem of embeddedness." *American Journal of Sociology* 91 (3): 481–510.

Gravel, Pierre Bettez. 1968. *Remera: A community in eastern Ruanda.* The Hague: Mouton.

Guichaoua, André. 2005. *Rwanda 1994: Les politiques du génocide à Butare.* Paris: Karthala.

Hardin, Russell. 1995. *One for all.* Princeton: Princeton University Press.

Hatzfeld, Jean. 2000. *Dans le nu de la vie: Récits des marais rwandais.* Paris: Seuil.

——. 2003. *Une saison des machettes.* Paris: Seuil.

Hedström, Peter, and Richard Swedberg. 1998. "Social Mechanisms: An introductory essay." In *Social mechanisms: An analytical approach to social theory,* edited by Peter Hedström and Richard Swedberg. Cambridge: Cambridge University Press.

Hinton, Alexander Laban, ed. 2002. *Annihilating difference.* Berkeley: University of California Press.

——. 2005. *Why did they kill?* Berkeley: University of California Press.

Hogg, Nicole. 2001. " 'I never poured blood': Women accused of genocide in Rwanda." LLM thesis, Law, McGill University.

Horowitz, Donald L. 2001. *The deadly ethnic riot.* Berkeley: University of California Press.

Jefremovas, Villia. 2002. *Brickyards to graveyards: From production to genocide in Rwanda.* Albany: State University of New York Press.

Jones, Bruce. 1999. "Civil war, the peace process, and genocide in Rwanda." In *Civil wars in Africa,* edited by Taisier M. Ali and Robert O. Matthews. Montreal: McGill-Queen's University Press.

——. 2001. *Peacemaking in Rwanda: The dynamics of failure.* Boulder: Lynne Rienner.

Kagame, Alexis. 1952. *Le code des institutions politiques du Rwanda précolonial.* Bruxelles: Institut royal colonial belge.

Kalyvas, Stathis N. 2003. "The ontology of 'political violence': Action and identity in civil wars." *Perspectives on Politics* 1 (3): 475–94.

——. 2006. *The logic of violence in civil war.* Cambridge: Cambridge University Press.

Kapferer, Bruce. 1988. *Legends of people, myths of state: Violence, intolerance, and political culture in Sri Lanka and Australia.* Washington DC: Smithsonian Institution Press.

Kaplan, Robert D. 1994. "The coming anarchy." *Atlantic Monthly*, February, 44–73.

Kaufman, Stuart J. 2001. *Modern hatreds: The symbolic politics of ethnic war.* Ithaca: Cornell University Press.

Kaufmann, Chaim. 1996. "Possible and impossible solutions to ethnic civil wars." *International Security* 20 (4): 136–75.

Kershaw, Ian. 1987. "The persecution of Jews and German popular opinion in the Third Reich." In *The persisting question*, edited by Helen Fein. Berlin: Walter de Gruyter.

King, Charles. 2004. "The micropolitics of social violence." *World Politics* 56 (April): 431–55.

Landesman, Peter. 2002. "A woman's work." *New York Times Magazine*, 15 September, 82–134.

Lemarchand, René. 1970. *Rwanda and Burundi.* New York: Praeger.

———. 1997. "The Burundi genocide." In *Century of genocide: Eyewitness accounts and critical views*, edited by Samuel Totten, William S. Parsons, and Israel W. Charny. New York: Garland.

———. 1998. "Which genocide? Whose genocide?" *African Studies Review* 41 (1): 3–16.

———. 2000. "Reflections on the Rwanda genocide: A backward glance into the past." Paper read at 43rd Annual Meeting of the African Studies Association, 16–19 November, at Nashville, TN.

Linden, Ian. 1977. *Church and revolution in Rwanda.* Manchester: Manchester University Press.

Lubkemann, Stephen C. 2005. "Migratory coping in wartime Mozambique: An anthropology of violence and displacement in 'fragmented wars.' " *Journal of Peace Research* 42 (4): 493–508.

Malkki, Liisa. 1995. *Purity and exile.* Chicago: University of Chicago Press.

Mamdani, Mahmood. 2001. *When victims turn killers.* Princeton: Princeton University Press.

Mann, Michael. 2005. *The dark side of democracy: Explaining ethnic cleansing.* Cambridge: Cambridge University Press.

McGovern, James R. 1982. *Anatomy of a lynching: The killing of Claude Neal.* Baton Rouge: Louisiana State University Press.

Migdal, Joel S. 1988. *Strong societies and weak states.* Princeton: Princeton University Press.

Mironko, Charles K. 2004. "Social and political mechanisms of mass murder: An analysis of perpetrators in the Rwandan genocide." Ph.D. diss., Yale University.

Monroe, Kristen Renwick. 1991. "John Donne's people: Explaining differences between rational actors and altruists through cognitive frameworks." *Journal of Politics* 53 (2): 394–433.

———. 1996. *The heart of altruism.* Princeton: Princeton University Press.

———. 2001. "Morality and a sense of self: The importance of identity and categorization for moral action." *American Journal of Political Science* 45 (3): 491–507.

———. 2004. *The hand of compassion.* Princeton: Princeton University Press.

Mueller, John. 2000. "The banality of 'ethnic war.' " *International Security* 25 (1): 42–70.

Nagengast, Carole. 2002. Inoculation of evil in the U.S.–Mexican Border Region: reflections on the genocidal potential of symbolic violence. In *Annihilating difference*, edited by Alexander Laban Hinton. Berkeley: University of California Press.

Newbury, Catharine. 1980. "Ubureetwa and Thangata: Catalysts to peasant political consciousness in Rwanda and Malawi." *Canadian Journal of African Studies* 14 (1): 97–111.

———. 1988. *The cohesion of oppression: Clientship and ethnicity in Rwanda, 1860–1960.* New York: Columbia University Press.

Newbury, David, and Catharine Newbury. 2000. "Bringing the peasants back in: Agrarian themes in the construction and corrosion of statist historiography in Rwanda." *American Historical Review* 105 (3): 832–77.

Newbury, Catharine, and David Newbury. 1999. "A Catholic mass in Kigali: Contested views of the genocide and ethnicity in Rwanda." *Canadian Journal of African Studies* 33 (2/3): 292–328.

Newbury, David. 1980. "The clans of Rwanda: An historical hypothesis." *Africa* 50 (4): 389–403.

———. 1981. "What role has kingship?" *Africa-Tervuren* 27 (4): 89–101.

———. 1995. "The invention of Rwanda: The alchemy of ethnicity." Paper read at 38th Annual Meeting of the African Studies Association, 3–6 November, at Orlando, FL.

———. 2001. "Precolonial Burundi and Rwanda: Local loyalties, regional royalties." *International Journal of African Historical Studies* 34 (2): 255–314.

Newbury, David S. 1999. "Ecology and the politics of genocide: Rwanda 1994." *Cultural Survival Quarterly* 22 (4): 32–35.

Nsengiyaremye, Dismas. 1995. "La transition démocratique au Rwanda (1989–1993)." In *Les crises politiques au Burundi et au Rwanda (1993–1994)*, edited by André Guichaoua. Paris: Karthala.

Nyiszli, Miklos. 1960. *Auschwitz: A doctor's eyewitness account.* Translated by Tibere Kremer and Richard Seaver. Greenwich, CT: Fawcett.

Peabody, Norbert. 2000. "Collective violence in our time." *American Ethnologist* 27 (1): 169–78.

Peritore, N. Patrick. 1990. "Reflections on dangerous fieldwork." *American Sociologist* (Winter): 359–72.

Petersen, Roger D. 2002. *Understanding ethnic violence.* Cambridge: Cambridge University Press.

Physicians for Human Rights (UK). nd. *Rwanda 1994: A report of the genocide.*

Portelli, Alessandro. 1991. *The death of Luigi Trastulli and other stories.* Albany: State University of New York Press.

Portes, Alejandro. 1998. "Social capital: Its origins and applications in modern sociology." *Annual Review of Sociology* 24: 1–24.

Posen, Barry R. 1993. "The security dilemma and ethnic conflict." *Survival* 35 (1): 27–47.

Prunier, Gérard. 1995. *The Rwanda crisis: History of a genocide.* New York: Columbia University Press.

Putnam, Robert D. 1993. *Making democracy work.* Princeton: Princeton University Press.

Rennie, J. K. 1972. "The precolonial kingdom of Rwanda: A reinterpretation." *Transafrican Journal of History* 2 (2): 11–53.

République rwandaise. 1991. *Recensement général de la population et de l'habitat au 15 août 1991, Résultats provisoires.* Kigali: Service National de Recensement.

République rwandaise. 1994. *Recensement général de la population et de l'habitat au 15 août 1991,* Résultats définitifs. Kigali: Service National de Recensement.

Reyntjens, Filip. 1985. *Pouvoir et droit au Rwanda.* Tervuren: Musée Royale de l'Afrique Centrale.

———. 1994. *L'Afrique des Grands Lacs en crise.* Paris: Karthala.

———. 1995a. "Akazu, 'escadrons de la mort' et autres 'réseau zéro': Un historique des résistances au changement politique depuis 1990." In *Les crises politiques au Burundi et au Rwanda (1993–1994)*, edited by André Guichaoua. Paris: Karthala.

———. 1995b. *Rwanda: Trois jours qui ont fait basculer l'histoire.* Vol. 16, *Cahiers Africains.* Paris: L'Harmattan.

Richards, Paul. 1996. *Fighting for the rain forest.* Oxford: James Currey.

———. 2005. "New War: An ethnographic approach." In *No peace, no war,* edited by Paul Richards. Athens: Ohio University Press.

Riches, David. 1986. "The phenomenon of violence." In *The anthropology of violence,* edited by David Riches. London: Basil Blackwell.

Ruzibiza, Abdul Joshua. 2005. *Rwanda: L'histoire secrète.* Paris: Éditions du Panama.

Sanders, Edith R. 1969. "The Hamitic hypothesis: Its origin and functions in time perspective." *Journal of African History* 10 (4): 521–32.

Saucier, Jean-François. 1974. "The patron-client relationship in traditional and contemporary southern Rwanda." Ph.D. diss., Columbia University.

Scott, James C. 1998. *Seeing like a state.* New Haven: Yale University Press.

Sémelin, Jacques. 2005. *Purifier et détruire.* Paris: Seuil.

Sluka, Jeffrey A. 1990. "Participant observation in violent social contexts." *Human Organization* 49 (2): 114–26.

Straus, Scott. 2001. "Contested meanings and conflicting imperatives: A conceptual analysis of genocide. *Journal of Genocide Research* 3 (3): 349–75.

———. 2004a. "How many perpetrators were there in the Rwandan genocide? An estimate." *Journal of Genocide Research* 6 (1): 85–98.

———. 2004b. "The order of genocide: Race, power, and war in Rwanda." Ph.D. diss., University of California, Berkeley.

———. 2006. *The order of genocide: Race, power, and war in Rwanda.* Ithaca: Cornell University Press.

Taylor, Christopher C. 2002. "The cultural face of terror in the Rwandan genocide of 1994." In *Annihilating difference,* edited by Alexander Laban Hinton. Berkeley: University of California Press.

Terry, Fiona. 2002. *Condemned to repeat? The paradox of humanitarian action.* Ithaca: Cornell University Press.

Tertsakian, Carina. 2008. *Le Château.* London: Arves Books.

Tilly, Charles. 1985. "War making and state making as organized crime." In *Bringing the state back in,* edited by Peter B. Evans, Dietrich Rueschemeyer, and Theda Skocpol. Cambridge: Cambridge University Press.

———. 2003. *The politics of collective violence.* Cambridge: Cambridge University Press.

Tolnay, Stewart E., and E. M. Beck. 1995. *A festival of violence: An analysis of southern lynchings, 1882–1930.* Urbana: University of Illinois Press.

Turyahikayo-Rugyema, Benoni. 1974. "The history of the Bakiga in southwestern Uganda and northern Rwanda, ca. 1500–1930." Ph.D. diss., University of Michigan, Ann Arbor.

Umutesi, Marie Béatrice. 2000. *Fuir ou mourir au Zaïre: Le vécu d'une réfugiée rwandaise.* Paris: L'Harmattan.

United Nations Department of Economic and Social Affairs / Population Division. nd. PRED bank 4.0 country profiles: Rwanda.

UNHCR. 2004. "Statistical yearbook 2002: Trends in displacement, protection and solutions." United Nations High Commissioner for Refugees.

Uvin, Peter. 1998. *Aiding violence.* West Hartford, CT: Kumarian Press.

Vansina, Jan. 1962. *L'évolution du royaume rwanda des origines à 1900.* Bruxelles: Academie Royale des Sciences d'Outre-Mer.

———. 2004. *Antecedents to modern Rwanda.* Translated by the author. Madison: University of Wisconsin Press.

Varshney, Ashutosh. 1997. "Postmodernism, civic engagement, and ethnic conflict: A passage to India." *Comparative Politics* 30 (1): 1–20.

Verwimp, Philip. 2005. "An economic profile of peasant perpetrators of genocide: Micro-level evidence from Rwanda." *Journal of Development Economics* 77 (2): 297–323.

Wagner, Michelle D. 1998. "All the bourgmestre's men." *Africa Today* 45: 25–36.

Waldorf, Lars. 2006. "Mass justice for mass atrocity: Rethinking local justice as transitional justice." *Temple Law Review* 79 (1): 1–87.

———. 2007. "Ordinariness and orders: Explaining popular participation in the Rwandan genocide." *Genocide Studies and Prevention* 2 (3): 267–69.

Walzer, Michael. 1965. *The revolution of the saints.* Cambridge: Harvard University Press.

———. 1977. *Just and unjust wars.* New York: Basic Books.

Warren, Kay B. 1998. *Indigenous movements and their critics: Pan-Maya activism in Guatemala.* Princeton: Princeton University Press.

Wood, Elisabeth Jean. 2003. *Insurgent collective action and civil war in El Salvador.* Cambridge: Cambridge University Press.

Index

Note: Italicized page numbers indicate tables and figures.

Abasinga: use of term, 116
Afro-Franco summit, 47n3
age: of Joiners, 130; of learning about ethnicity, 106–7; of respondents, 31, 115n8
agency: in face of coercion, 165–66; of group vs. individual, 157–58; minimized in interviews, 142, 182; "neighbor" level of, 18; situational explanations vs., 156
altruism study, 30
André, Catherine, 47n2
APROSOMA (Association pour la promotion sociale de la masse), 65–66, 70
Arusha Accords (1993), 52–53
assassinations: Habyarimana, 2, 15, 27, 53–55, 75, 80, 84, 89, 90, 132, 156; Ndadaye, 53, 74, 83–84, 88, 122; Rwabugiri's family, 62

Bahutu Manifesto, 65
Bakiga people, 59–60, 61
Balkan wars, 6, 35n6, 171
Beardsley, Brent, 54n9, 174n14
Belgium: coup of Gitarama facilitated by, 69–70; ethnic hierarchy imposed by, 118; Hutu supported by, 67, 68–69; identity card system of, 71, 109–11; Tutsi supported by, 62–65, 108
Bernard (pseud.), 107–8, 116–17
Bertrand, Jordane, 46n1
Biseruka, Stanislas, 73
Bisesero: resistance at, 87n6

blood pacts, 91–92, 131
Braeckman, Colette, 50n6
Bringa, Tone, 35n6
Browning, Christopher R., 178, 187–88
Brubaker, Rogers, 10
Brundage, William, 171n6
Bugesera: aid worker murdered in, 51; assumption about people from, 150, 151; attackers from, 86, 184
Burundi: Belgian rule of, 63, 65; fear of attackers from, 184; Ndadaye's assassination in, 53, 74, 83–84, 88, 122; Tutsi-controlled army of, 71
Butare: political protests in, 51; timing of genocide in, 56
Bwanakweri, Prosper, 67
bystanders: use of term, 8

Callixte (pseud.), 107
Cambodian genocide, 7, 171
Catholic Church, 62–65, 66, 71
CDR (Coalition pour la défense de la république), 52, 54n10
center-south region: assassination as trigger for genocide in, 89; north's rivalry with, 10, 26–27, 48, 56, 70, 72–73. *See also* Gitarama (town); MDR (Mouvement démocratique républicain); Ngali (pseud. for center-south site)
center to periphery generalizations, 9–10, 76

Charles (pseud.): on characteristics and
ethnicity, 112–13; group size and, 171; on
killings, 123–24, 172; on reason for
participation, 156–57
Chrétien, Jean-Pierre, 54, 122n12
Christianity, 62–65. *See also* Catholic
Church
clans as interethnic, 105–6
Classe, Léon, 61
CNS (Commission nationale de synthèse),
47, 48
Codere, Helen, 67
collaborators. *See* Joiners; perpetrators and
collaborators
colonial period: Belgian support for Hutu
in, 67, 68–69; Belgian-Tutsi rule (dual
colonialism) in, 62–65, 108; divisions in,
45–46; ethnicity constructed in, 63–64, 74,
103n1, 108–9, 118; identity card system of,
71, 109–11; prisons left from, 24–26; Tutsi
official histories supported in, 57–60
Commission Nationale de Synthèse (CNS),
47, 48
community ties. *See* friendship ties; local
ties; neighbors and neighborhood ties
confessions: interviews compared with,
146–47, 182; on killing process, 172–73;
motivations in, 142; strategic approach
to, 148
conflicts: among individuals, 181, 182–83;
as ethnic vs. political, 10; reframing of,
10, 45, 121–22; violence distinguished
from, 20
Congo: contamination via living in, 99;
refugees in, 132n5, 133
constructivist theory, 188–89
cows: eating of, 168; hidden from attackers,
92; loss of, 117–18, 124; pillaging of, 80,
87, 134, 160–61, 162; shared and
exchanged, 94, 97, 101, 131; Tutsi linked
to, 112, 114, 115, 116–17, 123; as wealth,
61

daily life: changing meanings of ethnicity in,
115–18; components of, 1, 98; individual's
multiple roles in, 16; interpreting narratives of, 41–44; learning about clans and
ethnicity in, 105–11; mobilization and
control of, 72–73; questions about, 41;
script distinguished from, 123; stereo∂t-
types contextualized in, 111–14; war's
effects on, 78–79. *See also* life history
narratives

Dallaire, Roméo, 53, 54–55
de Figueiredo, Rui J.P., 5
de Lame, Danielle, 86, 130n2
democratization: Belgians forced into, 65;
calls for, 74–75; international aid tied to,
46–47; massacres framed in context of,
51. *See also* political parties
denouncers: family members targeted by,
128–29, 136; role in script for violence,
175n15; in spectrum of responses, *30*
Des Forges, Alison, 50n6, 60, 147n10,
171n7, 173n13
divisionisme (genocidal ideology), 39,
181–82

economy: currency in, 168; decline of,
46–53
Édouard (pseud.): on ethnicity, 106–7;
group size and, 171; neighbor's killing
and, 1, 165; on reason for participation,
120–21, 155–56
education and schools: Hutu, at seminary,
64–65; learning about ethnicity in,
108–9; quota system for, 71, 109; Tutsi-
only, 63
egalitarianism, 64–65, 110
elites: as cognizant of local ties among
ethnic groups, 82–83; competition
among, 70; divisions among, 45–46, 74;
ethnicity as tool of, 103–4; generalizations about, 9; mobilization tactics of, 8;
political conflicts reframed as ethnic by,
4, 10, 45, 49–50, 52, 121–22; script created by, 12–13, 103, 121; situations used by,
90–91; stereotypes defined by, 124. *See
also* Hutu elites; Tutsi elites
Émilie (pseud.), 90–91, 108–9, 175n15
Ethiopians, 113–14
ethnic fear and hatred theses: components
of, 4, 5, 45, 89, 126; contamination explanation vs., 99–101; counterarguments to,
19–21, 77, 101–2, 185–86; friendship ties
vs., 143; group dynamics explanation vs.,
178–79; jealousy and greed explanation
vs., 95–98; legacies of past violence as
explanation vs., 93–95; limits of, 6, 9–10,
153; reconsideration of, 180–85; situational explanation vs., 89–93; testimony
on, 95–96; type of violence expected in,
74
ethnicity (*ubwoko*): absence of solidarity in,
84; ambiguity and complexity of, 121;
approaches to, 4–12; changing of,

115–18, 124–25; claim-making and, 123–25; collective categorization of, 187; colonial construction of concept, 63–64, 74, 103n1, 108–9; difficulty in distinguishing, 32, 33; elites' use of, 103–4; hierarchy of, 118; on identity cards, 71; Joiners' view of, 119; learning about, 106–11; official vs. lived history of, 57–62; political criterion of, 117–18, 126; as script, 13–14; situations vs. role of, 89–93; social interaction thesis and, 19–21, 185–86; status vs. hereditary criteria of, 115–17, 118; stereotypes in, 111–14; talk about, banned, 31–32, 35, 105, 119; talk about, political constraints on, 181–82; tensions based in, 96; war framed as based in, 4, 10, 45, 49–50, 52, 121–22. *See also* state-sponsored ethnicity; Hutu (label); Tutsi (label); Twa (label)

Eugène (pseud.): on attack process, 161–62; demeanor of, 139; on friendship and Interahamwe, 135, 140, 141–44; on reason for participation, 156, 162

evaders: in spectrum of responses, *30*, 130; tactics of, 137; use of term, 16

explanations for genocide: group dynamics, 178–79; jealousy and greed, 95–98; legacies of past violence, 93–95; logic of contamination, 99–101; situational basis, 89–93, 155–56, 162, 185–86. *See also* ethnic fear and hatred theses

family and family ties: betrayal of, 90–91; clan talk in, 105–6; in hiding targets, 151; inability to protect, 144; interethnic, 2–3, 91–92, 105–6, 131; jealousy and greed in, 96–97; in killing process, 172, 173–74; less role of, in north, 139; single *génocidaire* from, 128; as targets, 128–29, 135–37

FAR (Forces armées rwandaises), 14–15, 81, 89, 137

fears: changing object of, 120–21; variable sources of, 159–60, 184–85. *See also* ethnic fear and hatred theses

Fein, Helen, 3n2

Félix (pseud.): demeanor of, 139; on evading, 159–60, 165; on reason for participation, 122, 158–59

Fossey, Dian, 1

France: aid from, 47; peasant revolts in, 68

Frédéric (pseud.), 166–68, 181, 182

friendship ties: blood pacts in, 91–92, 131; components of, 140; contamination via,

99–101; genocide at level of, 152–53; group dynamics vs., 158–59; group ties compared with, 151; of Joiners, 139–44, 147; leaders' presence and, 128–29; persistence in face of violence, 92–93; shared values in, 168–70; strangers vs., 146–47

gacaca (community-based conflict resolution mechanism), 40, 43–44, 96

Gagnon, Chip, 6

gender: of author and interpreter, 34–35; of Joiners, 16n8; of respondents, 31, 34–35, 36

genocide: definitions of, 14; dynamic approach to explaining, 11–18; ethnicity in, 118–26; forms of, 6–7, 170–74, 178–79; limits of macro-level approaches to, 9–10; limits of standard categories in analyzing, 7–9; as means not end, 129; mechanisms at work in, 19–21; responses to, 5–6, 16, *30*, 130; "selective," of Hutu (1972), 71. *See also* Balkan wars; Cambodian genocide; Holocaust; Rwandan genocide (1994)

Germany: colonial rule by, 62–63; identity card system of, 110n4; indifference to deportations of Jews in, 6

Gisenyi (town): favoritism extended to, 73; timing of genocide in, 55–56; 1959 violence in, 68

Gitarama (town): coup of, 69–70; experience of war and genocide in, 27; Hutu elite party in, 10; interim government in, 132; political protests in, 51; prison in, 24–26; stereotype of, 126; 1959 violence in, 68. *See also* MDR (Mouvement démocratique républicain); Ngali (pseud. for center-south site)

Gitera, Joseph, 65–66, 69

Goffman, Erving, 12

Granovetter, Mark, 17–18, 128, 129, 131

Gravel, Pierre, 60

group dynamics: approach to, 154–55, 178–79; continuity of participation and, 174–78; form of killing and, 7, 170–74; group ties generated in, 186; motivations and constraints in, 155–62; negative cases of, 166–70; power and powerlessness in, 162–66; size of group and, 171, 177–78

group ties: agency of individual vs., 157–58; constitutive power in, 174–79; formation of, 86; of Joiners, 147–53; Joiners' explanations of, 155–70; killing as producing

group (*continued*)
and produced by, 154–55, 186; role in recruitment, 128–29
Gustave (pseud.), 168–69

Habyarimana, Agathe, 52
Habyarimana, Juvénal: assassination of, 2, 15, 27, 53–55, 75, 80, 84, 89, 90, 132, 156; as character in script, 122; circle and supporters of, 2, 27, 56, 86, 125; economy under, 46–47; identity card system under, 110; mobilization and control under, 72–73; peace agreement of, 52–53; political agreement of, 51–52; reform efforts of, 47–48; successors to, 121; threats to, 10, 48, 74–75; war framed as ethnic by, 49–50, 52
Hamitic hypothesis, 58–59, 114n5, 118
Hardin, Russell, 5, 111
hatreds: absent in reasons for killings, 120–21; among few rather than many, 95–98; implications of finding, 118–19. *See also* ethnic fear and hatred theses
history: *abiru* role in, 58; assassination precipitating violence in, 53–56; economic decline in, 46–47; learning about ethnicity in, 108–9; north-south rivalry in, 10, 26–27, 48, 56, 70, 72–73; official vs. lived, 57–62; origins of Hutu and Tutsi in, 56; political crisis in, 47–48; read backwards after 1994, 73–75; shift to Hutu power in, 67–72. *See also* colonial period; war (*intambara,* 1990–94)
Holocaust: characteristics of, 3, 7, 171; killers' status in, 178; lack of protest of, 6; peer and group contexts in, 187–88
households. *See* family and family ties
Hutu (label): colonial transformation of, 62–66; ethnicization of, 63–64, 74; learning about, 106–11; multifaceted nature of, 104, 111; politicization of, 61–62; regional and contextual variations in, 59–61; as social then ethnic label, 45–46
Hutu elites: Belgian support for, 67, 68–69; divisions among, 67; education of, 64–65, 71; hypercentralized state to control, 72–73; killings of moderate, 54; political revolution of, 67–72; separated from most Hutu, 66. *See also* Hutu Power/Hutu Pawa; MDR (Mouvement démocratique républicain); PARME-HUTU (Parti du mouvement de l'émancipation des Bahutu)

Hutu people: Burundi army's killing of, 71; Christian conversion of, 63; divisions among, 10, 66; family and clan ties of, 68–69; fears of, 120–21, 184–85; heterogeneity of, 59; killings of Tutsi by (1963), 70; official histories of, 57; response to Ndadaye's assassination by, 53; systematic discrimination against, 64–65; Tutsi differentiation of, 1–2, 183, 184–85. *See also* Rwandan genocide (1994)
Hutu Power/Hutu Pawa: recruitment by, 135–36; as slogan, 88, 172; ties to power of, 132; transformation into, 91

icyitso (accomplice; *ibyitso,* pl.): accusations of being, 77–79, 82, 123, 134, 136, 149, 152; desire to hunt down, 157; logic of contamination and, 100–101
identity card system, 71, 109–11, 124, 134
igisekuruza (lineage; *ibisekuruza,* pl.), 105
igitero (attack group), 171n10
Impuzamugambi (CDR militia), 54n10
individuals: agency of group vs., 157–58; conflicts among, 181, 182–83; hill as place of origin for, 40n11; multiple roles of, 16; privileges absent for, 178. *See also* interviews; life history narratives
Inkotanyi. *See* RPF (Rwandan Patriotic Front)
intambara. See war (*intambara,* 1990–94)
Interahamwe: as bad people, 95–96; changing meanings of, 87; constituting group identity of, 170, 175–78, 186; discipline of, 160–62; evading recruitment by, 137; family ties and, 135–36; fears of, 120–21; friendship ties and, 93, 141–44; killings by, 54–55, 85, 86, 148–49, 163–64, 170–74, 178–79; ties to power of, 132–37; Tutsi in, 124, 135, 143, 156; as "violence specialists," 87, 129–30
interethnic ties: blood pacts as, 91–92, 131; in clans, 105–6; in families, 2–3, 91–92, 105–6, 131; in friendships, 131; logic of contamination via, 100–101; targets based on, 80. *See also* social relations
international aid, 46–47, 51
interpreter: characteristics of, 32–34; questions about, 40; research explained by, 37–38, 39; role of, 17
interviews: assumptions about ethnicity in, 117–18n11; author's subjectivity in, 34–35; collecting and analyzing data of, 16–18; contextualizing data of, 41–44; ethnicity

as topic in, 119–20; gender imbalance in, 31; multiple visits in, 38–40; number and formats of, 28–30, *29*; other studies compared with, 186–88; protocol for, 35–41; questions in, 41; silence in, about sexual violence and pillaging, 150n12; sites and respondents for, 26–32, 36–38; trustworthiness of, 181–83. *See also* daily life; interpreter; life history narratives

intimate mass violence: characteristics of, 170–74; constructivist theory of, 188–89; questions about, 3, 7, 20–21; regional differences in, 88–89. *See also* Rwandan genocide (1994)

inyenzi (cockroach) raids, 70, 83, 149n11

Japanese and Japanese Americans, 5

jealousy and greed: family members targeted for, 136; genocide explained by, 96–98; imprisonment explained by, 138

Jean-Marie (pseud.), 108–9

Jefremovas, Villia, 130n2

Joiners: agency minimized by, 142, 182; bad people as, 95–96; on becoming Interahamwe, 170; Burundian refugees as, 84; contextualization of, 146–47; description of, 129–31; ethnicity as viewed by, 119; family ties of, 135–37; fears among, 120–21, 184–85; friendship ties of, 139–44, 147; gender of, 16n8; greed and jealousy of, 96–98; group dynamics and, 154–55; group ties of, 128–29, 147–53, 186; hatreds among, 118–19; hypocrisy of, 95–96; Interahamwe identity of, 174–78; killing practices of, 171–74; local power ties of, 131–39; logic of contamination applied to, 99–101; as murderers (pre-1994), 91; performances of, 121–27, 185; powerlessness claimed by, 162–66; profiles of, 129–31; reasons for participation, 119–21, 136, 138, 155–62; recruitment into, 85, 151–53; as rescuers, 130, 132, 144–45, 147; resisters compared with, 167–70; survival strategies of, 141–44; as targets, 150–51; typology of, 155–57; understanding of, 22; use of term, 15–16, 129, 130–31

Jude (pseud., leader in Ngali): claims counter to, 125; death of, 132n5; killings organized by, 85, 124, 148–49, 162; MDR linked to, 85, 132–33; MRND linked to, 167n3; others' fear of, 184; pillaged goods and, 160–62; power of, 126, 131,

132–37, 141, 143; resistance to, 167–68. *See also* Thérèse (pseud., wife of Jude)

Kagame, Alexis, 57–58, 61

Kagame, Paul, 55n12, 88, 94

Kalyvas, Stathis N., 5, 6, 9, 16, 19

Kanyarengwe, Alexis, 73

Karamira, Froduald, 88

Kayibanda, Grégoire: death of, 72; demise of regime, 71–72; home base of, 27; identity card system under, 110; political party of, 48, 65, 66, 67, 94n7; political tactics of, 69, 70–71

Kershaw, Ian, 6

Khmer Rouge, killings by, 7, 171

Kibirira: Tutsi massacred in, 50–51

Kigali (capital): killings in, 2, 15, 54–55, 76, 87; political rallies in, 49–50, 51; rural areas compared with, 9–10

Kigwa (ancestor), 67

killers: in spectrum of responses, *30*. *See also* Joiners; perpetrators and collaborators

Kimanzi (pseud. for north site): description of, 24–27, *25*; dramatis personae of, 191; friendship ties in, 131; genocide and war linked in, 78–79, 89, 122, 137; group dynamics in, 158; narratives of genocide in, 76–83, 88–89; number and identification of Tutsi in, 27–28, 119, 125–26; population of, *29*, 82; power centers in, 122, 131, 137–39; recruitment patterns in, 138–39; source of fear in, 184; targeting people of, 125–26; violence of pre-1990 vs. 1994 in, 15, 94–95

King, Charles, 19

Kinyamateka (periodical), 66

Kinyarwanda (language): *akazu* (little house) in, 52; distancing ties in, 85–86; "genocide" in, 15; Hutu and Tutsi terms in, 60–61; interviews in, 37; Pawa and power in, 88; *ubwoko* in, 105

kubohoza (forcible political recruitment), 83

Laitin, David, 10

leaders: family members targeted by, 128–29; as rescuers, 130; role of ties to, 131–39. *See also* Hutu elites; Jude (pseud., leader in Ngali)

Lemarchand, René, 66, 68

life history narratives: contextualizing data of, 41–44; of genocide at neighborhood level, 77–89; limits of, 89. *See also* daily life; interviews; script for violence

lineages, 105–6
Lizinde, Théoneste, 73
local, the: focus on, 27; insider knowledge of, 111; role in large-scale processes, 20–21; understanding of, 180
local authorities: *cellules* and, 28, 36; dispossession attempts and, 59–60; escalation in war as opportunity for, 79; feared by residents, 159–60; intimidation and arrest and, 68–70; mobilization by, 90–91, 122–23; power of, 124–25, 129; reconciliation after pre-1990 violence and, 94–95; timing of genocide and, 55–56
local ties: in central vs. rural areas, 9–10; divisions in, 45–46; of Joiners, 131; in multiple and single centers of power, 131–39; role in recruitment, 128–29; script for violence and, 12–13, 185–86; *ubuhake* and *ubureetwa* in, 64, 66. *See also* regional areas; rural areas
logic of contamination explanation, 99–101
Logiest, B. E. M. Guy, 68
lynchings, 7, 170, 171

Malkki, Liisa, 43
Mamdani, Mahmood, 49n4, 49n5, 103n1
masses: authorities' mobilization of, 90–91, 122–23; disaggregation of, 15, 18, 129–31, 153; ethnic appeals to, 56; generalizations about, 9; prejudices and fears of, 5; rational self-interests of, 3. *See also* Joiners
mass violence: ethnicity-based approaches to, 4–10; particularities in, 170–71. *See also* genocide; intimate mass violence
Maurice (pseud.), 93–94, 125
MDR (Mouvement démocratique républicain): establishment and goals of, 48; political agreement of, 51–52; Power wing of, 88, 132; rallies and protests of, 49–50, 51; ties to, 132–33
media: extremist rhetoric in, 4, 50, 52, 103–4, 187; political caricatures in, 122n12; political discourse in, 48
métisse (half Rwandan): author perceived as, 35
Michel (pseud.), 144–47, 156
militia: coups of, 71–72, 73; massacres by, 2–3, 54–55; war crimes of ex-FAR, 82. *See also* Interahamwe
Ministry of Internal Security (Ministère de la sécurité intérieure), 35–36
Ministry of Local Government, Community Development, and Social Affairs, 36

Mironko, Charles K., 171n7, 171n10, 174
"Mise au Point" (Statement of Views), 65
Monroe, Kristen, 30, 43
moral universe norms, 3
MRND (Mouvement révolutionnaire national pour le développement): members of, 72; opposition to, 48–50; on peace talks with RPF, 52; refusal to join, 167; regional support and tactics of, 55–56; tactics of, 50–51, 54, 88. *See also* Interahamwe
MSM (Mouvement social muhutu), 65, 66, 67
multipartyism. *See* political parties
Museveni, Yoweri, 49n4
Musinga, Yuhi (mwami), 62–63, 63
muzungu (foreigner: *bazungu*, pl.): use of term, 32n3, 34–35, 112, 113
Mwinyi, Ali Hassan, 53
My Lai massacre, 176

National Police, 2–3
Ndadaye, Melchior, 53, 74, 83–84, 88, 122
Nduga: Tutsi from, 59–60
neighbors and neighborhood ties: agency at level of, 18; effects of war on, 99; ethnicity known among, 104, 106–11; genocide at level of, 128–29, 143, 152–53, 165; group dynamics vs., 157–58; hypocrisy in, 95–96; jealousy and greed among, 96–98; perpetrators as perceived by, 81–83, 85–88; persistence of ties among, 86, 90–93; targets as perceived by, 77–81, 83–85. *See also* daily life; friendship ties; local ties
neutrality, 5–6, 33–34
Newbury, Catharine, 49n5, 60–61, 62
Newbury, David, 46–47n2, 49n5
Ngali (pseud. for center-south site): changing *ubwoko* in, 115–18, 124–25; description of, 23–27, *24*; dramatis personae of, 191–92; friendship ties in, 139–44; genocide and assassination linked in, 84, 89, 122, 132; group dynamics in, 158–59; narratives of genocide in, 76–77, 83–89; number of Tutsi in, 28; population of, *29*; power center in, 131, 132–37; rumors about war in, 83–84; source of fear in, 184; targeting people of, 122–25
Nicolas (pseud.), 97–98
north region: center-south rivalry with, 10, 26–27, 48, 56, 70, 72–73; group identities in, 59–60; war and genocide linked in,

14–15, 78–79, 89, 122, 137. *See also*
Kimanzi (pseud. for north site); MRND
(Mouvement révolutionnaire national
pour le développement); Ruhengeri
(town)
Nsanzimana, Sylvestre, 51
Nsengiyaremye, Dismas, 52
Ntaryamira, Cyprien, 53–54
Nyiginya clan, 57–59
Nyiszli, Miklos, 178

obedience thesis, 187–88
Olivier (pseud.): on avoiding violence, 123;
background of, 1–2; demeanor of, 148;
killings by, 2, 122, 148–49, 160–61; on
pillaging, 182; prison job of, 147–48; on
rescue attempt, 175, 177; as target,
150–51, 178
oral histories (*ibiteekerezo*), 57, 109. *See also*
interviews; life history narratives
organized resistance. *See* resisters

PARMEHUTU (Parti du mouvement de l'é-
mancipation des Bahutu), 48, 67–69, 70,
94n7
participants and participation in genocide,
11–18. *See also* Joiners; leaders
Paul (pseud.): demeanor of, 139; on Jude,
132, 133–34; on killing Hutu, 124; rescue
activities of, 125, 134–35, 140–41
Pawa. *See* Hutu Power/Hutu Pawa
PCD (Parti chrétien démocrate), 51
Peabody, Norbert, 9
peasant-to-*génocidaire* transformation: as
mostly impossible to predict, 90–91;
questions about, 3, 7, 20–21. *See also*
Joiners
performance. *See* script for violence
perpetrators and collaborators: households
of, 128; individuals' perceptions of,
81–83, 85–88; motivation of, 129; use of
term, 8, 16. *See also* Joiners
pillaging: admissions of, 150, 182; in killing
process, 173; organization of, 160–62;
silence about, 150n12; in spectrum of
responses, *30*
Platteau, Jean-Philippe, 47n2
PL (Parti Libéral), 48, 51
political parties: banned, 72; in early independence, 65–66; emergence of, 2,
47–49; end of war and economic crisis as
trumping, 51n7; extremists in, 2, 45,
52–53, 56, 85, 88, 103–4, 129, 132, 158;

recruitment into, 70, 83; as threat to
Habyarimana, 10, 48, 74–75; violence
linked to, 93–95, 183. *See also* power; *specific parties*
political violence: as always planned, 74;
form of, 7, 170–71; regime opposition
targeted in, 50–51; in retaliation for
inyenzi raids, 70; social embeddedness of,
20–21; in 1959–60 transformation, 31,
68–69, 93–94. *See also* Rwandan genocide
(1994)
politics: change of ethnicity based on,
117–18; crisis in, 47–48; genocide based
in, 2, 45, 54–56, 74–75; Hutu revolution
of, 67–72; use of term, 168, 169. *See also*
local authorities; political parties; political violence
Posen, Barry, 5
poverty, 46–47n2, 70–71, 74
power: Belgian-Tutsi abuses of, 63–65; in
group dynamics, 162–66, 174–78; Hutu
abuses of, 67–72; multiple vs. single centers of, 131, 132–39; of naming ethnicity
of another, 104; at neighbor level, 129;
reform process and, 47–48; rise of northern, 72–73; Rwabugiri's expansion of,
61–62; of script writing and claim-
making, 12–13, 103, 121, 124–25; slogan
of, 88. *See also* Hutu Power/Hutu Pawa;
political parties
Presidential Guard, 2, 54–55
prisons: confessions and, 29–30; description of, 24–26; interviews in, 37, 38,
39–40
Prunier, Gérard, 49n5, 50n6, 187n3
PSD (Parti social démocrate), 48, 51
Public Safety Groups, 71–72

quota system, 71, 72–73, 109

RADER (Rassemblement démocratique
réandais), 67, 70
Radio Rwanda, 50
Radio-télévision des mille collines (RTLM),
154n1
rationalist perspective, 3, 5
reconciliation: after earlier violence, 94–95;
mechanism for, 40, 43–44, 96
recruitment: face-to-face, 158–59; at family
level, 135–37; in killing process, 172,
173–74; limited hiding to avoid, 165; patterns in Kimanzi, 138–39; social relations
as basis for, 128–29

Red Cross, 26
refugees: Burundian, 83–84, 86; Rwandan, 49, 71, 99
regions: divisions in, 45–46; genocide's differences in, 55–56; meanings of Hutu and Tutsi differing by, 59–61, 66; narratives differing by, 76–89; Rwabugiri's expansion of power into, 61–62; Tutsification of, 63–64. *See also* center-south region; north region; rural areas
Rennie, J. K., 60
rescuers: blood pacts of, 91–92, 131; Joiners as, 130, 132, 144–45, 147; official documents used by, 134, 140–41; in spectrum of responses, *30*, 130; use of term, 8, 16
resisters: Joiners compared with, 167–70; in Ngali, 86–88; in spectrum of responses, *30*, 130; use of term, 16
Reyntjens, Filip, 50n6, 68, 110n4, 116n9
Richards, Paul, 17
riots, 7, 68, 170
roadblocks, 55, 122, 123, 145, 159
RPF (Rwandan Patriotic Front): attacks and invasions by, 1, 27, 49, 74, 77–80, 120, 122; fears of, 120–21, 184; forced conscripts of, 80–81; genocide intertwined with war of, 14–15, 78–79, 89, 122, 137; killing practices and atrocities of, 55n12, 81, 173n13, 182n2; names for, 149n11; peace agreement of, 2, 52–53; regime's rhetoric on, 49–51; respondents' comments about, 181–82; response to assassination, 54; rumors about, 83, 84, 87–88, 120, 156; soldiers killed by Joiners, 137–38; Tutsi exiles as members of, 48; Tutsi fears of, 118; victory of, 32, 56
Rudahigwa, Mutara (mwami), 63, 67, 117n10
Ruhengeri (town): in disfavor, 73; group identities in, 59–60; prison in, 24–26; RPF attack on, 27, 79–80; timing of genocide in, 50, 55–56; violence in (1959), 68; White Father mission in, 59–60, 61, 62. *See also* Kimanzi (pseud. for north site)
Rukeba, François, 67
rural areas: ambiguity and contradiction of violence in, 8–9; capital compared with, 9–10; focus on, 27; interpreter from, 33; regional differences in violence in, 2–3. *See also* Kimanzi (pseud. for north site); Ngali (pseud. for center-south site); regional areas
Rwabugiri, Kigeri (mwami), 61–62

Rwanda: administrative hierarchy of, 27, *28*; author's time in, 23, 26, 38n8; distance as conceived in, 86; first elections in, 65, 66; independence of, 47, 65–66, 67, 68, 69; map of, *xiv*; monetary exchange rate in, 168n4; place of origin as conceived in, 40n11; population of, 26, 56n15; research permission in, 35–36; returnees to, 32–33; violence in (1959–61), 31, 68–69, 94. *See also* colonial period; daily life; economy; history; Kigali (capital); political parties; state and state intervention; war (*intambara*, 1990–94)
Rwandan genocide (1994): approach to, 21–22; constitutive power of group killings in, 175–78; constructivist theory of, 188–89; contextualization of, 101–2, 145–47; ethnic divisions resulting from, 182, 183; events summarized, 2–3, 54–56; interpreting narratives of, 41–44, 88–89; intimidation tactics in, 68; killing practices in, 6–7, 54–55, 85, 86, 148–49, 163–64, 170–74, 178–79; lessons of, 188–89; matter-of-fact attitude toward, 148–49; momentum of, 160–61; multiple vectors in, 81; at neighborhood level, 128–29; not knowing about, 137; number killed, 56; number of perpetrators in, 6n4; past violence compared with, 93–95, 183; performance of, 121–26; political motivations for, 2, 45, 54–56, 74–75; public nature of, 7, 170–74; refusal to talk about, 43–44; regional differences in, 27; social embeddedness of, 17–18, 20–21, 128–29; studies of, 4n3, 186–88; terms for, 15; "work" as euphemism in, 154n1. *See also* explanations for genocide; interviews; Joiners; Kimanzi (pseud. for north site); Ngali (pseud. for center-south site); script for violence; social interaction thesis; social relations
Rwandan Patriotic Front. *See* RPF (Rwandan Patriotic Front)

Sanders, Edith, 58
script for violence: belief in vs. acting out of, 104; elites' rhetoric as, 12–13, 103, 121; local conseiller as deciding on, 134–37; in public killings, 172, 173–74; roles in, 174–78; social interaction thesis and, 19–21, 185–86; state-sponsored ethnicity as, 12–14, 19, 121–26; variations in following, 122–23, 126–27

sexual violence: group size and, 177–78; in killing process, 172, 174; participation in, 130, 137; silence about, 150n12

Sierra Leone: meaning of violence in, 17

silence (white space): about sexual violence and pillaging, 150n12; as clues, 41, 42–43; effects of, 5–6; ties to power and, 137

social interaction thesis: description of, 19–21, 185–86; implications of, 188–89. *See also* social relations

social relations: effects of environment as changing, 99–101; genocide embedded in, 17–18, 20–21, 128–29; historical accounts of, 57; implications, 19–21. *See also* family and family ties; friendship ties; group dynamics; group ties; interethnic ties; local ties; neighbors and neighborhood ties

socioeconomic status: change of ethnicity based on, 115–17, 118; meanings of Hutu and Tutsi terms in, 60–61

Sophie (pseud.), 95–96, 98, 115–16, 167

sports analogy, 176

state and state intervention: census of, 110–11; divisionistes pursued by, 39, 181–82; extremist control of, 2, 4, 45, 50, 52–53, 56, 85, 88, 103–4, 129, 132, 158, 187; hypercentralized, 72–73; *icyitso* category imposed by, 79; identity card system of, 71, 109–10; massacres jumpstarted by, 76–77; recruitment by, 158–59; talk about ethnicity banned by, 31–32, 35, 105, 119. *See also* education and schools; elites; political parties; state-sponsored ethnicity

state-sponsored ethnicity: concept of, 11, 12, 104; Hutu/Tutsi difference key to, 108–9; as script for violence, 12–14, 19, 121–26

Stefan (pseud.): background of, 151–52; group size and, 171; on motives and constraints, 155–57; neighbor's killing and, 152–53, 165; on reason for participation, 123

stereotypes: changes in, 115–18; everyday deployment of, 111–14; extremist rhetoric as fostering, 103; in Hamitic hypothesis, 58–59, 114n5, 118; killings based on, 123–24; regional, 125–26

Straus, Scott: on extremist rhetoric, 103–4; on form of killing, 171n7; on genocidal violence, 6–7; present work compared with, 186–87; on pre-1990 violence, 94;

on recruitment, 128; on RPF involvement, 55n12

subjectivity, 34–35

survivors: assumptions about, 36–37; on forced recruitment, 135–36; on president's assassination, 84; use of term, 16, 130

Tanzania: in peace negotiations, 52n8

targets: confusion about, 104; group members as, 147; individuals' perceptions of, 77–81, 83–85, 134; spouses of Tutsi as, 150–51

Thérèse (pseud., wife of Jude): on ethnicity, 117–18, 126; on jealousy and greed, 96–97; on Jude, 132–33; knowledge of, 136–37; Paul on, 134; on stereotypes, 113–14; on violence between neighbors, 90

ties. *See* social relations

Tilly, Charles, 19, 87, 154

Tutsi (label): colonial transformation of, 62–66; cows linked to, 112, 114, 115, 116–17, 123; ethnicization of, 63–64, 74; learning about, 106–11; multifaceted nature of, 104, 111; politicization of, 61–62; regional and contextual variations in, 59–61; as social then ethnic label, 45–46

Tutsi elites: Belgian alliances with, 62–65, 108; education of, 63, 71; resentment toward, 68; systematic discrimination by, 64–65

Tutsi people: cross-border raids by (1959–61), 31; fears of, 120–21, 184–85; hatreds against, 118–19; heterogeneity of, 59; Hutu differentiated by, 1–2, 183, 184–85; Hutu intimidation and arrest of (1959–61), 68–70; massacred in 1990–91, 50–51; Ndadaye assassinated by, 53, 74; official histories of, 57–60; population of, 27–28, 29; pre-1973 violence against, 46; stereotypes of, 55n13, 111–14. *See also* RPF (Rwandan Patriotic Front); Rwandan genocide (1994)

Twa (label), 106–11

Twa people, 56n15, 57, 112

ubuhake (voluntary vassalage), 64, 66

ubureetwa (involuntary vassalage), 64

ubwoko. See ethnicity (*ubwoko*)

Uganda: contamination via living in, 99, 101; in peace negotiations, 52n8; RPF bases in, 49, 53

umuganda (communal work duty), 72, 86, 128
umuhutu (pl., *abahutu*). *See* Hutu people
umukiga (person from Kiga), 125
Umutara (region): RPF invasion of, 77–78, 80, 120
Umutesi, Béatrice Marie, 33n4
umututsi (pl., *abatutsi*). *See* Tutsi people
UNAR (Union nationale rwandaise), 67, 68, 70
United Nations (UN), 53, 54, 65, 69
United States: Japanese internment in, 5; military (group) identity in, 176; in peace negotiations, 52n8; security rhetoric in, 158
Uvin, Peter, 46n1
Uwilingiyimana, Agathe, 54

values of resisters, 168–70
Vansina, Jan, 58
Verwimp, Phillip, 128
victims: use of term, 8
violence: center-to-periphery generalizations and, 9–10; conflict distinguished from, 20; constructivist theory of, 188–89; contradiction and ambiguity of, 8–9; in individual conflicts, 181; international donors' role in, 46n1; micropolitical approach to, 19–20; as organized social action, 17; of past vs. 1994, 93–95, 183; questions about, 3, 7, 20–21; scholarly explanations of, 17–18; self-reinforcement of descent into, 160–61; "specialists" and "riot captains" in, 87, 129–30. *See also* genocide; intimate mass violence; mass violence; political violence; sexual violence

Walzer, Michael, 3n2
war (*intambara*, 1990–94): events of, 49; framed as ethnic, 4, 10, 45, 49–50, 52, 121–22; genocide intertwined with, 14–15, 78–79, 89, 122, 137; peace agreement in, 52–53; references to, 14–15; regional differences in, 27, 88–89; Tutsi massacred in, 50–51. *See also* FAR (Forces armées rwandaises); RPF (Rwandan Patriotic Front)
Warren, Kay, 43
Weingast, Barry, 5
White Father mission and diaries, 59–60, 61, 62
witnesses: Joiner as, 163; role in script for violence, 175; in spectrum of responses, *30*, 130; use of term, 16
World War I, 63, 110n4
World War II, 5, 65. *See also* Holocaust